Gunboat
Democracy

Gunboat Democracy

U.S. Interventions in the Dominican Republic, Grenada, and Panama

RUSSELL CRANDALL

ROWMAN & LITTLEFIELD PUBLISHERS, INC.
Lanham • Boulder • New York • Toronto • Oxford

ROWMAN & LITTLEFIELD PUBLISHERS, INC.

Published in the United States of America
by Rowman & Littlefield Publishers, Inc.
A wholly owned subsidiary of The Rowman & Littlefield Publishing Group, Inc.
4501 Forbes Boulevard, Suite 200, Lanham, Maryland 20706
www.rowmanlittlefield.com

PO Box 317
Oxford
OX2 9RU, UK

British Library Cataloguing in Publication Information Available

Library of Congress Cataloging-in-Publication Data

Crandall, Russell, 1971–
    Gunboat democracy : U.S. interventions in the Dominican Republic,
Grenada, and Panama / Russell Crandall.
        p.   cm.
    Includes bibliographical references and index.
    ISBN-13: 978-0-7425-5047-6 (cloth : alk. paper)
    ISBN-10: 0-7425-5047-8 (cloth : alk. paper)
    ISBN-13: 978-0-7425-5048-3 (pbk. : alk. paper)
    ISBN-10: 0-7425-5048-6 (pbk. : alk. paper)
        1. Caribbean Area—Foreign relations—United States.   2. United States—
Foreign relations—Caribbean Area.   3. Intervention (International law—
History—20th century.   4. Dominican Republic—History—Revolution, 1965.
5. Grenada—History—American Invasion, 1983.   6. Panama—History—
American Invasion, 1989.   7. United States—Military policy—Decision-making.
8. National security—United States—Decision-making.   I. Title.
    F2178.U6C73   2006
    327.729073—dc22   2005029068

Printed in the United States of America

♾ ™ The paper used in this publication meets the minimum requirements of
American National Standard for Information Sciences—Permanence of Paper for
Printed Library Materials, ANSI/NISO Z39.48-1992.

This book is dedicated to the memory of teacher, mentor, and colleague Professor Fred Holborn. Blessed with an encyclopedic memory for the names, dates, and events of American foreign policy, Fred was an indefatigable teacher and ubiquitous presence on the campus of the Paul H. Nitze School of Advanced International Studies at Johns Hopkins University.

Fred's uncanny ability to sense the irony in history left a lasting impression on me; his willingness to read every page of my doctoral dissertation and subsequent books (including this one) went without saying. This book is one small step in returning the favor and saying thank you. A more lasting tribute to Fred would be for me to be as generous, patient, and supportive with my current and future students as he was with me.

Contents

Acknowledgments

This book represents the collected wisdom of numerous readers who provided much-needed "constructive criticism" to what was a much rougher initial draft. I am grateful to all of you, including the anonymous reviewers. There will be, of course, some colleagues and friends whom I will fail to thank for their work and attention, so please forgive me in advance.

I would like to give a special thanks to Davidson College colleagues Ralph Levering and Peter Ahrensdorf, two early and enthusiastic supporters of what was at that point just an idea for a book. I would like to thank other colleagues who read the manuscript: Chris Chivvis, Michael Shifter, Bob Snyder, and Denis McDonough.

As always, my wife and academic colleague Britta Crandall provided indispensable insight on the book's methodological approach and organization. Karin McDonough provided new meaning to the word "Panama," and I can't thank her enough for her assistance.

I am particularly blessed to have a seemingly inexhaustible well of eager and highly capable Davidson students to help me in my research. I would like to thank these current and former students for their excellent assistance and insight: Adam Chalker, John Foster, Rebecca Stewart, and Akilah Jenga. Andrew Rhodes and Josh Craft were two absolutely wonderful research assistants; their sweat and toil made the book infinitely better.

I completed this manuscript while on the International Affairs Fellowship sponsored by the Council on Foreign Relations. I owe a special note of gratitude to the Council's Elise Lewis and Aysha Ghadiali for their generous support.

At Rowman & Littlefield, I was fortunate to work with an excellent editor Laura Gottlieb, who provided me with constant attention during the publication process. Andrew Boney also provided much-needed assistance with the production process.

I also owe a note of appreciation to several colleagues who provided professional support during my fellowship year: Michael Mandelbaum, Eliot Cohen, Julia Sweig, Cynthia McClintock, Michael Shifter, Peter Rodman, Paul Wolfowitz, Tom Shannon, Kim Breier, Steve Shoemaker, David Shoemaker, Lt. Colonel Brian Kline, Brigadier General John Johnson, Brigadier General Robert Caslen, Lt. General Walter Sharp, and Lt. Colonel Burt Thompson.

As always, Riordan Roett, Diane Monash, Guadalupe Paz, Dorothy Sobol, and Anne McKenzie of the Western Hemisphere Program at the Paul H. Nitze School of Advanced International Studies (SAIS) provided me with wonderful hospitality over two summers in Washington, D.C. I also owe long overdue words of gratitude to Marc Chernick and Cynthia Arnson for support on an earlier project.

I am unbelievably fortunate to be affiliated with two institutions (Davidson and SAIS) that possess absolutely wonderful and professional library staff. I am indebted to both library staffs for their excellent research assistance, especially my endless interlibrary loan requests.

R. C.
Davidson, North Carolina

Introduction

"It was right out of *Apocalypse Now*," commented an American medical student residing in Grenada, who looked out his dormitory window to see a dozen U.S. helicopters zipping across the early dawn horizon. The helicopters that raced toward the medical school campus were part of the American invasion of Grenada in 1983. President Ronald Reagan told the American public that he had dispatched military forces to ensure that several hundred American students were not taken hostage as well as to liberate the Grenadian people from the clutches of a murderous, hard-line Marxist regime. And while the operation proved to be less of a cakewalk than expected, the Reagan administration largely succeeded in its goals: the visibly appreciative students were safely returned to the United States, over 90 percent of the Grenadian population supported the invasion, the regime was ousted, and democratic elections followed soon after.

Despite these apparent successes, the invasion came under enormous amounts of criticism. In fact, the American action in Grenada appeared odd to many. The island was a tiny one at the bottom of the Caribbean Sea. They asked incredulously why the almighty United States needed to invade such an unimportant country. Critics immediately questioned the Reagan administration's timing and motives, particularly since the invasion came just days after a bloody terrorist attack in Lebanon that killed hundreds of U.S. Marines in Lebanon. Words such as "stunt" or "sham" surfaced almost immediately.

As is the case with U.S. interventions in the Dominican Republic in 1965 and Panama in 1989, the decision to invade Grenada was predicated on a strongly held view that a serious security threat existed. In the Dominican Republic, the perceived threat was the spread of communism; in

1

Panama, it was the security of the canal and American citizens residing in the country.

In each case, U.S. policymakers firmly believed that they faced grave crises and that inaction was possibly more dangerous than action. Intelligence reports given to senior policymakers during the crises were often quite alarmist or even mistaken, warning that Communist takeovers and severe threats to American lives were distinct possibilities. For example, President Johnson's decision to send in the Marines into the Dominican Republic resulted from a series of frantic cables concerning the potential for a Communist takeover sent from the U.S. ambassador in the country's capital, Santo Domingo.

To be sure, one can question whether analysts and policymakers overestimated the dangers in the intelligence reports or that the intelligence sources were deliberately providing "convenient" information intended to confirm what policymakers already believed or wanted to hear. For this reason, it is paramount that we interpret the documents with a certain degree of skepticism, knowing that we can never fully establish the motives behind those who produced the reports.

In addition, any comprehensive analysis of the decision-making process that led to these interventions must also consider the counterfactual of what might have occurred had the United States *not* intervened. In all three episodes, a counterfactual argument can be made that the situations in the countries at hand could have become even more chaotic and violent, developments that could have provoked an even more aggressive response from Washington.

THE INTERVENTIONS IN CONTEXT

These instances of intervention by force were not new to U.S. policy in its traditional "backyard," the Caribbean and Central America. Rather, these U.S. interventions represented the continuation of the "Big Stick" that presidents such as Theodore Roosevelt and Woodrow Wilson wielded so actively and unapologetically in the first few decades of the twentieth century. Indeed, the United States has routinely invaded countries in Central America and the Caribbean for reasons that it would have never even considered in just about any part of the world.

Following World War II and the establishment of the United Nations, the democratic practices and the principle of nonintervention became important parts of the international system, especially as they related to the Western Hemisphere. The creation of the Organization of American States in 1948 and Rio Pact in 1947 were U.S.-led initiatives that promoted multilateral responses to crises and the promotion of democracy. Thus, unlike previous eras when the Big Stick was used with virtual impunity, during the Cold War and afterward greater restraints existed on how U.S. military force could be used to promote outcomes in Washington's favor. Colonial-era occupations were out; state sovereignty and self-determination were more prominent. To be sure, Washington still wielded its Big Stick, but it had to do much more to justify or even disguise its use.

In many ways, the Dominican Republic, Grenada, and Panama interventions represent the schizophrenic nature of U.S. policy in the Caribbean and Central American during and after the Cold War: the United States wanted stability, democracy, anticommunism, and multilateralism. Yet as these three episodes demonstrate, at times they could not have all of these at once. Compromises would have to be made. Often this meant sacrificing the agreed-on principles of nonintervention to guarantee that communism or chaos did not take root in an area of the world where the United States had long felt the need and obligation to ensure order—whether it was invited or not. When in doubt, American boots on the ground ensured an outcome to Washington's liking.

Contrary to what is sometimes assumed, these interventions were anomalies that represent departures from normal U.S. policy toward Latin America during the Cold War and afterward. Outright U.S. military interventions in the region following World War II were actually quite rare relative to prior eras. In fact, aside from the noncombat interventions in Haiti in 1994 and 2004, the episodes studied in this book represent the only instances.

This is not to say, of course, that during this period the United States did not meddle, cajole, or overtly and covertly support governments or opposition movements. On the contrary, the historical record—for example, the 1954 CIA-backed overthrow of Jacobo Arbenz in Guatemala, the 1961 Bay of Pigs operation in Cuba, covert efforts to undermine the government of Salvador Allende in Chile during the early 1970s, and support for Nicaraguan counterrevolutionary groups in the 1980s—is replete with instances when the United States has been deeply involved in the internal affairs of its Latin American neighbors.

Overall, the episodes such as the previously mentioned Chile and Cuba examples that reinforce the culpability or mischievousness of the United States tend to get the most attention in our understanding of the evolution of the U.S.–Latin American relations. Thus, revisiting the "Dominican Republics," "Grenadas," and "Panamas," along with the usual "Chile 1973s" and "Guatemala 1954s," we will begin to broaden our existing interpretation of the history and nature of U.S. policy toward Latin America as well as American foreign policy more broadly.

DEMOCRATIC LEGACY

Most portrayals of the Dominican, Grenada, and Panama interventions stop their historical narratives soon after the United States has invaded the country in question. Yet a final verdict on the necessity, wisdom, and even morality of these interventions must also consider what occurred in these countries following the intervention. For example, if a particular U.S. intervention directly led to the installation of a tyrant, then we should consider that fact in our evaluation of the intervention. Conversely, we should also consider if an intervention helped to usher in a more positive political or economic system.

What is particularly fascinating for our purposes is that in these three cases some of the most vocal critics believed that interventions could not or should not lead to democracy. For example, immediately following the invasion of Grenada, Senator Patrick Moynihan (D-N.Y.) commented, "I don't think we can go around promoting democracy at the point of a bayonet." Right after the Panama invasion, Senator Ted Kennedy (D-Mass.) argued that the United States does not have the right to "roam the hemisphere, bringing dictators to justice or installing new governments by force or other means. Surely, it is a contradiction in terms and a violation of America's best ideals to impose democracy by the barrel of a gun in Panama or any nation."[1]

One big reason for this widely held belief that the United States cannot promote democracy by force stems from the painful experience in Vietnam.[2] Yet while Vietnam is clearly a case of failed democracy promotion and nation building, in the cases studied in this book there is more than scattered evidence to suggest that democracy actually emerged stronger following the U.S. intervention than before. Indeed, we must ask whether U.S. bayonets helped lead to more democracy, not less.

The *Vietnam syndrome* is a phrase used to describe the impact of the Vietnam War on U.S. foreign policy—the fear that interventions abroad will invariably lead to quagmires and end in failure and disgrace. In 2005, Ted Kennedy tied the ongoing war and nation-building efforts in Iraq with the American effort in Vietnam, suggesting that America should know better than trying to promote democracy through force:

> We thought that victory on the battlefield would lead to victory in the war, and peace and democracy for the people of Vietnam. We did not understand that our very presence was creating new enemies and defeating the very goals we set out to achieve. We cannot allow that history to repeat itself.[3]

There is no question that the Vietnam War served to radically alter the foreign policy positions of many American liberals, especially those in positions of power within the Democratic Party. During the 1965 Dominican crisis and well before Vietnam had become a lost cause, the Johnson administration's top foreign policy positions were staffed with Kennedy-era Democrats such as McGeorge Bundy, Robert McNamara, and Dean Rusk. Above all else, they were "cold warriors," firmly committed to containing communism anywhere on the globe.

Jump forward to 1983, when, after many liberals had taken from the Vietnam experience to view American power with great skepticism and suspicion, the Democratic Party's foreign policy leadership in Congress now almost instinctively condemned the Reagan administration's invasion of Grenada. To these liberals, the raw use of American power almost by definition was counterproductive and/or immoral. This stance was largely repeated during the Panama invasion six years later.

It ultimately was the Yugoslavia crisis (especially the NATO-led military operation in Kosovo) during the 1990s that forced a split within liberal and Democratic Party ranks about the efficacy and morality of U.S. military power. Yet this division did not start with Yugoslavia; rather, it had been brewing ever since Grenada in 1983, when the American intervention did not turn into the quagmire or moral quandary that some liberals believed was inevitable.

INTERVENTION AND SOVEREIGNTY
American power lies at the core of these invasions. If the United States had not yielded overwhelming power, then these interventions would have

likely not occurred. At the same time, however, the fundamental role of power alone does not undermine the justifications that the United States gave for going in or its intention to adhere to these justifications.

In all three cases, the ability of the United States to act collided with the principle (and international law) of nonintervention that posits that one state does not have the right to violate the sovereignty of another state. Political scientist Stephen Krasner has called sovereignty a form of "organized hypocrisy," meaning that in reality power is much more important to understanding the international system than is any hopeful belief in the preeminence of sovereignty.[4] Sovereignty might appeal to many observers, but ultimately it is much more fleeting than we might think. That is, whether we like it or not, violations of sovereignty take place all the time for a variety of reasons. Some are more justifiable and legitimate than others.

Instead of focusing exclusively on sovereignty to evaluate the legitimacy of an intervention, a more helpful evaluation of interventions should incorporate the operation's purposes and consequences.[5] What motivated the country or countries to use military force? How did it use these forces? What were the results of its actions?

Thus, for example, in his reference to the Panama invasion, international legal scholar Alfred Rubin is incorrect to conclude that the United States *always* loses "respect and influence" and that democracy will never strike "deep roots" when it uses force against "weak neighbors."[6] This is not to say, of course, that the United States *cannot* lose respect and influence when it invades; rather, it often depends on the specific details of the case at hand.

While sovereignty as a key principle of the international system was paramount during the time of these three invasions, it became less important in U.S. foreign policy following the end of the Cold War. Today, especially among Western nations, it is increasingly acceptable for a state or group of states to intervene in the affairs of another country.[7] The United States and many other countries no longer worry obsessively about violating sovereignty when deciding whether to send in military forces. Most often, however, these "humanitarian interventions" are at least in part prompted by massive violations of human rights, famine, or ethnic cleansing and genocide. Examples include Somalia in 1993, Haiti in 1994, Bosnia in 1995, and Kosovo in 1999.

The sheer scale of human suffering of many humanitarian crises has made the interventions in these instances relatively easy to justify in terms of any violation of sovereignty. Less studied, however, are instances of intervention, such as the three cases involved in this book, that were not directly humanitarian. Thus, a critical question to ask is if, when, and how interventions not linked to humanitarian crises are warranted and/or justified. In this sense, the cases of the Dominican Republic, Grenada, and Panama hold lessons for the legitimacy and necessity of "nonhumanitarian" interventions in the post–Cold War era.

This study of these three American interventions will by no means produce concrete answers to these extremely delicate and critical questions. Yet it is hoped that it will allow us to see these episodes of U.S. interventions in a broader context, one that will help us revise our historical understanding of the motivations and outcomes of U.S. policy toward Latin America as well as the nature and necessity of interventions in the post–Cold War era. The concepts of "regime change" and "democracy by force" are largely associated with the wars in Afghanistan in 2001 and Iraq in 2003. Yet, as we will see, the antecedents for these operations lie in the lessons learned from the Dominican Republic, Grenada, and Panama. But before we can address these interventions in detail, we must first briefly review the historical evolution of U.S. policy toward Latin America.

NOTES

1. Kennedy quoted in "The Panama Invasion," 101st Cong., 2nd sess., *Congressional Record* 136, no. 1 (January 23, 1990).

2. The Dominican crisis obviously came before the United States was deeply involved in Vietnam.

3. Quoted in Rick Klein, "Kennedy Calls on U.S. to Begin Troop Pullout," *Boston Globe*, January 28, 2005, 1.

4. Stephen Krasner, *Sovereignty: Organized Hypocrisy* (Princeton, N.J.: Princeton University Press, 1999), 6.

5. Richard Haass, *Intervention* (Washington, D.C.: Carnegie Endowment Press, 1994), 50.

6. Alfred Rubin, "Reason and Law Reject Our Panama Invasion," *New York Times*, January 2, 1990, 18.

7. See Martha Finnemore, *The Purpose of Intervention* (Ithaca, N.Y.: Cornell University Press, 2003), 85–140.

1

The Evolution of U.S. Interventions and Occupations in Latin America

In his critique of then President George H. W. Bush's decision to invade Panama, journalist Michael Massing argued that the United States should not consider invading a Latin American country but rather return to the "principle of nonintervention" in the region. Whatever the efficacy of the doctrine of nonintervention, Massing failed to mention that America's principle of nonintervention in Latin America was the exception to the rule during the twentieth century. On the contrary, the twentieth century was in fact a period of American meddling and cajoling in numerous nations of the Western Hemisphere.

Perhaps a more accurate characterization of American policy in Latin America comes out of the tradition of the "Big Stick." Ever since President Theodore Roosevelt uttered the phrase "speak softly and carry a big stick," the Big Stick as a policy has loomed large in terms of how the United States conducts its relations with the nations of Latin America.[1] Implicit in the idea of the Big Stick foreign policy is how successive American governments have used military force to determine outcomes. And Latin America, in particular the Caribbean basin, is the region most associated with the use of American military force in part because of its proximity and relative lack of external constraints on American power.

But while Roosevelt's adventures in the Caribbean are now fodder for diplomatic historians, the Big Stick as a concept in contemporary U.S. policy toward the region remains. While in certain ways quite different from its "traditional" version at the start of the twentieth century, the Big Stick was alive and well during the three interventions examined in this book.

First, though, we must clarify a number of things about the nature of the historical presence of the United States in Latin America. For starters, scholars of the region have used the term "intervention" far too liberally. Political scientist Peter Smith, for examples, notes that the United States intervened in the Caribbean region over thirty times between 1898 and 1934.[2] But not all instances of U.S. interference were operationally similar, even during the vaunted era of "gunboat diplomacy" at the beginning of the twentieth century. At times, military intervention involved overwhelming force, such as the over 20,000 troops used to invade Panama in 1989. In others, such as during an occupation of Cuba in the early 1900s, U.S. forces did little other than infrastructure reconstruction or electoral supervision. As we will see, over time, and particularly in the post–World War II era, American leaders opted to move toward less visible methods of exercising American power in the region.

An important issue for understanding U.S. policy toward the region concerns the motives of the United States for its interventions. Some scholars have argued that a number of nefarious motivations, such as race, economic gain, and the urge for empire, drive U.S. actions and interventionism.[3] Others have argued that U.S. policy has been determined solely by the legitimate need to defend the region from outside interference.[4] No doubt all these factors have some relevance, but a substantial number of scholars agree that the core motivation was securing America's strategic interests.[5] To be sure, the threats addressed may have at times been largely imaginary and the actions taken misguided or unnecessary, but most American administrations acted in a manner through which they addressed legitimate national security interests (albeit at times with "side benefits," such as access to foreign markets or military bases).[6]

Before proceeding, we must also take into account some important concepts that will shape this chapter. First, the three cases addressed in *Gunboat Democracy* focus on military interventions in the Caribbean basin, not Latin America as a whole. While U.S. policymakers and historians often do not differentiate between areas in Latin America, the distinction is a critical one with regard to the use of force. The countries in Central America and the Caribbean are much closer and generally politically and economically weaker than many of the countries in South America. This grants the United States much greater latitude in using its power in the Caribbean basin, a fact not lost on generations of U.S. officials.[7] Thus, it is not surprising that the Caribbean basin has been the area where the United States has conducted the overwhelming majority of its interventions.[8]

In a certain sense, the ability to maintain a secure and pro-U.S. Central America and Caribbean became an indicator of America's broader self-identification in the world. As former president Ronald Reagan once said, "If we cannot defend ourselves [in the Caribbean basin], we cannot expect to prevail elsewhere. Our credibility would collapse, our alliances would crumble, and the safety of our homeland would be put in jeopardy."[9] But no matter if there were more global considerations involved, American presidents have rarely hesitated to order the use of force when security concerns arise in its backyard. In this sense, strategic concerns, more often than economic ones, served to link the concerns of American administrations from Roosevelt to Kennedy to Reagan.

Yet, while there was a significant amount of continuity among the respective presidential administrations, the types of force used varied throughout the twentieth century. The Big Stick normally meant active intervention in Caribbean affairs, but it did not necessarily lead to the same type of action each time. And contrary to what is sometimes understood by students of the topic, almost all presidents, even "Mr. Big Stick" himself, Theodore Roosevelt, most often preferred nonmilitary means, such as customs receivership and diplomacy, to achieve their goals.

When the United States actually had a hand in military actions in the Caribbean, such actions often took on two forms. First was action by proxy, where the United States funded and trained its opposition forces, such as in the Bay of Pigs in 1961 and support for the *contrarevolucionarios* (*contras*) in Nicaragua in the 1980s. The second was direct military intervention, which was more common in the first part of the century and less used in the second.

THE RISE OF THE BIG STICK

The period known as "gunboat diplomacy" lasted from the late nineteenth century to the first two decades of the twentieth. The key event that

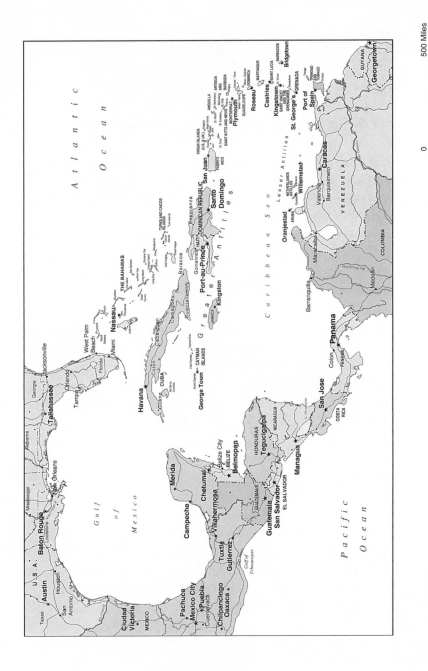

Atlantic Ocean

U.S.A.

Texas

San Antonio

Austin

Houston

Baton Rouge

Louisiana

Mississippi

New Orleans

Alabama

Georgia

Tallahassee

Jacksonville

Orlando

Tampa

West Palm Beach

Florida

Miami

Nassau

THE BAHAMAS

Freeport

Gulf of Mexico

MEXICO

Ciudad Victoria

Pachuca

Mexico City

Cuernavaca

Puebla

Chilpancingo

Oaxaca

Tuxtla Gutierrez

Villahermosa

Gulf of Tehuantepec

Campeche

Chetumal

Merida

Belize City

BELIZE

Belmopan

Guatemala

GUATEMALA

San Salvador

EL SALVADOR

HONDURAS

Tegucigalpa

NICARAGUA

Managua

COSTA RICA

San Jose

PANAMA

Colon

Panama

Pacific Ocean

Havana

CUBA

George Town

CAYMAN ISLANDS

Camagüey

Guantánamo

Baracoa

JAMAICA

Kingston

Greater Antilles

TURKS AND CAICOS ISLANDS

HAITI

Gonaïves

Port-au-Prince

DOMINICAN REPUBLIC

Esperanza

Santo Domingo

San Juan

PUERTO RICO

VIRGIN ISLANDS (U.S. & U.K.)

ANGUILLA

Lesser Antilles

GUADELOUPE

ANTIGUA AND BARBUDA

MONTSERRAT

Plymouth

SAINT KITTS AND NEVIS

DOMINICA

Roseau

MARTINIQUE

Castries

SAINT LUCIA

SAINT VINCENT AND THE GRENADINES

Kingstown

BARBADOS

Bridgetown

GRENADA

St. George's

Port of Spain

TRINIDAD AND TOBAGO

Lesser Antilles

Oranjestad

ARUBA

NETHERLANDS ANTILLES

Willemstad

Caribbean Sea

Maracaibo

Barranquilla

COLOMBIA

Medellín

Barquisimeto

Valencia

Caracas

VENEZUELA

GUYANA

Georgetown

0   500 Miles

0   500 KM

Parallel scale at 20° N 0° E

ushered in this period was the American decision in 1898 to go to war with Spain to end the Spanish occupation of Cuba. Fueled by the "yellow journalism" of the era, many Americans were convinced that Spain had blown up the USS *Maine*; popular and political pressure thus convinced President William McKinley to wrest Cuba free of Spanish rule.[10] The Spanish-American War represented the first serious instance of the United States' use of sizable military power in the Caribbean basin. After easily defeating the Spanish, over the following decades the United States intervened frequently in the Caribbean and Central America, often to combat "chronic instability" and the perceived threat of European incursion.

The development of American hegemony in the Caribbean region continued when Theodore Roosevelt assumed the presidency in 1901. Many scholars believe that Roosevelt was motivated to use American power in the Caribbean for two principal purposes. First, Roosevelt hoped to secure a U.S.-controlled canal route through Central America. The second, more immediate cause was a debt crisis in Venezuela in 1902 that prompted significant attention by British and German bankers. Roosevelt decided that America must create a policy that would deter future encroachment by Europe in the U.S. sphere of influence. Secretary of War Elihu Root announced what became the "Roosevelt Corollary" at a speech in May 1904:

> Any country whose people conduct themselves well can count upon our hearty friendliness. If a nation shows that it knows how to act with decency in industrial and political matters, if it keeps order and pays its obligations, then it need fear no interference from the United States.[11]

But many nations in the Caribbean basin did not heed Root's call, leading Roosevelt to put U.S. boots on the ground. The message of the corollary was clear: unlike the Monroe Doctrine, which told other powers simply to "stay out," Washington now reserved the right to intervene in the internal matters of nearby countries to address instability. Quickly, Washington discovered that "gunboats" were an effective and relatively cost-free way of determining outcomes in a region that was increasingly under America's sphere of influence. For the first three decades of the twentieth century, barely a year went by when the United States was not conducting some sort of intervention in a Central American or Caribbean country.

As was stated earlier, these interventions ranged widely in their duration and extent of the occupation. Haiti, Nicaragua, Cuba, Honduras, Panama, the Dominican Republic, and Mexico constitute some of the countries that were touched by the Big Stick. Again, a historical debate continues as to the significance of these episodes. It is safe to say, however, that U.S. occupations often did not lead to the lasting development of stable domestic political and economic institutions that was often hoped for. Another competing view is that it was the instability *before* American interventions that was usually the underlying problem and that, if anything, U.S. occupations helped alleviate some of the misery and instability.[12]

These sorts of debates aside, Washington dispatched warships, troops, and political advisers to allow countries to supervise elections, build infrastructure, structure and enforce debt payments, quell insurrections, and even establish democracy. Many interventions took on a familiar shape: large-scale deployments of American forces for short periods of time, followed by short-term occupations that regulated elections and financial issues. The United States often left quickly after elections occurred or debt restructuring was under way, not eager to annex any of the Caribbean nations.

It merits mention that the three presidents most identified with gunboat diplomacy—Theodore Roosevelt, William Howard Taft, and Woodrow Wilson—all used similar tools to advance their goals in Latin America. Above all, three presidents firmly believed that the United States had a right and at times a duty to intervene in the region. While Taft's legacy is inextricably linked to the notion of "dollar diplomacy" (the term is meant to imply more of an emphasis on economic interests in the region), his "dollar diplomats" nevertheless did not hesitate to use American troops when it best suited their needs.[13]

Similarly, Woodrow Wilson, whose missionary zeal led him to detest colonial rule, was also quite comfortable using military force. In fact, Wilson intervened more often—and his occupations ended up lasting much longer—than his two predecessors. To be sure, Wilson wanted democracy or, in his words, "to teach the South American republics to elect good men." But Wilson squarely put security before democracy, a prioritization that led him into several interventions in Mexico and the Caribbean basin. In this sense, Wilson is similar to future presidents, such as John F. Kennedy, Lyndon Johnson, and even Ronald Reagan, who ultimately placed security before democracy in the region.

THE ERA OF THE GOOD NEIGHBOR

By the end of the 1920s, the priorities of the United States had shifted significantly. Following the carnage of the World War I, the concepts of anti-imperialism and isolationism were becoming increasingly popular among the American public. The Great Depression forced the U.S. government to look inward and find ways to reform its shattered economic institutions. On top of that, popular resentment of American occupations in countries such as Haiti and Nicaragua were growing. A sort of "intervention fatigue" had set in Washington. It was time for a less intrusive strategy, one that would promote hemispheric solidarity and lower America's burden of intervention and occupation. Thus, while it was certainly as much strategic and self-serving as it was altruistic, by the late 1920s the era of the "good neighbor" was about to begin.

Although Franklin D. Roosevelt is credited for creating the "Good Neighbor Policy," the beginnings of nonintervention in the Americas started during the presidency of Herbert Hoover. Facing growing popular opposition to U.S. intervention at home and abroad, Hoover and his advisers expressed interest in easing American occupation in the Caribbean. Hoover himself publicly stated that "it ought not to be policy of the United States to intervene *by force* to secure or maintain contracts between our citizens and foreign states or their citizens."[14] Later, a memorandum by his undersecretary of state, Reuben Clark, repudiated the Roosevelt Corollary, although Hoover later distanced himself from the statements.[15] In addition, Hoover supported efforts to end the seemingly intractable American occupation of Nicaragua.

An interest in moving away from active military action in Central America and the Caribbean was one of the few things that Hoover and Roosevelt held in common politically. It ultimately was Franklin Delano Roosevelt who formally argued that the United States should move away from the Big Stick and toward a new, less intrusive policy in the region. In an article in the journal *Foreign Affairs* in 1928, Roosevelt argued for a new version of the Monroe Doctrine. "Single-handed intervention by us in the internal affairs of other nations must end; with the cooperation of others we shall have more order in this hemisphere and less dislike," he wrote.[16] After his election, Roosevelt and his advisers remained committed to the goal of nonintervention, a position aided by the lack of immediate security threats abroad. At an address on March 4, 1933, Roosevelt stated,

> In the field of world policy, I would dedicate this nation to the policy of the good neighbor—the neighbor who resolutely respects himself and, because he does so, respects the rights of others—the neighbor who respects his obligations and respects the sanctity of his agreements in and with a world of neighbors.[17]

The Good Neighbor Policy emphasized trade and cooperation in the hemisphere over unilateral military intervention and occupation. It broadly defined U.S. policy for the next twenty years.

Roosevelt's first move in the direction of noninterference was completing the withdrawal of U.S. troops from Nicaragua in 1933. He did not, however, switch to entirely peaceful means to achieve his policy goals. For example, later that year, widespread instability and protest broke in Cuba. Roosevelt came under intense pressure from his advisers to order American soldiers to quell the problem. The president declined to send troops but ordered U.S. warships posted in front of the island.[18] In this case, the gunboats were not used but still remained close at hand.

Cuba proved to be the only major test to the Good Neighbor, however. Instead of American boots on the ground, Washington now eyed the new gathering threat of Nazism and fascism, which appeared to be spreading to Latin America. Paradoxically, the onset of World War II reinforced a softer American approach toward its backyard. Washington needed allies in its war against fascism, and Latin America's proximity made it the logical place to look for them. Also knowing that the region was a key source for precious raw materials, the Roosevelt administration aggressively worked to forge strong relations with Latin American countries. So, for example, when Mexican President Lázaro Cárdenas nationalized several oil companies owned by foreign investors, Roosevelt held off on using force and compromised on the oil expropriation.[19]

Roosevelt's Good Neighbor Policy was an important change in U.S. policy. For the first time, Washington deemphasized the military option as a way of achieving desired results in its neighboring countries. But the policy was not an ideological one. Roosevelt saw it as a prudent and pragmatic way of attaining good relations with Latin America at a time when the United States desperately needed to focus on winning World War II. Nonetheless, the Good Neighbor at times turned a blind eye to the growth of dictatorship in countries such as Nicaragua and the Dominican Republic.

But even with the lack of boots on the ground, U.S. policy still underwent an important shift. At the Pan-American Conference at Bogotá in 1948, the United States expressed for the first time its concern about communist penetration into Latin America. In that the Organization of American States was founded to provide for the collective security of the hemisphere, Washington was now using the Good Neighbor tools (noninterference, hemispheric cooperation, and multilateralism) to promote more realistic ends: anticommunism. Whatever the case, as it had done during the 1930s, the United States spearheaded a number of initiatives aimed at directly creating multilateral institutions and indirectly continuing its growing battle against communism. In 1950, the assistant secretary of state for inter-American affairs laid out a new version of the Good Neighbor Policy:

> The fact is that the doctrine of nonintervention [under the Good Neighbor] never did proscribe the assumption by the organized community of a legitimate concern with any circumstances that threatened the common welfare. On the contrary it made the possibility of such action imperative. Such a collective undertaking, far from representing intervention, is the alternative to intervention. It is the corollary of nonintervention.[20]

No matter what the full intentions were in promoting more multilateral approaches and institutions in the hemisphere, as the years went by, fighting communism became the preeminent security (and, by extension, foreign policy) concern in the region. After a tour of the region in the early 1950s, veteran U.S. diplomat George Kennan, one never particularly impressed with Latin America, offered an extremely pessimistic assessment of the fight against communism in the region. Arguing that the Communist foe was a vicious one, Kennan urged that the United States should not hesitate "before police repression by the local government" if such policies helped check Soviet influence.[21] In essence, anticommunism had eclipsed the Good Neighbor. The shift in focus to *internal threats* from within the hemisphere now made the use of force much more likely. In time, the Big Stick would make its comeback.

THE BIG STICK IN THE COLD WAR ERA

The Good Neighbor era might have ended following Kennan's visit to Latin America. His dire warnings of communist expansion resonated in a country that was becoming terrified of communism's seemingly inexorable spread across the globe. First it took over in Eastern Europe, then Berlin, and then Korea. It was only a matter of time before Latin America was under siege, many policymakers believed.

The first real instance of the Big Stick in its Cold War, anti-Communist form took place in Guatemala. New president Dwight D. Eisenhower, while a Republican, initially looked to pursue much the same policies as Truman had. Deterring communism was at the center of the new administration's Latin America policy. While Secretary of State John F. Dulles treaded carefully, saying that the United States did not support "interference in the internal affairs of any republic," he was clear that the administration would not tolerate the presence of "political institutions which serve alien masters."[22] Diplomat Richard Paterson set a benchmark for intervention with his "quacks like a duck" test, whereby regimes that resembled Soviet ideology but were not openly pro-Soviet still represented a significant security threat to America.[23]

Eisenhower's fears about leftist governments in the Caribbean basin came to a head after the election of President Jacobo Arbenz in Guatemala in 1950. While Arbenz was not himself a Communist, his advocacy of land reform, nationalization of economic activities, and the number of leftists in his government greatly worried the United States.[24] Secretary Dulles and brother CIA chief Allen Dulles also allegedly pushed action because of their extensive ties to the United Fruit Company, which had extensive operations in Guatemala. Most important, however, was the fear that the new government's economic nationalism (and its incipient relations with the Soviet Union and Eastern bloc countries), would move it inexorably toward communism. To a Washington in the throes of anticommunism, Arbenz was a duck. He needed to go.

The American-backed coup in Guatemala provides an interesting new take on U.S. military intervention in Latin America. Guatemala was at the heart of America's "sphere of influence," so outright invasion was possi-

THE EVOLUTION OF U.S. INTERVENTIONS IN LATIN AMERICA

ble, but Eisenhower chose a coup by proxy instead. Fascinated by the idea of covert operations, the administration authorized the CIA to engineer the removal of Arbenz.[25] A relatively small group of anti-Arbenz fighters led by Colonel Castillo Armas entered the country from Honduras and, backed by CIA bombing operations, managed to frighten the army into removing Arbenz from his post in favor of a military junta. Armas's new regime, neither democratic nor reformist, satisfied the U.S. demands for strict anticommunism.

This episode provides an interesting twist on the traditional gunboat method of U.S. policy. Rather than commit to an invasion or other sort of occupation, as was often the case in the early decades of the century, this time Washington opted for a covert operation, allowing it to exert power less visibly and without involving the use of American troops. It is not difficult to see why the United States began to experiment with this approach: it provided all the benefit of the Big Stick without the glaring association with American interventionism and heavy-handedness that had marked prior eras.[26]

Intervention by proxy thus attempted to blend some of the aspects of the most successful policy tools of the United States. Nevertheless, "regime change" in Guatemala proved to be enormously unpopular in the hemisphere. Governments across Central and South America complained bitterly about the replacement of Arbenz with a military dictatorship.[27] In a visit to Venezuela in 1958, Vice President Richard Nixon's motorcade was pelted by crowds throwing stones. The next administration decided that a new approach to Caribbean policy was needed.

AN ILL-FATED ALLIANCE AND THE RETURN OF THE BIG STICK

Latin America, somewhat surprisingly, became a major issue for John F. Kennedy as he ran for president. Before his election in 1960, the political situation in the Caribbean basin and Central America had been altered dramatically by the successful leftist revolution in Cuba in 1959. Now the American backyard contained a Communist regime with growing military and political ties to the Soviet Union. Kennedy criticized his predecessor's approach to Latin America, suggesting that Eisenhower had failed to address the roots of the Cuban insurrection. Kennedy saw his task as to head off both. It is difficult to underemphasize the impact that Fidel Castro's rapidly consolidated Marxist revolution in Cuba had on American policymakers. And there was good reason to be greatly concerned about Cuba. In 1962, the United States and Soviet Union came to the brink of global nuclear war over the question of nuclear missiles positioned on the island.

In its unyielding position of placing the combat against Communist expansion above all other priorities, the Kennedy administration demonstrated a remarkable amount of continuity with Eisenhower in the Americas. Calling Latin America "the most dangerous area of the world," Kennedy believed his first priority was to check the anti-U.S. revolutionary tide in the region and secure the United States against external threats in its traditional backyard. Like his predecessors, Kennedy also believed strongly that Washington had the right to intervene if the threat of a communist takeover was imminent. While attempting to show deference to Roosevelt's Good Neighbor Policy, the president announced that if "any Latin country be driven by repression into the arms of the Communists, our attitude on nonintervention would change overnight."[28] Troops would be dispatched to promote critical American interests if need be.

And indeed Kennedy did intervene militarily to support his objectives. Hoping to dispatch Cuban leader Fidel Castro quickly and inheriting a plan started while Eisenhower was still in office, the Kennedy administration hoped to enact regime change with a CIA-backed coup carried out by Cuban exiles.[29] Like Guatemala in 1954, the Bay of Pigs invasion of 1961 was an example of U.S. power by proxy rather than the direct military ventures of earlier days. Washington supported and financed the operation, but no American soldiers took part in the fighting. Unlike the Arbenz coup, however, the Bay of Pigs proved to be a disaster. Castro held much stronger support on the island than government officials had estimated, and his supporters put down the invading forces. Embarrassed by its failures, the Kennedy administration eased off the pressure on Castro and stayed away from the direct use of force to prevent communism throughout the rest of the hemisphere.[30]

Kennedy's major innovation in Latin America policy was in his Alliance for Progress. Realizing that revolution could not be stopped solely by force, Kennedy saw the need to aggressively promote structural economic and democratic reforms as an alternative to socialist upheaval. In a speech on March 13, 1961, he announced,

Unless necessary social reforms, including land and tax reforms, are freely made—unless we broaden the opportunity of all our people—unless the great mass of Americans share in increasing prosperity—then our alliance, our revolution and our dream will have failed.[31]

In this sense, while still idealistic, at their core Kennedy's democracy-building initiatives were primarily about using noncoercive means to stop communism. Thus, the United States once again attempted to involve itself deeply in the affairs of its neighbors but this time through diplomacy and millions of dollars in development aid. Kennedy's "Marshall Plan" for the Americas proposed that $100 billion be spent on economic development.[32] The Kennedy administration also attempted to groom socially progressive, non-Communist reformers, such as Rómulo Betancourt in Venezuela and José Figueres in Costa Rica. The Alliance for Progress was an enormous effort to exert what is now known as "soft power."

Overall, though, the Alliance failed to produce the democratic, stable Latin America that Kennedy had hoped for.[33] This failure resulted from a number of different political and economic factors. First, the number of leaders with whom Kennedy could work remained fairly small, especially in the Caribbean/Central America region. Most countries had few democratic institutions and were often controlled by military regimes. In addition, Washington was ill prepared for such a large venture in a set of very different cultures.

Finally, the political imperative of anticommunism undermined the initiative as well. Kennedy often found it necessary to support stable regimes, which were at times repressive, to ensure the defeat of Communist elements.[34] Foreign aid, perversely enough, served to uphold the status quo as much as it promoted drastic social change. Like the earlier part of the century, nonmilitary means proved unable to advance the type of development and stability that Washington desired.

Kennedy left a confused legacy for U.S. policy in the hemisphere. He found that no certain means of affecting change existed for hemispheric affairs. Military intervention, even if it was limited, failed to unseat Castro. So the Big Stick was not always a wise option, as it risked public relations and diplomatic disasters without guaranteeing success. But the failure of the Alliance for Progress made policymakers realize that soft-power measures, such as aid and diplomacy, could be equally problematic. Whatever the approach, a bipartisan consensus had formed about the need to keep Communist movements in the Caribbean at bay that would last until the Vietnam War.

Whatever chance of success for Kennedy's "revolutionary dream" for Latin America was cut short by his assassination in Texas in 1963. Vice President Lyndon B. Johnson took over the reins as the American president. Johnson's accession to the presidency first seemed to have little effect on policy, as he too was committed to addressing Communist threats in the region.

Yet under the surface, a major shift had occurred. Despite his public affinity for impoverished peoples, Johnson had little interest in Latin America, focusing mostly on events in southern Asia. Further, even though many of Kennedy's key advisers remained in the Johnson administration, the idealism from the Kennedy era had largely dissipated. For example, now the conservative pragmatist Thomas Mann took charge of Latin America policy and competed for influence with Kennedy's more liberal advisers, such as Arthur Schlesinger Jr. Mann encouraged Johnson's inclination to move away from the Alliance for Progress, signaling the beginning of the end of U.S. heightened interest in inter-American economic and social development.

But events in the Dominican Republic prevented Johnson from completely ignoring the Caribbean basin. As we will discuss in detail shortly, in 1965 Johnson ordered over 20,000 American troops into the capital of Santo Domingo. The intervention, the first instance of American boots on the ground in the Caribbean since the 1930s, appeared to signify a shift back to the "traditional" Big Stick. With little time or patience for nonmilitary diplomacy, Johnson saw the need to achieve his goals through overt military force. The newly emerging "Johnson Doctrine" had no instinctive preference for the gunboat diplomacy of earlier decades; rather, as we will see shortly, Johnson's only concern for a country as seemingly irrelevant as the Dominican Republic centered on the strategic interest of keeping Communists out of America's backyard.

THE NIXON–FORD–CARTER LULL
While the Johnson administration largely achieved its goals in the Dominican crisis, the war in Vietnam had an entirely different outcome. In this sense, the success in the Dominican Republic might have led some U.S.

policymakers to believe that the same thing could be accomplished in Vietnam. Whatever the case, mired in a war in Asia that he saw no way out of, President Johnson decided not to pursue a second term.

The staunchly anti-Communist Richard Nixon took his place. Nixon, along with his highly influential foreign policy adviser Henry Kissinger, had even less interest in Latin America than Johnson. Firmly committed to negotiating with the world's great powers, the Nixon team focused on large-scale foreign policy initiatives in Vietnam, Russia, and China. Still, though, like his predecessors, Nixon was committed to seeing that communism in Latin America did not expand under his watch. Ultimately, and somewhat ironically since the region was not a priority, the Nixon–Kissinger years became some of the most controversial in terms of U.S.–Latin America relations because of the administration's involvement in the political chaos that ensued in Chile in the early 1970s.

After the socialist candidate Salvador Allende was democratically elected in 1970, Nixon expressed a desire to block him from taking office.[35] Many critics also point out that Washington subsequently funded efforts to assassinate Allende and destabilize the Chilean economy, a topic that is today still fiercely disputed.[36] While it is certainly not the purpose of this book to resolve the controversy surrounding this episode, we can conclude that Nixon's response to Allende's socialist government in Chile represented one instance of the return to the more covert approach to influencing outcomes in the region.[37] It is also a time when Washington feared the situation enough to turn its attention to what was taking place far away in the Southern Cone of South America as opposed to its normal area of hemispheric strategic concern: Central America and the Caribbean.

The incident showed that Nixon took heed of Kennedy adviser Arthur Schlesinger's advice to avoid believing that America could always enforce its superiority through military intervention.[38] As seen in Chile with the efforts to undermine Allende's government, the Eisenhower–Dulles method of intervention by proxy forged in Guatemala had survived the Bay of Pigs debacle and remained an important part of the U.S. policy arsenal in Latin America.[39]

The only major action of the Nixon presidency involving the Caribbean basin was the beginning of negotiations over the status of the Panama Canal. As we will see shortly, fearing that Panamanian nationalism would erupt as a result of American control of the canal, Kissinger worked to start negotiations to decrease American authority over the canal. Although the negotiations did not reach fruition until the Carter years, the episode could perhaps be compared to Herbert Hoover's general rethinking of the need for intervention to achieve policy goals in the early 1930s.

The Nixon era of relative "benign neglect" in U.S.–Latin American relations illustrates a number of important facts about American intervention in the hemisphere. Most importantly, U.S. presidents, even in the throes of Vietnam, were still willing to authorize efforts to prevent perceived external influences, especially Communist ones, from gaining a foothold in the hemisphere. But for the long-term, a different version of Big Stick foreign policy was in vogue. Indeed, naked intervention of the Johnson type became increasingly infrequent in the 1970s and the 1980s.

Both Nixon and Kissinger preferred to keep their involvement in Chile muted so as not to provoke outcry from the American public or Latin American governments. The resulting policy was a confused one, as U.S. policymakers firmly believed that U.S. involvement in the region was necessary but wanted to minimize the negative publicity. Future U.S. presidents struggled with these new political realities, especially as Central America boiled over in the late 1970s.

After the fall of Allende in 1973, events "settled down" in Latin America. A series of repressive, military-authoritarian governments in countries such as Argentina, Chile, Brazil, and Uruguay firmly held onto power through the 1970s and into the following decade. The most important events that altered American foreign policy toward the world occurred in the United States and not abroad. Rocked by Nixon's Watergate scandal and the failure of Vietnam, Americans began to question their government's foreign policy, especially military intervention in the Third World. A number of liberal Democrats advocating a new foreign policy were swept into power in Congress.[40]

In effect, the Ford and Carter years served as a definitive interlude where successive administrations sought to move away from anticommunism to other priorities. Jimmy Carter entered office in the wake of national scandal promising a new era of honesty and integrity in government. His foreign policy approach marked a major departure from Johnson and Nixon. Taking a keynote from Kennedy, Carter expressed a great deal of interest in Latin America. He also took the focus of American foreign policy away from anticommunism and realism to one of human rights.

Carter, a polymath with strong and public religious convictions, proposed a more honest foreign policy and one that respected human rights and the self-determination of other nations.[41] Arguing that previous administration had "been willing to adopt the flawed and erroneous principles and tactics of our adversaries," Carter believed that the best way to win the Cold War was to lead by example and not by force.[42] A new type of noninterventionism came to Washington. Indeed, Carter appeared to be once and for all putting the Big Stick to rest.

Carter generally avoided making policy decisions that required direct military force. Instead, he continued Nixon's effort to renegotiate ownership of the Panama Canal, spending significant political capital to get Congress to ratify an eventual handover of the canal. He also pushed for a more conciliatory stance toward Castro's Cuba, advocating a loosening of travel and trade restrictions.[43] Additionally, Carter attempted to press military or autocratic regimes in Latin America on human rights violations. While the latter initiatives largely failed, in 1978 the Senate did vote to hand over control of the canal to Panama by the end of the century.

The most critical change in U.S. policy was Carter's strong emphasis on human rights as a goal of U.S. foreign policy. In a speech in May 1977, the president stated that "we have reaffirmed America's commitment to human rights as a *fundamental tenet of our foreign policy*" (emphasis added).[44] This meant that the United States would promote democratic practices and stand up to governments that repressed and tortured their own citizens. In actuality, Carter's belief in the importance of human rights was quite new to American foreign policy. One favorable observer argued, "No Carter administration policy affecting Latin America is as dramatically new as its stand on human rights."[45] The Caribbean basin seemed like the perfect testing ground for the new human rights policy. The United States had enormous power over the region, and aside from Cuba, it appeared free of Communist influence.[46]

The administration had a tremendously difficult time finding a workable human rights policy, however. Carter wanted to play the role of both Franklin Roosevelt and Kennedy, reining in American meddling in Latin American affairs while simultaneously altering internal events in the other American republics. Presidential National Security Council Directive 30 of February 17, 1978, outlined the methods and mechanisms of the human rights policy. The memorandum explicitly ruled out the use of American military power, pointing to methods such as private diplomacy, linking foreign assistance to human rights performance, and public denunciations as the way to unseat repressive governments.[47]

More problematic, however, was that the Cold War still raged between the United States and the Soviet Union, and, no matter its human rights commitment, the Carter administration had no desire to lose this global struggle. By the late 1970s, the security environment in Latin America had changed rapidly. Strong Marxist movements challenged governments in Central America, arousing great concern in Washington.[48] The Carter White House wanted to both distance itself from unsavory reactionary regimes and avoid hostile leftist revolutions.

In Latin America, the Carter administration was torn between its human rights policy and Cold War realism. It could not effectively prioritize one over the other. The result was a sometimes conflicted policy of halfhearted and often counterproductive policies. Above all, events in Central America proved to be the spoiler for Carter's human rights policy. After decades of repressive rule and underdevelopment, regimes in El Salvador and Nicaragua faced credible challenges from revolutionary leftist insurgencies.

Carter originally sought to deal with these efforts through diplomacy. For example, in Nicaragua, Carter never could settle on an appropriate balance between the seemingly imminent victory of the leftist Sandinista forces or the continued Somoza dictatorship.[49] Once the Sandinistas seized power in 1979, Carter attempted diplomacy to keep the situation under control. He even invited the newly formed Sandinista junta to the White House to show that Washington was sincere in working with the new government.

But the United States was still in the midst of the Cold War, and both political and strategic pressures forced Carter to turn away from human rights to an older, more traditional focus on stability and security. Carter's idealism ultimately fell prey to his inability to implement and reconcile his goals for a stable Latin America through solely diplomatic means. The stage was set for fierce ideological conflict in America's backyard throughout the 1980s.

It is clear that the Carter administration was unable to sway Central

American nations such as Nicaragua and El Salvador from their inexorable path toward clashes between the old political and economic elite and their increasingly revolutionary and militant leftist opponents. Interestingly enough, one wonders if Carter would have been more successful at achieving his goals had he been more willing to use a little more Big Stick and if, counterintuitively, such action could have remained consistent with his cherished human rights policies. Nonmilitary means of persuasion once again disappointed U.S. policymakers. But for Carter, military or other forms of direct American involvement were an unacceptable *means* that had no place in America's foreign policy arsenal in its backyard.

REAGAN AND BUSH: FROM COMMUNISM TO DRUGS

The early 1980s altered the course of U.S.–Latin American relations significantly. By 1980, Marxist forces controlled Nicaragua, had made significant gains in El Salvador, and continued to rule in Cuba and Grenada. The fundamental causes of the instability, according to former Assistant Secretary for Inter-American Affairs Viron Vaky, were "poverty, severe socioeconomic inequalities and maladjustments, frustrations about the latter which translate into political strains, and the potential for radicalization."[50] In the context of increasing strain between the United States and the Soviet Union, that potential for radicalization became a major concern for U.S. policymakers. The conservative Committee on Santa Fe declared that the Caribbean basin was "becoming a Marxist-Leninist lake."[51]

On the other side, the political landscape had shifted to the right in the United States. Feeling humiliated by the Iranian hostage crisis in 1979 and bullied by the Soviets in Afghanistan, in 1980 the American public overwhelmingly chose Republican Ronald Reagan over Carter.[52] Reagan proposed a much more assertive anti-Communist policy, feeling that decades of containment had merely allowed the United States to fall behind its Communist rival. Competition in the Third World was a major part of new policies. National Security Decision Directive 17, issued in January 1983, outlines the new White House's thinking on anti-Soviet policy well:

The U.S. must . . . support effectively those Third World states that are willing to resist Soviet pressure or oppose Soviet initiatives hostile to the United States. . . . The U.S. efforts in the Third World must involve an important role for security assistance and foreign military sales, as well as readiness to use U.S. military where necessary to protect vital interests and support endangered Allies and friends.[53]

President Carter's lack of success in the Caribbean helped shape the case for Reagan's more forceful approach to containing and even rolling back global communism. In addition, the Carter administration's tragic failure to rescue American hostages being held in Iran and the Soviet invasion of Afghanistan convinced many voters that he was unable to restore America's strong role on the world stage.

Reagan then became the first Republican president since the beginning of the century to focus strongly on Latin America. Firmly committed to keeping the communism out of America's backyard, Reagan was on offense, not defense, when it came to combating communism in Latin America.

Reagan soon deemphasized Carter's focus on human rights, fearing that it would overshadow the ultimately much more important goal of combating communism. He often employed compelling (if at times exaggerated) rhetoric to demonstrate to the American people what the stakes were in the region. Reagan firmly believed this was a moral struggle of good versus evil. His rhetoric and anti-Communist sentiments aside, Reagan employed a variety of tactics to achieve the goal of a secure Caribbean basin. This has led some more sympathetic observers to compare Reagan's legacy to that of Kennedy's in that both leaders were uncompromising in the belief that America would not wait for events to get out of its control in the region.

The Reagan administration put the use of American forces on the table in Latin America once again. But it was geared less toward direct intervention and more toward a return to the proxy strategy similar to what Eisenhower pursued in Guatemala. Reagan wanted to avoid controversy, so a major thrust of his worldwide anti-Communist policy became to create and support anti-Communist movements within Third World countries.[54]

The convergence of an aggressive foreign policy in the United States and leftist insurgency would make the small region "the main battleground of political and ideological war of the 1980s."[55] The two most visible battles occurred in Nicaragua and El Salvador. In Nicaragua, the Reagan administration faced a consolidated leftist regime friendly to Soviet and Cuban interests. El Salvador was different. It had a relatively moderate government but faced threats from the right-wing oligarchy and leftist insurgents receiving aid from the Sandinistas.[56] In both countries, U.S. policymakers wanted to prevent a Castro situation where anti-American Communist elements held power.

Reagan officials had no tolerance for subversive Marxist activity in the hemisphere, and its responses to these crises demonstrated that they had no qualms with intervention in the affairs of its neighbors. In its own form of subversive activity, the administration decided to support covertly a growing but largely unknown military force of *contras* training in Honduras in the early 1980s. The hope was that the *contras'* military success would put pressure on the Sandinistas to negotiate and end their aid to Salvadoran rebels.[57] This effort appeared at least somewhat like past efforts to arm and train proxies to destabilize Jacobo Arbenz in 1954 and Fidel Castro in 1961.

Policy in El Salvador differed significantly. There Reagan pushed the government to implement political reforms and clean up the unprofessional and often abusive military, hoping to prevent "another Cuba," but also to secure at least the basic elements of electoral democracy.[58] The only instance of Big Stick diplomacy to occur in the Caribbean basin during Reagan's term in office was in Grenada in 1983, as will be discussed later.

As was the case in the past, an intervention fatigue set in during the second Reagan term. By 1984, popular and congressional opposition to Reagan's policies in El Salvador and Nicaragua grew as it appeared to many that neither conflict would subside soon. This was only accelerated by the public scandal over the discovery of the White House's illegal arms sales to Iran to provide monetary support for the *contras*. Reagan had also found a partner in the Soviet Union's Mikhail Gorbachev, and formal diplomacy once again came back into favor in Washington.

The Reagan years provided a new twist on the Big Stick, as administration officials attempted both to speak loudly and to use military means to achieve its goals. On the one hand, Central America remained violent during the 1980s, to which critics argued that Washington's policies did little to ease. They believed that Reagan's "knee-jerk anti-Marxism" may have foreclosed diplomatic policy choices during his first term.[59] On the other hand, while this fact is often not cited in his legacy on Latin America policy, Reagan's almost Wilsonian commitment to promoting electoral democracy in his second term helped rid the region of one its most notorious authoritarian dictators, Chile's Augusto Pinochet. Supports also held up El Salvador as a model of a gradual but lasting democratic transition that isolated extremists on both the left and the right.

Historically, the Reagan era resembled a return to past U.S. policies of intervention. Like Kennedy and Johnson before him, Reagan believed in the use of military intervention to achieve its goals in the Caribbean region. But it also stridently avoided using U.S. troops where possible, especially when it proved politically costly. Scholars will continue to debate Reagan's impact on Central America, but his presidency did not represent nearly the return to military adventurism in the hemisphere that many often associate with his legacy.

BUSH DEALS WITH DRUGS AND THUGS

By the late 1980s, one would have thought that the U.S. policymakers and the public at large would have been happy with the state of U.S.–Latin American relations. Revolution in Central America was slowing, with the Sandinistas receiving a surprising and resounding defeat against the center-right candidate Violeta Chamorro and the civil war in El Salvador coming to a negotiated peace. Even better, Soviet leader Gorbachev had pledged to new president George H. W. Bush that his country would refrain from further aid to leftist groups in the region at a conference at Malta in 1989.[60] Democracy and pro-U.S. governments were on the rise in all countries in the Caribbean region except for Castro's Cuba.

Indeed, Bush's posture toward the region was not unlike that of Lyndon Johnson's, desiring to wipe his hands clean of the region in favor of other foreign policy goals. Bush initially backed off from Big Stick measures, aiding Costa Rican President Oscar Arias in brokering peace agreements in El Salvador and presidential elections in Nicaragua. With no clear external or internal security crises in the works, Bush appeared free to pursue his goal of the economic integration of North America. But an entirely "kindler and gentler" Bush policy in the hemisphere was not to be.[61]

During the late 1980s, a new foreign policy threat rose to the forefront of the public mind: drugs. In September 1989, polls recorded that 64 percent of Americans believed that drugs were the nation's number-one problem.[62] William Bennett, Reagan's head of the newly created Office of National Control Policy, stated, "Drugs are a major threat to our national security."[63] American politicians of all stripes attempted to do something about this seemingly out-of-control drug scourge. And because Latin American nations supplied the vast majority of cocaine to the United States, the southern republics reemerged as a major foreign policy concern.

Not surprisingly, in its redoubled efforts to fight the war on drugs, the Bush administration looked to Panama, where strongman General Manuel Noriega's ties to drug lords and his repressive regime were embarrassing the president. After a period of foot dragging, Bush ordered Noriega captured and his military forces destroyed in a massive invasion involving over 20,000 troops.

CONCLUSION

In the years following the Cold War, the rationale for U.S. policy in Latin America moved away from the older paradigm of a strict focus on security and stability toward dealing with humanitarian crises and narcotics.[64] Yet, as we just observed with the case of Panama in 1989, Washington reserved the right to yield its Big Stick when it thought necessary. More recently, however, Latin America and the Caribbean have fallen off the list of U.S. foreign policy priorities. Outside of trade and investment agreements, Latin America received relatively little attention during either the Bill Clinton or the George W. Bush years. The only major military actions by the United States in the hemisphere have been in Haiti (1994 and 2004) and indirectly in Colombia. These policies are consistent with the lower-priority interests in the region, such as upholding democratic rule (Haiti) and stopping narco-terrorism (Colombia).

The Big Stick has been largely silent in recent years. Yet this is not to mean that it is no longer in American's foreign policy arsenal for the region. Rather, it is dormant. If history is at all predictive, instability in the Americas (the Caribbean basin in particular) may call on the American government to utilize military force to succeed in its goals. From Theodore Roosevelt to George W. Bush, American administrations have sought to preserve American power and credibility through either direct or indirect military action.

Perhaps the most important insight of the history of U.S. military action in the Caribbean and Central America may be that the majority of American presidents and their advisers have viewed the region as a strategic imperative for the country. As a regional (not to mention global) hegemonic power with the ability to project overwhelming military force, the United States has often viewed the existence of security threats, whether internally or externally generated, as unacceptable. Largely because of the tremendous gap in power between the United States and its Caribbean neighbors, America has reserved the right to deploy its military forces to ensure stability favorable to its interest. Almost no American president has refused outright to invade or intervene when events appear to make such an action the safest policy option.

NOTES

1. Quoted in Max Boot, *The Savage Wars of Peace: Small Wars and the Rise of American Power* (New York: Basic Books, 2002), 149.

2. Peter Smith, *Talons of the Eagle: Dynamics of U.S.-Latin American Relations,* 2nd ed. (Oxford: Oxford University Press, 2000), 50.

3. For an example, see Lars Schoultz, *Beneath the United States: A History of U.S. Policy toward Latin America* (London: Harvard University Press, 1998), xv.

4. See Walter F. Hahn, ed., *Central America and the Reagan Doctrine* (Washington, D.C.: United States Strategic Institute, 1987).

5. Both Max Boot's *The Savage Wars of Peace* and Nancy Mitchell's *The Danger of Dreams: German and American Imperialism in Latin America* (Chapel Hill: University of North Carolina Press, 1999) focus largely on power and security as the reason for U.S. interventions.

6. David Healy, *Drive to Hegemony: The United States in the Caribbean, 1898–1917* (Madison: University of Wisconsin Press, 1988), 97. For a more skeptical but similar viewpoint, see Mitchell, *The Danger of Dreams,* 225–26.

7. Robert Pastor, *Whirlpool: U.S. Foreign Policy toward Latin America and the Caribbean* (Princeton, N.J.: Princeton University Press, 1992), 23.

8. Harold Molineu, *U.S. Policy toward Latin America: From Regionalism to Globalism* (Boulder, Colo.: Westview Press, 1986), 55.

9. Quoted in Pastor, *Whirlpool,* 32.

10. Dana G. Munro, *Intervention and Dollar Diplomacy in the Caribbean, 1900–1921* (Princeton, N.J.: Princeton University Press, 1964), 24–25.

11. David Healy, *Drive to Hegemony,* 107.

12. For a sample of this perspective, see Boot, *The Savage Wars of Peace.*

13. Boot, *The Savage Wars of Peace,* 141–48.

14. Bryce Wood, "The Making of the Good Neighbor Policy," in *Neighborly Adversaries: Readings in U.S.-Latin American Relations,* ed. Michael LaRosa and Frank O. Mora (Lanham, Md.: Rowman & Littlefield, 1999), 108.

15. Irwin Gellman, *Good Neighbor Diplomacy: United States Policies in Latin America, 1933–1945* (Baltimore: Johns Hopkins University Press, 1979), 5.

16. Gellman, *Good Neighbor Diplomacy,* 110.

17. Quoted in Michael Kryzanek, *US-Latin American Relations,* 2nd ed. (New York: Praeger, 1990), 53.

18. Frederick B. Pike, *FDR's Good Neighbor Policy: Sixty Years in Generally Gentle Chaos* (Austin: University of Texas Press, 1995), 173.

19. Schoultz, *Beneath the United States*, 306–11.

20. Quoted in Walter LaFeber, *Inevitable Revolutions: The United States in Central America* (New York: Norton, 1983), 94.

21. Quoted in LaFeber, *Inevitable Revolutions*, 107.

22. J. Lloyd Mecham, *The United States and Inter-American Security, 1889–1960* (Austin: University of Texas Press, 1961), 441.

23. LaFeber, *Inevitable Revolutions*, 114.

24. Piero Gleijeses, *Shattered Hope: The Guatemalan Revolution and the United States, 1944–1954* (Princeton, N.J.: Princeton University, Press, 1991), 226–27.

25. Stephen Schlesinger and Stephen Kinzer, *Bitter Fruit: The Untold Story of the American Coup in Guatemala* (Garden City, N.Y.: Doubleday, 1982), 99–100.

26. Piero Gleijeses, *Shattered Hope: The Guatemalan Revolution and the United States, 1944–1954* (Princeton, N.J.: Princeton University Press, 1991), 247.

27. Kryzanek, *US-Latin American Relations*, 58.

28. Stephen G. Rabe, *The Most Dangerous Area in the World: John F. Kennedy Confronts Revolution in Latin America* (Chapel Hill: University of North Carolina Press, 1999), 13.

29. LaFeber, *Inevitable Revolutions*.

30. See Arthur M. Schlesinger Jr., *A Thousand Days: John F. Kennedy in the White House* (Cambridge, Mass.: Houghton Mifflin, 1965).

31. Quoted in Kryzanek, *US-Latin American Relations*, 63.

32. LaFeber, *Inevitable Revolutions*, 148.

33. Jerome Levinson and Juan de Onis, *The Alliance That Lost Its Way: A Critical Report on the Alliance for Progress*, in LaRosa and Mora, *Neighborly Adversaries*, 189–202.

34. Rabe, *The Most Dangerous Area in the World*, 168; LaFeber, *Inevitable Revolutions*, 151.

35. Mark Falcoff, "Kissinger and Chile: The Myth That Will Not Die," *Commentary*, November 1, 2003, www.aei.org/include/news_print.asp?newsID = 19385 (accessed June 23, 2004).

36. See exchange between William D. Rogers and Kenneth Maxwell, "Fleeing the Chilean Coup: The Debate over U.S. Complicity," *Foreign Affairs* (January/February 2004): www.foreignaffairs.org/20040101faresponse83116/william-d-rogers-kenneth-maxwel l/fleeing-the-chilean-coup-the-debate-over-US-complicity.html (accessed July 19, 2004).

37. Falcoff, "Kissinger and Chile"; see also Rogers and Maxwell, "Fleeing the Chilean Coup."

38. Arthur Schlesinger Jr., "The Lowering Hemisphere," *The Atlantic*, January 1970, www.theatlantic.com (accessed August 2, 2004).

39. Kryzanek, *U.S.-Latin American Relations*, 73.

40. Robert Kagan, *A Twilight Struggle: American Power and Nicaragua, 1977–1990* (New York: Free Press, 1996), 29.

41. Seyom Brown, *Faces of Power: Constancy and Change in Foreign Policy from Truman to Clinton* (New York: Columbia University Press, 1994), 311–12; Gaddis Smith, *Last Years of the Monroe Doctrine, 1945–1993* (New York: Hill & Wang, 1994), 140.

42. Jimmy Carter, "Human Rights and Foreign Policy," in *Public Papers of the*

Presidents of the United States: Jimmy Carter, vol. 1 (1977), Basic Documents in Democracy, United States Information Agency, 954, http://usinfo.state.gov/usa/infousa/facts/democrac/demo.htm (accessed August 20, 2004).

43. Robert Pastor, *Whirlpool: U.S. Foreign Policy toward Latin America and the Caribbean* (Princeton, N.J.: Princeton University Press, 1992), 46–47; Abraham Lowenthal, "Jimmy Carter and Latin America," in *Eagle Entangled: U.S. Foreign Policy in a Complex World*, ed. Kenneth Oye, David Rothchild, and Robert Leiber (New York: Longman, 1978), 291.

44. Carter, "Human Rights and Foreign Policy," 954.

45. Lowenthal, "Jimmy Carter and Latin America," 293.

46. Lars Schoultz, *Human Rights and United States Policy towards Latin America* (Princeton, N.J.: Princeton University Press, 1981), 372.

47. Jimmy Carter, "Human Rights/Presidential Directive/NSC-30," 17 February 1978, Jimmy Carter Library, www.jimmycarterlibrary.org/documents/pd30.pdf (accessed August 20, 2004); Brown, *Faces of Power*, 324–27.

48. Pastor, *Whirlpool*, 55.

49. Robert Pastor, *Condemned to Repetition: The United States and Nicaragua* (Princeton, N.J.: Princeton University Press, 1987), 202–7.

50. Viron P. Vaky, "Hemispheric Relations: Everything Is Part of Everything Else," *Foreign Affairs* 59, no. 3 (1980): 623.

51. Pastor, *Whirlpool*, 67.

52. Kagan, *A Twilight Struggle*, 168.

53. Ronald Reagan, "National Security Decision Directive 75," January 17, 1983, Federation of American Scientists Intelligence Resource Program, www.fas.org/irp/offdocs/nsdd/nsdd-075.htm (accessed August 20, 2004).

54. James M. Scott, *Deciding to Intervene: The Reagan Doctrine and American Foreign Policy* (Durham, N.C.: Duke University Press, 1996), 16; Kagan, *A Twilight Struggle*, 204.

55. Kagan, *A Twilight Struggle*, 171; Brown, *Faces of Power*, 460.

56. Pastor, *Whirlpool*, 68.

57. Pastor, *Condemned to Repetition*, 244–45.

58. Thomas Carothers, "The Reagan Years: The 1980s," in *Exporting Democracy: The United States and Latin America*, ed. Abraham Lowenthal (Baltimore: Johns Hopkins University Press, 1991), 92–97; William Leogrande, Douglas C. Bennett, Morris J. Blachman, and Kenneth E. Sharpe, "Grappling with Central America: From Carter to Reagan," in *Confronting Revolution: Security through Diplomacy in Central America*, ed. Morris J. Blachman, William M. Leogrande, and Kenneth Sharpe (New York: Pantheon Books, 1986), 312–13.

59. Brown, *Faces of Power*, 460.

60. Pastor, *Whirlpool*, 84.

61. Brown, *Faces of Power*, 558.

62. Pastor, *Whirlpool*, 91.

63. Quoted in Smith, *Talons of the Eagle*, 287.

64. See Smith, *The Last Years of the Monroe Doctrine, 1945–1993*, 211–14. Smith makes the distinction between the end of the Monroe Doctrine, which he argued ended after the Cold War, and the use of force, which has stayed on to face threats of a different nature.

The Dominican Intervention, 1965

After reading a series of hysterical classified cables from his ambassador in Santo Domingo and on the near unanimous recommendation of his most senior advisers, on the evening of April 30, 1965, President Lyndon Johnson made the decision for the U.S. military to intervene in an incipient civil war that had broken out in the Dominican Republic almost a week earlier. When viewed in the light of repeated interventions by the United States in Central America and the Caribbean—including the Dominican Republic (in 1905 and 1916)—in the first three decades of the twentieth century, this decision should not have raised many eyebrows. Indeed, the physical involvement of the United States in what were overwhelmingly domestic Dominican affairs could be viewed as an extension of American "Big Stick" hegemonic policies in its traditional neighborhood.

Yet, while there is no doubt that the traditional method of the United States of responding to conflict and potential threats was learned in previous decades and in previous adventures, the Dominican case is also instructive in that by 1965 it represented a marked departure from the norms of interhemispheric relations established leading up to and after World War II.[1] As was discussed in the previous chapter, President Franklin Roosevelt's "Good Neighbor Policy" began a retrenchment from direct intervention and occupation in Latin America, replaced by the creation of an interwoven set of multilateral treaties that supported the concepts of state sovereignty and nonintervention.

Thus, the Dominican intervention represented a return to an approach that had been dormant for over thirty years. Again, this is not to say that

during this time the United States refrained from meddling in domestic
Latin American affairs—the overthrow of Jacobo Arbenz in Guatemala in
1954 and the Bay of Pigs operation in 1961 are two important examples.
Rather, until Johnson ordered the first batch of 400 or so Marines to land
outside of Santo Domingo, direct intervention had been dormant.

The reappearance of the Big Stick as the chief weapon in the U.S. arsenal is the main reason that so many historians and political scientists have
condemned the 1965 intervention. Abraham Lowenthal, for example, in
his seminal work on the U.S. intervention, writes that it was "a tragic
event, costly to the Dominican Republic, to the United States, and to
inter-American relations."[2] For diplomatic historian Piero Gleijeses, U.S.
intervention ended the "five glorious days" of a democratic uprising.[3]

Many critics concluded that the heavy-handed and military response to
what was largely an internal crisis manifested the unwillingness of the
United States to allow Latin Americans to control their own destinies.
They also maintained that the United States was interested solely in its
own, narrowly defined national interests and was willing to sacrifice the
principles of democracy, sovereignty, and nonintervention in the process.

While the United States certainly acted in its own self-interest in the
Dominican case, it is also true that the methods and goals desired by the
Johnson administration had changed noticeably since earlier "golden"
eras of U.S. interventions in the region. In addition to the nonintervention
principles of the Good Neighbor Policy, as we saw in the last chapter the
advent of the Alliance for Progress in 1961 had shifted U.S. priorities away
from combating instability (read communism) by supporting progressive
reformers in the region.

In fact, the very political figure (Juan Bosch) that the United States
opposed during the events of 1965 was seen as an archetypal reformer
back in 1962, when he was democratically elected president of the Dominican Republic. In other words, the Johnson administration's decision to
intervene was one made reluctantly, knowing full well that the preference
would have been for Bosch to have remained president after his election
and to have implemented the necessary social and economic reforms that
would have preempted any efforts for more radical elements to foment a
Communist takeover.

What is also overwhelmingly clear is that, democracy or no democracy,
Bosch or no Bosch, the Johnson administration was not going to allow

"another Cuba" in the Dominican Republic. Gleijeses has written that the underlying reason for the intervention was that Washington could not stand to see a returned Bosch, who, while not in Castro's camp, was a reformer who remained fiercely independent from U.S. economic and political hegemony.[4] As we will see, this conclusion is debatable. Rather, the Johnson administration would have likely tolerated an independent and stable Bosch government as the Kennedy administration did back in 1962; it certainly had bigger fish to fry with the looming issue of Vietnam. Yet what it would not stomach was a victory for the pro-Bosch revolt that then turned into a Communist takeover.

Some will continue to make the case that Washington ended "five glorious days" of leftist revolt in Santo Domingo. But any balanced analysis of the crisis must also ask what could have transpired had the United States not intervened. It is not unreasonable to ponder that without U.S. intervention there also could have very easily been 500 "glorious days" of violent civil war or five or fifty "glorious" years of communism.

Gleijeses convincingly shows that Dominican Communists were largely marginal players in the pro-Bosch revolt and might not have been able to commandeer the revolt even if the United States had not intervened. Yet this fact does not change the reality that Washington perceived the threat to be serious, even if there was a significant amount of internal debate inside the administration about its exact extent.

Perhaps a better way of viewing the situation is to accept that at least *some* risk of a Communist takeover existed and that it was enough of one that Washington was going to act to ensure that it did not come to life. The relative ease of intervening in the Dominican Republic (because of its size, geographic proximity, and lack of significant hostile opposing force) made the military option appealing compared to doing nothing or relying on negotiations to ensure a favorable outcome.

This is particularly true in the case of the Dominican crisis as the situation was moving tremendously fast and reporting from Santo Domingo was sporadic and incomplete. Several authors have argued that intense diplomacy by U.S. officials in Santo Domingo could have defused the crisis and ensured the creation of a non-Communist Bosch government. Yet as we will see, there is insufficient evidence to suggest that this outcome could have been guaranteed. Moreover, if there was any guarantee, it certainly did not have the assurances that the Marines and 82nd Airborne gave to the Johnson administration.

A strong case can be made that the Johnson administration overreacted in the Dominican Republic. The often-argued point is that the initial dispatch of Marines to protect U.S. citizens was warranted, but the subsequent decision to send the 82nd Airborne into the heart of the fighting in Santo Domingo was when Washington went too far. The difficulty with this reasoning is that it had been made after the United States actually successfully ended most of the fighting and, after a period of several months of difficult negotiations, brokered an agreement that led to democratic elections in 1966.

In fact, Bosch's supporters were more receptive to the final U.S.-brokered agreements than were the anti-Bosch forces. We do not know what would have happened if the United States had stayed out of the fray entirely or just relied on diplomacy. There is good reason, though, to believe that the situation could have been much worse, as both pro- and anti-Bosch forces were far from defeated. An all-out civil war was not out of the question.

Given the type of intelligence that top U.S. officials were receiving and the innate fear of a second Cuba, President Johnson's decision to intervene in the Dominican crisis becomes more understandable. Yet the manner in which the Johnson administration portrayed this action to the American public had important costs that would eventually severely damage Johnson's more important foreign policy concerns, namely, Vietnam.

Seeing as how one legitimate—but certainly not the major—reason for the intervention was the protection of American lives, the Johnson administration used the rescue of Americans as its first public explanation for the operation. Soon after, however, it decided to focus on the Communist threat and often made exaggerated claims to reinforce the perceived danger. Thus, a "credibility gap" opened up when many of the administration's allegations about Communist involvement in the revolt were refuted. Indeed, many journalists and members of Congress—Arkansas Senator and Foreign Relations Committee Chairman J. William Fulbright chief among them—started to sense something was wrong with the Dominican intervention not long after the invasion had occurred. Distrust of the administration's motives and promises grew.

Yet, while the Johnson administration's often disingenuous or incorrect remarks hurt its credibility with Congress and the American public, this fact alone does not undermine the initial motives that prompted the administration to intervene in the Dominican Republic. Exaggeration or not, President Johnson and his advisers were terrified of a Communist takeover and believed that a swift intervention was their most effective response. What is unfortunate is that the Johnson administration did not need to resort to hyperbole to make a convincing case that an intervention by the United States would protect American lives, quell the violence, prevent a Communist takeover, and usher in relatively free elections in just over a year. In fact, all of that happened. To understand the events of 1965, we first need to review the Dominican Republic's tumultuous history leading up to this critical year, especially its relationship with the United States.

THE UNITED STATES, THE DOMINICAN REPUBLIC, AND THE RISE OF TRUJILLO

In the decades following its independence in 1844, the Dominican Republic was ravaged by domestic revolts and foreign plunder. In fact, before the dictator Rafael Trujillo came to power in the early 1930s, the Dominican Republic had no fewer than 123 rulers, including French and Spanish governors, a Colombian governor and president, and Haitian presidents.[5] Rebellions and counterrebellions dominated the domestic political scene; externally, both U.S. and European power coveted the island nation's economic riches.[6] In something that will be an important element in the U.S. intervention of 1965, political instability had been the norm in the Dominican Republic, not the exception. The Dominican Republic was also increasingly valued for its strategic location, above all the Samaná peninsula, which could be used as a coaling station for warships.

Often during the second half of the nineteenth century, U.S. officials negotiated with their Dominican counterparts over various treaties that would grant special concessions for U.S. interests.[7] None of these attempted efforts proved lasting until, on November 29, 1869, a U.S.–Dominican bilateral treaty was signed that called for the Dominican Republic's annexation to the United States. Dominican leader President Buenaventura Báez ordered an immediate plebiscite on the annexation issue and warned that opposition to the treaty could mean imprisonment, forced exile, and even death.[8]

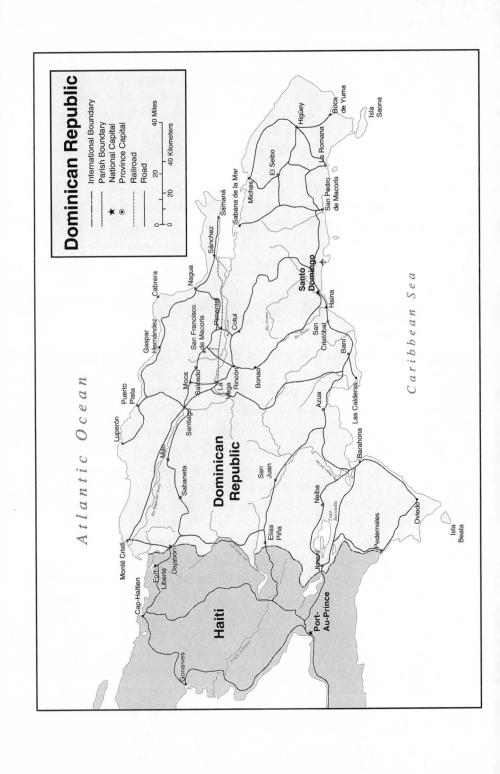

Dominican Republic

International Boundary
Parish Boundary
★ National Capital
⊙ Province Capital
Railroad
Road

0   20   40 Miles
0   20   40 Kilometers

Atlantic Ocean

Caribbean Sea

Cap-Haïtien
Fort-
Liberté
Dejabón
Monte Cristi
Gonaïves
Haiti
Port-
Au-Prince

Luperón
Puerto
Plata
Gaspar
Hernández
Cabrera
Nagua
Santiago
Mao
Sabaneta
Moca
Salcedo
La
Vega
Rincón
San Francisco
de Macorís
Pimentel
Cotuí
**Dominican
Republic**
Bonao
San
Juan
Elías
Piña
Jimaní
Neiba
Lago
Enriquillo
Azua
Baní
San
Cristóbal
Haina
Las Calderas
Barahona
Pedernales
Oviedo
Isla
Beata
Santo
Domingo
San
Sánchez
Samaná
Sabana de la Mar
Miches
El Seibo
San Pedro
de Macorís
La Romana
Higüey
Boca
de Yuma
Isla
Saona

Río Grande
Río Yuna

On February 19, 1870, Dominicans supported the proposed annexation by a vote of 16,000 in favor and 11 against. The treaty then went to the U.S. Senate, where a bitter, protracted debate ensued. Senator Charles Sumner, chairman of the Senate Foreign Relations Committee, led the opposition. According to Sumner, "Kindness, assistance, aid, help, protection, all this is implied in good neighborhood, this we must give freely, bountifully; but [the Dominican people's] independence is as precious to them as is ours to us, and it is placed under the safeguard of natural laws which we cannot violate with impunity."[9] The support of half of the fifty-six senators was not enough, and the annexation treaty was defeated.

In the years following the treaty's defeat, the Dominican Republic continued its now routine pattern of revolts and instability. On September 1, 1882, General Ulisés Heureaux was inaugurated as president, marking only the second time in the Dominican Republic's history that a president was elected and inaugurated according to the constitution.[10] While his first term was relatively uneventful, Heureaux's attempts to extend his term in office led him to become increasingly repressive. In fact, Heureaux can be compared to the country's most brutal twentieth-century dictator, Rafael Leonidas Trujillo Molina.

By the end of the nineteenth century, two separate rebellions began against Heureaux's rule. In 1899, President Heureaux was assassinated by one of the leaders of the opposition, General Ramón Cáceres. That same night, another rebellion leader, General Horacio Vásquez, along with about two dozen followers, declared the revolution of July 26, 1899. Following the murder, rebel groups fought wars against each other; various governments came and went for the next several years. Political and economic stability remained elusive, even though the hated dictator had been removed. To gain a strategic upper hand, various Dominican leaders requested U.S.-protectorate status. In one particular case, a Dominican president reopened the annexation question, to which then president Theodore Roosevelt famously responded, "As for annexing the island, I have about the same to desire to annex it as a gorged boa constrictor might have to swallow a porcupine wrong-end-to."[11]

While Roosevelt's colorful language demonstrated a genuine American reluctance to irrevocably take over political control of the island, this is did not mean that the United States did not maintain political and economic interests in the Dominican Republic. Above all, U.S. policies focused on the collection of debts owed to U.S. creditors and the perceived strategic challenge from European nations, especially Germany.[12] Indeed, President Roosevelt's famous "corollary" to his annual speech to Congress in 1904 set out an aggressive U.S. stance in Central America and the Caribbean, one focused on stamping out "chronic wrongdoing" (especially fiscal wrongdoing toward U.S. creditors) committed by Latins themselves.

One of the first applications of the Roosevelt Corollary came in the Dominican Republic in 1905, when, in an operation that was decidedly more "fiscal" than military, the United States established a customs receivership in the country.[13] American authorities quickly began to administer key elements of Dominican society in order to satisfy foreign creditors' claims. In something that seems remarkable viewed from today, the United States decided that it would carry out debt collection itself and distribute the revenue to the Dominican government and its creditors, both American and European.[14] That debt collection would also allow U.S. officials to keep an eye on the feared German naval presence in the Caribbean was an additional advantage not lost on Washington.

Cáceres became president of the Dominican Republic in 1906, and the following five years became the longest period of stable government in the country's history up until that point. Cáceres's government built roads and schools and reformed public institutions and quelled several revolts without resorting to widespread repression. His tenure as president was cut short when he was assassinated on November 19, 1911. The country went into chaos. The U.S. government responded to the deteriorating situation by becoming increasingly involved in Dominican affairs.[15]

In April 1916, another civil war broke out on the island. In a foreshadow of the events of 1965, on orders given by President Wilson with the "deepest reluctance," a month later U.S. troops came ashore and occupied Santo Domingo with the initial goal of protecting American lives.[16] Wilson's Dominican policy had started out in the beginning of his first term as electoral intervention and by 1916 had evolved into military intervention and ended with a military occupation.[17] Then, on November 29, 1916, Captain Harry S. Knapp announced from his ship the USS *Olympia* that the United States would be occupying the Dominican Republic, an operation that would last eight years.[18]

Knapp's orders were to pacify the country, which he achieved by disarming it. Amazingly, Knapp proved quite successful in confiscating guns and ammunition largely by his willingness to use force to do this.[19] In addition to pacifying the country, the United States wanted to put an end to the regional caudillos who were responsible for much of inveterate instability and violence. In an effort to establish a professional, apolitical military force that could ensure stability once the U.S. occupation ended, the U.S. military also dissolved the Dominican army and established a national guard that came to be known as the Policia Nacional Dominicana (PND). Yet, while the pacification policy was largely successful, U.S. Marines had a more difficult time in the eastern provinces, such as Seibo and San Pedro de Macrorís. Many Dominicans resisted the disarmament campaign and instead took to the hills. The Marines considered them bandits and hunted them down. Atrocities were committed on both sides.[20]

In addition to its military-led pacification campaign, the U.S. military built a number of roads, schools, post offices, piers, and telegraph systems; increased teachers' salaries and agricultural production; improved sanitation; and reformed the country's financial system.[21] While U.S.-built public works are an undisputed fact of the occupation, some historians argue that the motives for these works were far less than altruistic. One has written that almost all the roads built were done so for military purposes. Another interpretation of the occupation is that it allowed U.S. economic interests to take over the Dominican Republic's one key industry: sugar.[22] John Martin, who was the U.S. ambassador during Juan Bosch's presidency, probably said it best when he wrote,

> In sum, it is probably fair to say that our occupation of the Republic was neither so bad as Dominican nationalists picture it nor so good as our own used to picture it and that, coupled with the Marine occupations of Nicaragua and Haiti, it damaged our position in the Hemisphere more than in the Dominican Republic itself.[23]

Military personnel dominated the U.S. presence in the Dominican Republic during the eight-year occupation. The quality of officers, though, was not always the best, as many were often sent to fight in Europe following the American commitment to World War I. The U.S. Department of State officials were often political appointees who lacked even rudimentary language skills and experience in the region.[24] Yet the nature of the occupation changed markedly in the early 1920s as seasoned diplomats such as Sumner Welles began to gain control of the political and economic administration on the island.

In 1922, Welles was named the commissioner to the republic with the rank of envoy extraordinary and minister plenipotentiary, and he had one main task: to secure the withdrawal of the occupation forces. After an extremely difficult time balancing the various political factions, in preparation for upcoming presidential elections in 1923 a provisional government was installed, electoral laws were implemented, voters were registered, and polling places were created. The aging general Horacio Vásquez won the election held on March 15, 1924, and for the first time in Dominican history the losing candidate congratulated the winner.[25]

The idea of removing the Marines started soon after the end of World War I, yet it ended up taking years of fighting among various Dominican factions and years of negotiation with U.S. authorities before an acceptable settlement and framework was reached.[26] By the time it ended in November 1924, the occupation had left behind an elected government, a professional police force, a stronger financial position, and seeming internal stability. The PND had now become a modern, centralized force that held a virtual monopoly over the use of lethal force.[27]

For American policymakers, the withdrawal of the Marines and the establishment of a democratic government in Santo Domingo indicated a successful policy. Welles wrote that "a new era of liberty and independence had commenced."[28] At the same time, though, the occupation created considerable bitterness throughout the local population. As we will see, only six years after the end of the U.S. military government, the Dominican Republic's "democracy" fell to the long-term Trujillo dictatorship.[29]

THE MARINES GO HOME AND TRUJILLO RISES TO POWER

The rise of dictator Rafael Trujillo is often portrayed as a direct result of the U.S. military's establishment and training of local police forces that, on the American departure, turned into institutions of political repression and autocratic rule. For example, Peter Smith writes that in the U.S. occupation of the Dominican Republic (as well as Haiti and Nicaragua),

Washington supervised the creation of local constabularies that would eventually become the agents of dictatorial repression. Not only did the United States fail to promote democratic development in Latin America; it could even be argued with considerable reason that U.S. military interventions tended to retard the prospects for political democracy.[30]

Yet what Smith overlooks is that the Dominican Republic never enjoyed even the semblance of "political democracy" that could have been retarded by the U.S. occupation. A more balanced interpretation is that, in an era when Washington was moving away from direct intervention in the region, U.S. indifference following the 1924 withdrawal (such as its unwillingness to intervene to prevent the fraudulent 1930 elections) helped allow a schemer such as Trujillo to take advantage of the still fragile political situation.[31] In this sense, it is perhaps more U.S. involvement and meddling, not less, that kept a figure such as Trujillo at bay.[32]

Trujillo entered the newly formed PND in 1918 and took advantage of the social mobility that it offered to a mulatto (or mixed-blood Dominican) such as him.[33] Trujillo quickly ingratiated himself with American officers and soon found himself promoted to major in 1924, the same time that American forces were withdrawing from the island. American military officers described Trujillo as "calm, even-tempered, forceful, active, bold, and painstaking . . . one of the best in the service."[34]

In December of that same year, newly elected president Vásquez promoted Trujillo to lieutenant colonel and assigned him as chief of staff of the national police. Within a year, Trujillo was named commander of the national police force. In 1927, Vásquez reorganized the police as the Dominican National Army and put Trujillo in command as a brigadier general. By 1929, the Dominican Republic had both an army and a secret police, and Trujillo was in charge of both. His military power consolidated, Trujillo now turned on his benefactor Vásquez.

Originally elected to a four-year term in 1924, Vásquez organized a constitutional convention to dubiously amend the constitution to allow him to extend his tenure in office until 1930.[35] Dissatisfied with this extension, Vásquez then announced his intention to be a candidate in the May 1930 presidential elections. In February 1930—three months before the slated elections—an insurgent movement opposed to Vásquez's creeping authoritarianism erupted in the city of Santiago de los Caballeros. After consulting with U.S. officials, Vásquez agreed to resign.

The U.S. mission in Santo Domingo mediated between the insurgents and the remaining government, and an armistice was brokered. Rafael Estrella Ureña, leader of the uprising, became the provisional president pending the upcoming elections, and Washington quickly recognized the new government. Lurking behind the scenes was Trujillo, who had backed Estrella Ureña's insurrection knowing that his support would ensure Vásquez's downfall. Trujillo soon forced Estrella Ureña to step aside in favor of him as a presidential candidate and accept the position as his running mate. Trujillo then won by a vote margin of 223,731 to 1,883 in the May 16, 1930, presidential election, from which all his opponents withdrew. The U.S. minister reported back that the number of votes "far exceeds" the number of voters in the country.[36]

Inaugurated on August 16, 1930, "President" Trujillo immediately turned his efforts toward repressing his political opponents. Virtually all political opposition was banned, and the Dominican Republic turned into an authoritarian, conspiratorial society. The regime used violence, fear, and terror as ends in themselves.[37] Relying on his intricate espionage network, Trujillo set out to consolidate his rule throughout the cities and countryside.

Yet Trujillo was not content to govern as just one more autocratic ruler in the Dominican Republic's long line of autocratic rulers. Rather, Trujillo set out to establish himself as the sole figure controlling not only Dominicans' political and economic activities but also their social and cultural ones. Soon into his rule, a province was named for him, and Congress passed a resolution declaring him the "Benefactor of the Fatherland." In 1936, Santo Domingo, the oldest of European cities in the Caribbean, was renamed "Cuidad Trujillo."[38] Trujillo held over forty different titles, including "Genius of Peace," "Father of the New Fatherland," "Protector of Fine Arts and Letters," and "The First and Greatest of Dominican Chiefs of State." One figure put monuments to Trujillo in Ciudad Trujillo at 1,800.[39] Estimates hold that the Trujillo family held nearly two-thirds of the national wealth.

Throughout the 1930s, 1940s, and 1950s, Trujillo continued to be reelected in one election or another, or he was "succeeded" by a puppet president. Well aware of the continued influence that the United States had in the Dominican Republic and the region more broadly, Trujillo

deftly positioned himself as a strong opponent of European fascism leading up to World War II and communism after the advent of the Cold War.

Trujillo spent incredible sums of money employing top-shelf political
lobbyists in Washington and entertaining the endless procession of U.S.
congressional delegations that came to Santo Domingo to view the "Truji-
lloist miracle."[40] Indeed, to use the often-quoted aphorism, Trujillo might
have been a "son of a bitch," but he was Washington's son a bitch, and he
did everything to remind Washington of this fact. And there is no denying
that the U.S. government's support for Trujillo's sultanistic regime—or
even just the willingness to tolerate its many excesses—hurt Washington's
credibility when it claimed to be supporting democratic solutions to
Dominican crises such as the one in 1965.

Fidel Castro came to power in Cuba in 1959, and the two dictators soon
became ideological and regional rivals. It did not go unnoticed in Havana
when former Cuban strongman Fulgencio Batista fled into exile in Trujillo's Dominican Republic. However, always the opportunist, Trujillo continued to sell arms sales to Castro's Cuba even after the United States had
ceased its military assistance.[41]

In what was a bold move considering that his own revolution was only
six months old, in June 1959 Castro ordered an invasion of the Dominican
Republic by groups of insurgents of various nationalities.[42] Trujillo's forces
soon apprehended the invaders and killed them in what he labeled a "rab-
bit hunt." Some insurgents who were not immediately killed were taken
to the San Isidro Air Base, where Trujillo's son Ramfis tortured them.
Only five guerrillas survived the invasion.[43] While he easily stomped Castro's plot, Trujillo still played up the threat of a Communist insurrection
to his increasingly concerned American counterparts.

Yet, ironically, it was Castro's successful revolution and consolidation
of a Marxist–Leninist regime in Cuba that signaled the end of Washington's unqualified support—or at least tolerance—for its trusty antifascist
and anti-Communist ally in Santo Domingo. Sobered by the images of
throngs of euphoric Cubans supporting Castro and his young, idealistic,
and bearded "compadres" as they descended out of the Sierra Maestra
Mountains (and the subsequent debacle at the Bay of Pigs in April 1961),
the Kennedy administration began to reconsider its support for "sons of
bitches" such as Trujillo.

With the logic of "Batista is to Castro what Trujillo is to . . .," the Ken-

nedy administration began to distance itself from Trujillo and instead supported the efforts of social democratic reformers such as the Venezuelan
president Rómulo Betancourt. In fact, it was the 1960 Trujillo-hatched
effort to assassinate Betancourt that led the Kennedy administration to the
decision by the Organization of American States (OAS) to slap economic
sanctions on the Trujillo government.[44]

Faced with crushing OAS sanctions, in the early 1960s Trujillo sought
to downplay his role in the Dominican government, allowing figureheads
or members of his family to nominally serve in his place. Yet, faced with
an unsympathetic ear in Washington and increasingly bold domestic
opposition, Trujillo's days were numbered. In a secret memo dated May
29, 1960, President Kennedy authorized a plan to assist in the assassination of Trujillo. With support from the U.S. Central Intelligence Agency
(CIA), a group of eight conspirators assassinated Trujillo on May 30, 1961,
as his chauffeur was driving him alone outside of Santo Domingo.[45] Yet,
while Trujillo was now dead, "Trujillismo" remained alive and well as
members of his family, such as son Ramfis, continued to call the shots in
Santo Domingo.

Then, in November 1961, two of Trujillo's brothers, Hector and Aris-
mendi, returned from exile and challenged Ramfis's control over the military and family wealth. Still reeling from the recent Bay of Pigs debacle in
Cuba the previous April, President Kennedy had no patience for a return
to the "status quo" in the Dominican Republic. He immediately dispatched a naval task force to anchor off the coast of Santo Domingo to
send a strong message to Trujillo's "wicked uncles" that they had better
think twice about ousting Joaquín Balaguer, who had been Trujillo's fig-
urehead president and had taken over following the assassination.[46]

Yet Balaguer was still not out of the woods just yet. Tarred by his longtime association with the Trujillo dictatorship, Balaguer was continuously
attacked by emerging political groups. The United States eventually per-
suaded Balaguer to share power with a seven-person Council of State,
which took office on January 1, 1962. In addition to Balaguer, who
remained head of state, the council was made up of members of the private sector, the Catholic Church, and the two surviving assassins of Trujillo: Luis Amiama Tió and Antonio Imbert Barrera.[47]

Balaguer was overthrown by General Rafael Echevarría on January 15,
1962, and immediately sent into exile. Under pressure from the Kennedy

administration, which once again dispatched a task force to issue a more than subtle warning to the Dominicans, Echevarría was arrested and forced into exile; Captain Elías Wessin y Wessin constituted a second Council of State, one that governed until democratic elections took place in December 1962.[48]

THE RETURN, ELECTION, AND REMOVAL OF JUAN BOSCH

Following Trujillo's murder, Dominican society descended into a state of uncertainty and continued fear, one where few political leaders knew how to govern a country that had been so traumatized by more than three decades of tyrannical rule. In addition, caught up in the turbulent global political environment of the 1960s, the Dominican Republic teetered between far-left and far-right political poles.

From Washington's perspective, the post-Trujillo political instability in the Dominican Republic made it a prime target for Communist expansion. In May 1961, Kennedy made it clear that, while he moved away from rightist dictators such as Trujillo and promoted social reform in order to prevent them, stopping communism was the number-one priority of the United States in the region:

> Should it even appear that the inter-American doctrine of non-intervention merely conceals or excuses a policy of nonaction—if the nations of this hemisphere should fail to meet their commitments against outside Communist penetration—then I want it clearly understood that this government will not hesitate in meeting its primary obligations which are to the security of our nation.[49]

In the Dominican Republic specifically, Kennedy is believed to have said that there were three potential outcomes for that country, "in descending order of preference: a decent democratic regime, a continuation of the Trujillo regime, or a Castro regime. We ought to aim for the first but we can't really renounce the second until we are sure we can avoid the third."[50] When Balaguer was head of the Council of State, this meant that Kennedy wanted him to understand that Washington was interested in "progress of anti-communist laws in [the] Dominican Congress, measures taken [to] exclude [the] return [of] Communist and Castroist exiles, and other actions taken [to] prevent infiltration and agitation by Communist-Castroist elements."[51]

With presidential elections slated for December 1962, Bosch, the charismatic leftist and member of the Dominican Revolutionary Party (Partido Revolucionario Dominicano [PRD]), returned to the Dominican Republic in 1961 from twenty-five years of exile.[52] Bosch won the Dominican Republic's first democratic election since 1924 (the year that the Marines left the island) in a landslide, taking 648,000 votes out of roughly one million votes cast and beating his closest competitor, Viriato Fiallo of the National Civil Union (Union Cívica National), by a two-to-one margin. The PRD won twenty-two of twenty-seven seats in the Senate and forty-eight of seventy-four seats in the Chamber of Deputies.[53] President-elect Bosch made a visit to the Kennedy White House, and Vice President Lyndon Johnson attended Bosch's inauguration on February 27, 1963.[54]

Hoping and believing that Bosch would be able to transform the Dominican Republic into the "pearl of the Caribbean" or the "showcase for democracy" and not "another Cuba," the Kennedy administration quickly poured over $100 million in U.S. assistance into the country. Three hundred technical experts and Peace Corps volunteers came to the country during Bosch's tenure as president.[55]

Yet Bosch turned out to be a disappointing president, one unable to follow up on the many promises made during his campaign. Part of Bosch's problems stemmed from the basic fact that he was the first democratic president following the Trujillo era, and the Dominican Republic was not fully prepared for democratic politics. Another mortal blow stemmed from the fact that, while he himself was not a Communist, Bosch allowed Communists to operate openly in the country. This permissive position antagonized elements within the Dominican military and conservative elements in political class.

American ambassador in Santo Domingo John Bartlow Martin was originally a strong supporter of Bosch, hoping that he could be the democratic force that could unite Dominicans behind a progressive yet non-Communist government. Yet like his boss John Kennedy, Martin all the while remained dubious that Bosch was indeed the type of reformer Washington had hoped for. For example, on reflection, Martin recalled that with respect to Bosch, in our own interest, we could not ignore several possibilities—that Bosch himself was a deep-cover Communist (I did not and do not believe it); that he would lose cover control of his PRD to the Castro/Communists; that if he failed to meet the people's expectations he might be overthrown.[56]

As the months after Bosch's inauguration passed, the Kennedy administration moved from a policy of cautious support for Bosch to one of damage control, one where policy decisions were increasingly focused on ensuring that Bosch's tenure did not lead to another military coup or, much worse, a Communist takeover. Lyndon Johnson offered his perception of Bosch from when he was Kennedy's vice president:

> We continued to hope that Bosch would be able to do for his people what President Rómulo Betancourt had done for Venezuela after dictatorship had been overthrown there. But Bosch was no Betancourt. While his aspirations were admirable, his performance was weak. . . . He lacked the capacity to unite under his leadership the various elements that wanted progress and constitutional government—elements of the non-Communist left and center. Nor was he able to control or satisfy the rightists, including powerful elements in the military, who looked on him with suspicion.[57]

One of Kennedy's top officials, George Ball, was a little less diplomatic than Johnson in his description of Bosch but perhaps closer to the administration's consensus view. To Ball, Bosch was

> unrealistic, arrogant, and erratic. I thought him incapable of running even a small social club, much less a country in turmoil. He did not seem to me a Communist . . . but merely a muddle-headed, anti-American pedant committed to unattainable social reforms.[58]

Bosch's increasingly tenuous grip on democratic power offered a dilemma for policymakers in Washington: they wanted to support the democratically elected and constitutional government in the Dominican Republic, but they were also worried about political instability and whether it would allow Communist forces to take advantage of the situation.

One scholar has written that Washington's growing defensive posture was attributed to a reflexive fear of communism in the country, seeing Dominican Communists "not as weak and fragmented dissidents, but as potential agents of extra continental power."[59] Yet it is also important to point out that, given the tense and uncertain climate at the time (including Castro's stunning revolution in Cuba in 1959 and his equally stunning decision to align Cuba with the Soviet Union soon after) the fear of a Communist takeover in the Dominican Republic was not at all unreasonable.

With rumors of a coup circulating throughout Santo Domingo, on September 24, 1963, a desperate Bosch asked Ambassador Martin to request immediate military assistance from Washington. Bosch wanted not a full-scale invasion but rather a naval task force off the coast similar to what Washington had done against Trujillo's family in November 1961 and the Echevarría coup in January 1962.

Martin went ahead and asked that the United States "alert a carrier as requested," but Washington rejected his recommendation. Martin was then told that "little more can be done by us to maintain [Bosch] in office against the forces that he himself has created."[60] Yet, while Martin publicly opposed the coup and had requested a task force, he nonetheless cabled Washington to report that "I have no desire to return him, or his Cabinet or PRD to power."[61]

The Dominican army, backed up by some conservative political groups, led the bloodless coup that ousted Bosch. The rationale given by the coup plotters was that Bosch was too soft on communism and therefore could not be allowed to continue as president. One of the chief architects of the coup was once again General Wessin y Wessin, who commanded the Armed Forces Training Center located at the San Isidro air base outside Santo Domingo.[62] The coup leaders immediately banned Communist groups, promised to hold free elections, and declared Bosch's 1963 constitution (which was highly progressive by Dominican standards) "nonexistent."[63]

Supporters of the coup believed that Bosch's perceived tacit support for communism justified the ousting of the country's first democratically elected president in almost forty years.[64] Bosch fled into exile in Puerto Rico, and a year later, Donald Reid Cabral, who had earlier served in the Council of State before Bosch's election, headed a three-person civilian junta.[65]

President Kennedy was unhappy with the coup, as he realized that it damaged Washington's policies of promoting democratic social change.

THE DOMINICAN INTERVENTION, 1965   53

The U.S. and OAS efforts to support a democratic "third way" in the Dominican Republic had failed. On October 4, 1963, Kennedy ordered Secretary of Defense Robert McNamara to create contingency plans for a possible military intervention in the Caribbean. While the hoped for Bosch-led "peaceful revolution" had disintegrated under U.S. impatience and Bosch's incompetence, Kennedy did not want to see the country revert back to the Trujilloistas.[66]

Washington initially withheld diplomatic recognition of the newly installed junta, but by November, Kennedy had decided that the United States needed to deal with reality in the Dominican Republic, not dreams. Kennedy thus made the decision to recognize the junta known as the Triumvarite, although the American president was assassinated before this order went through. The Johnson administration recognized the government on December 14, 1963, based on the agreement that it would hold national elections in 1965.

Many observers directly link the crisis of 1965 to the overthrow of Bosch in 1963. The thinking is that incipient Dominican democracy was truncated by rightist political and military elements. They maintain that if the United States had worked harder to support Bosch's presidency, he would not have been overthrown and there would, logically, never have been a revolt to return him to power in 1965.[67] This is certainly an interesting historical counterfactual question—what might have occurred if the United States had not allowed Bosch's removal? But once again, it also suggests that more U.S. intervention was needed, not less. The removal of Bosch and subsequent instability in the Dominican Republic reinforces an important counterintuitive fact: that during these years, the Dominican Republic was at its most violent and chaotic when the United States was *not* directly involved in events.

THE REID CABRAL ERA AND THE REVOLT OF APRIL 1965

With the question of support for a democratic social reformer rendered moot by Bosch's ouster in September 1965, the Johnson administration assumed the Kennedy-era policy of preventing a Communist takeover its priority in the Dominican Republic. And for over a year, while certainly no showcase for democracy, the Dominican Republic remained relatively stable under the junta headed by Reid Cabral. Content to observe from afar and keep its eye out for any "chronic wrongdoing," the Johnson administration's foreign policy concerns could not have been further than the Dominican Republic, as U.S. involvement in a civil war in Vietnam was coming to dominate the White House's time and efforts.

This is not to suggest, however, that most Dominicans considered the Cabral junta to be legitimate or effective. On the contrary, the pro-coup alliance that worked to remove Bosch was probably less cohesive than Bosch's government had been.[68] Over a period of several months following the September 1963 coup, two of the original members of the Triumvarite stepped down, paving the way for Cabral to become its president.[69] Cabral's tenure as president of the junta was a dismal failure. With his country mired in an economic recession in 1964 and 1965, Cabral implemented International Monetary Fund–supported economic austerity measures, a move that won little favor with large sectors of the Dominican population who were desperate for immediate economic expansion.[70] Another large part of Cabral's problems stemmed from his efforts to reform the military. Cabral cut fringe benefits to officers, shut down smuggling rings, and reduced the military budget.[71] Not surprisingly, many officers felt threatened by these moves and began devising coup plots to remove Cabral.

Cabral announced in late 1964 that scheduled elections would be postponed and held in September 1965. Yet few Dominicans believed that Cabral would ever allow former presidents Balaguer of the Reformist Party (Partido Reformista) or the PRD's Bosch to return from exile to run against him.[72] It should also be noted, however, that while there was little chance that the Dominican Republic was going to experience democratic elections in September 1965—as Cabral had promised—following the U.S. intervention democratic elections did take place in June 1966. This fact alone does not justify the U.S. intervention, but it does show how U.S. involvement led to democratic practices that were often only window dressing in Dominican politics.

By the spring of 1965, a CIA poll indicated that Cabral enjoyed 5 percent public support, compared to five times as many Dominicans who favored Bosch and ten times as many who favored Balaguer.[73] This poll also indicated that, unlike some historians' characterization of his support, in the months before the pro-Bosch revolt of April 1965, Bosch was not an overwhelmingly popular political figure. In fact, the advantage that

Balaguer held over Bosch as indicated in polling done in early 1965 largely held up when Balaguer defeated Bosch in the post-U.S. intervention elections in 1966.

By April 1965, Cabral could count on very little support from the military or even conservative political elements. Even Washington, which normally was willing to give Cabral the benefit of the doubt since he might provide "stability," was beginning to sour on his rule.[74] Cabral sealed his fate when he indicated his desire to rule beyond the date of the certain elections. Yet, while there was a growing consensus that Cabral had to go, there was very little agreement at all as to whom or what should replace him. The military, for one, was split between the officers who solely wanted Cabral and others who wanted him out and others in. According to one characterization, "Thus, the Generals, though unwilling to fight for Reid, were willing to kill their own countrymen to prevent Bosch's return. They told the rebels they would attack at once unless a military junta was established."[75]

Various political groups jousted to oust Cabral, including those who wanted Bosch to return as president without elections, those who wanted to establish a new junta so that later Bosch and Balaguer could run in an election (the scenario that most resembled what resulted following the U.S. intervention), and those who wanted to oust Cabral and establish a military junta without any political preconditions.[76]

On Saturday, April 24, 1965, while U.S. Ambassador W. Tapley Bennett Jr. was in Savannah, Georgia, visiting his sick mother, the anti-Cabral coup went forward. General Marcos A. Rivera Cuesta, chief of staff of the Dominican army, notified Cabral that officers were plotting against his government. In a move that he later described as "stupid," Cabral sent Rivera to army headquarters without an armed guard to arrest the coup plotters.[77] By 12:30 P.M. of that same day, Rivera Cuesta and his deputy were prisoners.[78]

Suddenly, Santo Domingo's streets were full of residents (some armed, some not) and soldiers allied to various factions. The U.S. embassy was reporting that two-thirds of the army stationed in Santo Domingo was in revolt and providing arms to civilians. Buoyed by thousands of civilians who had surrounded the presidential palace, former Cabral adviser and recently turned Constitutionalist military commander Colonel Francisco

Caamaño Deñó seized the palace, arrested Cabral, and affirmed his support for Bosch. [79]

The Constitutionalists soon took the capital city without a fight, and it appeared as though Bosch's triumphant return to power was only a question of time. That afternoon Radio Santo Domingo announced that the Constitutionalists—a set of diverse groups ranging from various military troops and officers, PRD members, democratic socialists, orthodox Communists, and opportunists—should support PRD leader José Molina Ureña, who had just declared himself "provisional constitutional president." (The name "Loyalists" described the anti-Constitutionalist forces.)

The situation in Santo Domingo was deteriorating rapidly as increasingly civilians were arming themselves and allying with the rebels. Law and order had vanished. Communist groups such as the pro-Castro "IJ4" and the Dominican Popular Movement (Movimiento Popular Dominicano) joined the rebels, complicating the ability to understand if the revolt was largely anti-Cabral, pro-Bosch, or Communist in nature.[80] *New York Times* reporter Tad Szulc observed that "submachine guns, rifles and side arms were being issued to anyone who asked for them at army headquarters (now Constitutionalist controlled) in Santo Domingo, and yesterday all the military patrols in the capital were accompanied by armed civilians." An estimated 15,000 homemade gas bombs were in the hands of civilians.[81]

The common denominator that united the opposition forces in the early hours of the revolt was an intense dislike of the Cabral junta. Yet, as was probably to be expected, once Cabral was out of the picture, the situation became more complicated. Indeed, some historians have suggested that intense diplomatic pressure (and not an intervention) from Washington could have ensured an ideal outcome where the violence was quelled and Bosch reinstalled as president. Yet this worthwhile historical counterfactual argument is rendered less convincing when analyzed in light of the chaotic situation engulfing Santo Domingo at the time and the alarmist reports that policymakers in Washington were receiving.

Several key elements of the military—many of whom had passively stood by as Cabral was being removed—reacted with horror to the now openly pro-Bosch and seemingly pro-leftist and Communist revolt. Generals such as Wessin y Wessin (who had led the 1963 coup against Bosch) and the air force's Juan de los Santos Céspedes responded with alacrity in an effort to prevent an outcome that would lead to Bosch's return as president. On April 28, Loyalist commanders formed a junta under the head of Colonel Pedro Bartolomé Benoit that worked out of the San Isidro base just to the west of the capital.[82] What started as an anti-Cabral coup and had evolved into a pro-Bosch revolt was now an incipient civil war.

Loyalist commanders subsequently ordered Dominican air force F-51 planes to strafe the presidential palace, where Molina Ureña was serving as the disputed provisional president.[83] On Monday, April 26, Wessin and de Los Santos requested the assistance of U.S. troops, but the U.S. embassy told them not to expect anything. Nonetheless, on April 27, General Wessin's troops left the San Isidro base and crossed the key Duarte Bridge over the Ozama River, the main western approach to the city. His forces then advanced several blocks into the city in what was the bloodiest battle in Dominican history.[84] It appeared as though the Loyalists had all the momentum and that, in a dramatic turn of events, a new reality was imminent where Cabral was out of power, the pro-Bosch forces were defeated, and a military junta was in power. Yet, remarkably, Constitutionalist forces began to push General Wessin's troops back toward the river; the Constitutionalist forces lived to fight another day.

THE FATEFUL MEETING AT THE EMBASSY

Early on in the fighting, Constitutionalist leaders met with U.S. embassy officials at the presidential palace. During those conversations, William Connett, U.S. charge d'affaires, was in charge of the embassy as Bennett was out of the country. From the first contact with the rebel leaders, the embassy never seriously considered the notion of supporting a solution that ended with Bosch's immediate return to power. Confident that the Loyalist forces would prevail and thus U.S. military action was not necessary, Connett reported back to Foggy Bottom that the Communists were moving with tremendous speed to convince the Dominican people that Bosch should be restored.

Yet after several more days of fierce fighting, it appeared as though the revolt had been defeated. Elements of the army had gone over to the Constitutionalist side, but the navy and air force remained loyal. Late on the afternoon of April 27, Constitutionalist officers led by Molina Ureña went over to the U.S. embassy in order to get an end to the air attacks. Ambassador Bennett, who had just returned from the United States, refused to grant this request and repeated his concern about Communists involved in the revolt and that the United States would only work to achieve a cease-fire.[85]

Bennett did, however, make it clear to the rebel leaders that the United States had supported Bosch's presidency in 1963 and had condemned the coup that removed him. The ambassador also told them that he thought the PRD was a democratic movement but that they had allowed Communists to exploit the situation.[86] Ureña and other Constitutionalist leaders accepted Bennett's request to surrender and immediately sought asylum in foreign embassies.[87] It is worth noting that U.S. officials would later use Ureña's withdrawal from the Constitutionalist side as an example of the radicalization of the pro-Bosch camp. He also reported that the Ureña "government" was not able to control all of the rebel factions.[88]

The pro-Bosch revolt appeared finished. Yet, angered by Bennett's refusal and indignant about accusations of Communist involvement in the revolt, Colonel Caamaño (who was not the highest-ranking Constitutionalist officer) left the embassy and returned to the front, where he ordered his troops to cross the Duarte Bridge. It was here that they defeated General Wessin's tanks that were attempting to cross over from San Isidro. By the end of the day, the tables had turned once again. On the morning of April 28, the Constitutionalists went on the offensive and attacked and seized the Loyalist holdout at the Ozama fortress, the main depository of weapons in the city.[89]

Following the Constitutionalists' stunning turn of fortunes, the U.S. embassy in Santo Domingo began to view the events with increasing alarm, especially the fear that mob violence or civil war could pave the way for a Communist takeover. Ambassador Bennett was completely taken by surprise by the strength of the Constitutionalists' counterattack. In the previous days when Ambassador Bennett was in Georgia, Connett began reporting back to Washington that "in view [of] extremist participation in [the] coup and announced communist advocacy of Bosch's return as favorable to their long-term interests," there was cause for concern. Connett also wrote that the Loyalist decision to attack the palace was the only "course of action having any real possibility of preventing Bosch's return and containing growing disorders and mob violence."[90] By April 28, the U.S. embassy was becoming alarmed over this battle, which to them was one between "Castro-types and those who oppose them."[91]

There is no question that the Constitutionalists' military resurrection is what prompted the embassy to radically alter its perception of the conflict in Santo Domingo. In fact, on the same day that Caamaño was scoring his stirring victories against Wessin's forces, Bennett sent a cable announcing that the Loyalists had formed a military junta under the command of Colonel Pedro Bartolomé Benoit, an indication that he believed the situation had stabilized.[92] But within minutes of this cable, Bennett sent another one that indicated that two police stations had fallen to the Constitutionalists. It is safe to say that had there been no imminent Loyalist defeat, Washington would not have ordered any military intervention that went beyond evacuating U.S. nationals. Yet it is also worth mentioning that Washington did absolutely nothing to prevent Cabral's removal in the first place.

A lot has been written about what might have happened if the U.S. embassy officials had acted differently during these critical meetings with the Constitutionalist military and political leadership. The conventional interpretation is that aggressive U.S. diplomacy and even intervention could have resulted in a negotiated settlement, one that would have likely included Constitutionalist participation in any eventual government. For example, Abraham Lowenthal has written that "no attempt" was made by American officials to promote a possible compromise.[93] Other observers have written that by not openly supporting the pro-Bosch forces, Washington lost a prime opportunity to be on the right side of history. Theodore Draper wrote that

> if the United States had acted quickly and firmly enough, Bosch would have returned to Santo Domingo with a minimum of bloodshed. Wessin y Wessin's forces would not have been formed, and the Communists would not have had time, even if we credit the official story, to take advantage of the temporary setback to the pro-Bosch cause of the fourth day, Tuesday, April 27. It was as if, after Adolf Hitler had committed suicide in 1945, the Allies had decided to back Air Force Marshall Hermann Goering as the man to save Germany from Communism.[94]

In another article, Draper argues that Bosch's "bid for power" would have certainly been "bloodless" except for U.S. intervention and that Communists could not have hijacked the revolt since they had already "missed the boat."[95] Piero Gleijeses has also written about how events in Santo Domingo would have turned out had the United States acted differently:

Thus, insofar as history allows us to speculate, one can conclude that the success of the countercoup would have resulted in a moderate answer to the Dominican dilemma. A new Bosch administration would have sought social reforms while rejecting "radical" or "hasty" solutions. It would have been anti-Communist, but respectful of political democracy. It would have felt no sympathy for the "totalitarian" solutions of Cuba and the Soviet bloc, but would have opposed U.S. imperialism in the Western Hemisphere and asserted the national sovereignty of the Dominican Republic. In short, it would have been a government of the "democratic left"—not of that "democratic left" that enjoyed Washington's favor.[96]

It is no doubt valuable to posit such counterfactuals. What if the embassy had rallied around the pro-Bosch forces? Would Bosch have returned to lead a peaceful and democratic Dominican Republic? Unfortunately, though, we will never know the answers to these questions. It is important to keep in mind that, as the polling indicated, Bosch was by no means an overwhelmingly popular figure. Thus—and given the Dominican Republic's history of political instability—there is little to conclude that his return to power would have been bloodless. Another question we can ask, however, is what motivated the United States to not support the pro-Bosch forces? Why did not the embassy support the rebel forces if at this point in time a Constitutionalist victory would have meant Bosch's return and an end to the violence?

The simple answer is that U.S. officials believed that, no matter the good intentions of some of the rebels, a pro-Bosch victory would increase the likelihood of a Communist takeover. And the United States was not going to risk communism for the hope that Bosch's return would lead to stability and democracy. After "losing" Cuba to communism, the stakes were just too high in the Dominican crisis. As we will see, U.S. intelligence reports were unequivocal in their belief that the Constitutionalist side was heavily influenced by Communist elements.

For example, even as late as almost a month after the U.S. intervention, a CIA intelligence memorandum wrote that "Communists continue to play an important role in the rebel movement, although since 4 May their part has not been an obvious or dominant one . . . Communists did, in fact, clearly dominate the rebel movement between 28 April and 2 or 3 May."[97] Piero Gleijeses is correct to conclude that Washington feared a

Dominican "democratic left" that did not enjoy its favor, but what he should add is that for Washington this type of "democratic left" was considered to be communism.

To its credit, the embassy's interpretation of events was not totally unwarranted. American officials believed that while a number of officers had joined the revolt since they were bitterly opposed to Reid, they would have defected once it became apparent that Bosch was returning to the capital. Therefore, they feared that a Bosch return would not have led to a peaceful and democratic solution but would have fueled greater fighting in Santo Domingo and possibly throughout the countryside. Rightly or wrongly, many U.S. officials believed that a pro-Bosch victory very well could have meant full-scale civil war.

The "what might have been" question concerning the U.S. embassy's dealings with the Constitutionalist forces became a major point of contention in congressional hearings a few months after the events in late April. For example, in testimony that was classified until 1990, Senate Foreign Relations Chairman J. William Fulbright asked Johnson adviser Thomas Mann, the undersecretary of state for economic affairs, why the United States did not back the rebels in the early stages of the revolt. Mann responded by stating that Bosch was by no means the consensus political figure, that his return did not guarantee a return to stability. He continued by testifying,

> Senator, the possibility of having the PRD crowd set up a provisional government on the 25th and 26th, 24th, 27th, is absolutely zero. This is precisely what caused the military and a large segment of the Dominican opposition to split away from the rebel side, let's say the anti-Reid side. They split over the issue of Bosch.[98]

Two days later, Fulbright asked Ambassador Bennett whether the United States had missed an opportunity to promote a peaceful outcome by supporting the Constitutionalist forces. Bennett responded, "I don't think so," because by that point the Communists had sufficiently infiltrated the Constitutionalist forces so that a Bosch return could have led to a Communist takeover. Bennett then went on to lecture Fulbright about the stakes at play during these critical meetings:

What would have been the reaction in Latin America if we had not taken
the action and the place had gone completely bad and we had allowed
another Cuba or incipient Cuba to develop there? I am sure we would have
been more heavily criticized than we have been.[99]

Fulbright then followed up his question by asking Bennett whether it was
his opinion that a Constitutionalist victory would have led to a Communist regime. Bennett replied, "It is mine, and I think almost every single
observer on the scene, the Papal Nuncio, the British Embassy, most of the
Latin American embassies, the Colombian, the Peruvian, the Guatemalan,
the Brazilian."[100] It is also interesting that Fulbright, who by September
1965 would go public with a harsh attack on Johnson's Dominican policy,
agreed with the assessment that there was significant Communist involvement in the pro-Bosch revolt. In later remarks to William F. Raborn,
director of the CIA, Fulbright stated,

I think likely the CIA established there was a significant Communist
involvement among the rebels. You have documented it this morning. The
question that interests me very much is not whether the Communists were
influential, which I think you have made clear, but whether they were dominant and, more importantly, whether we tried to exert a countervailing
moderate influence on the rebel leadership.[101]

Fulbright's remarks reveal that even the Johnson administration's chief
critic on the Dominican intervention agreed with the perception of Communist infiltration but simply questioned if the United States could have
moderated it.

THE WHITE HOUSE RESPONDS TO THE CRISIS
Beginning on the morning of Saturday, April 24, the day of the anti-
Cabral coup, President Johnson began to discuss and receive intelligence
concerning events in Santo Domingo. What emerges from the transcripts
of Johnson's deliberations—both in the early hours of the crisis and
through his decision to send in U.S. troops almost a week later—is that
the Johnson White House was concerned about the consequences of
Bosch's return to power and the potential for Communists to take advantage of the chaos or Bosch's return in order to seize power.

Indeed, the evidence suggests that while he would have likely still ordered the Marines into the country to assist with the evacuation of U.S. nationals, if there had been no perceived Communist threat, then Johnson would certainly have not ordered the intervention. Like Theodore Roosevelt over sixty years earlier, Johnson's position toward the situation in the Dominican Republic was a reluctant conclusion that no other viable options short of intervention would be sufficient to ensure an outcome that suited the United States.

On April 27, Johnson ordered the Marines ashore to coordinate a nonmilitary evacuation of U.S. nationals that lasted through the following day.[102] Captain James A. Dare led the Marines' Caribbean Ready Amphibious Task Group—a rotating force of Marines stationed on warships.[103] On the night of Saturday, April 24, Dare had moved his 1,700 Marines and 3,000 sailors under his command into the vicinity of Santo Domingo. The Marines were sent into the Hotel Embajador, where Americans had been gathering. The task was to get the citizens from the hotel to the sugar port at Haina seven miles away, where they were to be loaded onto two ships (the *Wood County* and the *Ruchamkin*) from the task force that was moored there.[104]

The 1,172 evacuees ended up going to Haina by bus, truck, helicopter, and even embassy automobiles. After boarding the ships, the evacuees were transported to Puerto Rico.[105] The evacuation went off largely without incident other than one episode when a group of Constitutionalists barged into the hotel, said they were looking for "counterrevolutionaries," and forced American citizens to line up against a wall. Eventually, though, the Constitutionalists left, and no Americans were hurt.[106]

In his first recorded conversation on the crisis on the day of the first evacuation, President Johnson demonstrated his belief that the United States might have to intervene to guarantee stability. In a conversation with Thomas Mann, Johnson concluded, "We're going to have to really set up that government down there and run it and stabilize it some way or other. This Bosch is no good. I was down there." Mann responded by saying, "And if we don't get a decent government in there, Mr. President, we get another Bosch. It's just going to be a sinkhole."[107]

Mann, who had previously served as assistant secretary of state for inter-American affairs, emerged as one of Johnson's most trusted and influential advisers during the course of the Dominican crisis. More conservative than Johnson's other advisers, such as National Security Advisor

McGeorge Bundy or trusted friend Abe Fortas, Mann had Johnson's ear for most of the crisis, a fact that meant that, especially in the early days of the revolt, Johnson received briefings and advice that tended to focus on the potential for a Communist takeover.

Yet no matter what they were telling Johnson, his advisers themselves were receiving intelligence reports from Santo Domingo that described a threatening situation. On April 26, Bundy received an intelligence report that listed

> evidence of participation in the movement to restore Bosch by Communists and other extreme leftists has continued to come to light. The reprisal threats among other indications point to increasing extremist domination of the movement. . . . Some of the military leaders [rebel leaders] now appear to realize they were duped by the Bosch supporters and the extremists.[108]

The next day, the CIA delivered a report to Secretary of State Dean Rusk that stated,

> Should the forces of General Elías Wessin y Wessin, supported by the major elements of the air force and elements of the navy over the next several hours or days be unable to defeat that revolution that started last Saturday, the Dominican Republic in my opinion will be so far on the way to becoming another Cuba that the tide may well not be able to be turned back, unless the U.S. takes prompt and strong action. Pro-Communist—if not Communist—people are emerging as members of the "cabinet" of "provisional president" Molina Ureña. Communists are gathering arms and reportedly have a real "in" with at least one arsenal. They set up strong points within the city.[109]

Two days later, right before Johnson ordered armed combat-ready Marines onto the island, another CIA cable reported,

> Early in the present insurrection it became apparent that the well-organized Dominican communists and associated extremists were committing their full resources to the rebel effort . . . the well-armed mobs now resisting the hard-pressed Loyalist forces are largely controlled by the Communists and other extremists. . . . While there is no evidence that the Castro regime is

directly involved in the current insurrection, it is nevertheless clear that
Cuban trained Dominican extremists are taking an active part.[110]

As the events of the days following Reid's removal indicate, President
Johnson was constantly peppered with reports about the Communist
threat implicit in a Bosch return. This is what led him to decide to move
beyond the much less controversial evacuation of American nationals and
to intervene politically and militarily in the Dominican civil war in order
to prevent the Communist scenario from unfolding.

In fact, while Johnson implored his advisers to make it clear to the U.S.
media that the administration was "not supporting one [side] against the
other" in the conflict; it was already apparent on the first day of the revolt
that the United States had serious reservations about any outcome that
included Bosch's immediate return to power. This is not to say, however,
that at this point the Johnson administration would not tolerate a Bosch
presidency. Rather, the conversations indicate that the worry was over
what Bosch would lead to. In a conversation on April 27 at 7:17 A.M.,
Johnson asks Mann what a Bosch return would indicate: "Does it mean,
you think, that this is another Castro government?" Mann responds,

> Not yet, no. Hard to tell what comes out of one of these messes, who comes
> out on top. We don't think that this fellow Bosch understands that the com-
> munists are dangerous. We don't think that he is a communist. What we
> are afraid of is that if he gets back in, he'll have so many of them around
> him—and they're so much smarter than he is—that before you know it,
> they would begin to take over.[111]

Yet, while it was clear that the administration was above all concerned
about where Bosch's return would take the Dominican Republic, Johnson
made the fateful decision to go public with the line that U.S. actions were
geared entirely toward protecting American lives and using diplomacy to
stop the fighting. In the same April 27 conversation, Johnson asked Mann
what he should say at a scheduled 4:00 P.M. press conference, and Mann
responded by recommending that Johnson state that "the situation is
fluid. That we are evacuating Americans. . . . And we're in touch with both
sides, hoping to do what we can do to stop the bloodshed."[112]

It is worth noting that Johnson was not asked a single question about the Dominican Republic during this press conference, a fact that reflects how still at this point on April 27 U.S. actions were seen as largely related to the rescue mission. This decision came back to inflict irreparable damage on the Johnson administration's credibility, as it quickly became apparent that the single most important goal of the U.S. intervention was to ensure an outcome that did not lead to Bosch's immediate return. But while Johnson was deciding to tell the American public that the White House was solely concerned about evacuating Americans, his advisers continued to brief him on what they believed was a growing threat of Communist involvement in the Constitutionalist revolt.

For example, Jack Hood Vaughn, the assistant secretary of state for inter-American affairs, told Johnson right before the press conference that "the involvement, sir, of the Communist elements is becoming clearer and clearer."[113] Indeed, the fear of a Communist takeover came to dominate the White House's view of the revolt in the days leading up to Johnson's decision to send in the Marines on April 28 and the 82nd Airborne on April 30. During the highpoint of the crisis from April 25 to May 2, Johnson held dozens of meetings with National Security Adviser Bundy, Secretary of Defense Robert McNamara, and Secretary of State Rusk.[114]

JOHNSON ESCALATES THE INTERVENTION

Starting on April 28 and continuing through the next day, Johnson and his top advisers were in constant contact with Bennett in the embassy in Santo Domingo.[115] Bennett reported to Washington that "I regret we may have to impose a military solution to a political problem. . . . While leftist propaganda will fuzz this up as a fight between the military and its people, this issue is really between those who want a Castro-type solution and those who oppose it."[116] Bennett's tone left little doubt that the ambassador's interpretation of events in the capital city gave the White House very little room to maneuver. Seen through Bennett's lens, Johnson quickly concluded that American inaction in the face of a formidable Communist threat was antithetical to its interests.[117] Yet, despite this dire warning, even at this point the White House was reluctant to intervene unless the outcome was in doubt. This fact is one more indication that there was one overriding factor driving the decision to launch a full-scale intervention: fear of a pro-Communist outcome.

One question that historians have largely overlooked is this: If Washington was bent on stopping a Bosch presidency then why did not Johnson order the invasion sooner? The violence in Santo Domingo and threat to American lives were more than enough to allow Johnson to justify a military intervention. Yet in reality, Johnson waited for the situation to unfold, hoping that an intervention would not be necessary.

SECOND MARINE OPERATION

On April 28, Ambassador Bennett's alarming cables continued, and he pleaded to Washington that "the time has come to land the Marines."[118] Bennett's main concern was that Marine forces secure the embassy, as it was under sniper fire. Stating that his embassy staff was unanimously behind this recommendation, using the urgent classified CRITIC cables, Bennett asked that Rusk request that Johnson approve the "immediate landing" of Marines to continue to protect American citizens and also assist at the embassy.[119] During the evening, Johnson approved the plan. Within two hours, 526 Marines landed near the hotel, and 200 evacuees were flown to the USS *Boxer*. A platoon of Marines then went in taxis and private automobiles to the embassy to reinforce it.[120] It was the first time since 1928 that American Marines had landed in Latin America for military purposes.

About twenty minutes after Marines had received their order to go ashore, President Johnson met with congressional leaders at the White House to brief them on the operation and solicit their support. At 7:15 P.M., dressed in pajamas and holding a drink, Johnson told the congressmen that "I want you to know that I have just taken an action that will prove that Democratic presidents can deal with Communists just as strong as Republicans."[121] Senate Minority Leader Everett Dirksen (R-Ill.) in turn urged the president to take actions that were "vigorous and adequate." House Minority Leader John McCormack (R-Conn.) asked rhetorically whether the United States could afford "another Castro of this sort." Senator Fulbright told Johnson that "this has been the most informative meeting we have ever had. I feel much better informed. I support you fully."[122] Following his meeting with the members of Congress, Johnson informed Latin American ambassadors by telephone. At 8:51 P.M., the president made an announcement on national television that hundreds of Marines had landed in the Dominican Republic to protect the lives of Americans and other foreigners.[123]

A force of 500 Marines was Johnson's "Dominican policy" on April 28; this was hoped to be enough. Johnson agreed to more troops only after Bennett made it exceedingly clear to him that the situation required a much more robust U.S. force if Washington wanted to guarantee a non-Communist outcome.

As the dust began to settle after the first Marine landing the previous evening, Bennett continued to send frantic cables to Washington. In Bennett's estimation, the initial dispatch of Marines was not enough "in order to prevent another Cuba from arising out of the ashes of this uncontrollable situation."[124] By early afternoon on April 29, Johnson ordered the rest of the Marines aboard the *Boxer* to go ashore; one hour later, the Joint Chiefs of Staff ordered the remaining elements of the 6th Marine Expeditionary Unit aboard the Caribbean Ready Group (1,580 men) to go ashore.

82ND AIRBORNE OPERATION

Late on Monday night, April 26, the 82nd Airborne was placed on high alert in the eventuality that the initial decision to land the Marines did not prove adequate.[125] It was after this point that the White House's considerations were moving beyond evacuation of American nationals and toward an intervention that would quell the revolt and ensure that Wessin's forces were not totally defeated. The shooting and snipers at the U.S. embassy throughout the day on April 29 and the ambassador's heated cables had led policymakers in Washington to conclude that both the second Marine dispatch and the 82nd Airborne's deployment were needed.[126]

Some of Johnson's key advisers strongly believed that the insufficient use of forces at the Bay of Pigs in Cuba in 1961 had been a fatal mistake. During that operation, Cuban forces horribly outgunned CIA-trained Cuban exiles. President Kennedy then ordered the U.S. military not to provide air and sea cover for the beleaguered invading force. Johnson's team was not about to make the same mistake in the Dominican Republic, and for this reason they recommended sending a relatively large force into Santo Domingo.[127]

Following the landing of the entire amphibious force earlier that day, by the night of the April 29 the White House had concluded that a sizable force was needed, and this meant the 82nd Airborne. One hundred and forty C-130 transports flew from Pope Air Force Base in North Carolina

to San Isidro, which was still held by Loyalist forces.[128] Even just the location of the Airborne's landing demonstrably showed which side the U.S.
military was on. The operation did not go off without hitches, though, as
San Isidro's small area forced the transports to land instead of having the
troops jump.

At 2:30 A.M. on Friday, April 30, 2,000 paratroopers of the 82nd Airborne began landing at San Isidro. On that same day, U.S. paratroopers
departed San Isidro toward the Duarte Bridge, where they secured it and
moved across into Constitutionalist-held areas within the city. This action
prevented the Constitutionalists from crossing over the river to attack
Loyalist forces at San Isidro, one more manifestation of which side the
U.S. forces were supporting. By May 1, there were 6,200 U.S. troops in the
Dominican Republic. Within ten days, the U.S. military's buildup reached
23,000 men, half as many as were serving in Vietnam.[129]

Once the Marines and 82nd Airborne paratroopers were in place, the
Marines moved out from around the hotel areas and occupied nine square
miles in the western part of the capital to set up the OAS-sanctioned international security zone, a rectangular perimeter that ran along the ocean
from near the Hotel Embajador and then went into the old part of the city
to include the United States and most of the other foreign embassies.[130]
On May 3, troops from the 82nd Airborne continued to move west from
the Duarte Bridge and linked up with the Marines who had created the
international security zone beginning in the eastern end of the city. This
allowed the two U.S. forces to establish a corridor that stretched across the
city.

The U.S. military considered it a "line of communication," but there is
no doubt that this connectivity greatly enhanced the U.S. military position
vis-à-vis the Constitutionalists.[131] In addition to the communication concern, the public justification for the corridor was that it separated the two
sides; in reality, an additional reason was that the corridor served to isolate
the Constitutionalists from the rest of the city. This is exactly what the
United States wanted to happen: to quarantine the rebels so that the revolt
would not spread.[132]

What was also readily apparent is that, unlike the first and even second
Marine operations, there was no rescue or humanitarian value to the 82nd
Airborne's mission. Its primary task was to prevent a Loyalist defeat. At
the same time, though, Johnson's advisers did not want U.S. troops to be

directly involved in the fighting if this could at all be avoided. Fears of a "Budapest in the Caribbean," where U.S. troops were killing civilians just as Soviet troops did in Hungary, and the international damage to America's prestige that these images would produce remained at the forefront of policymakers' minds.

In short, Washington wanted to prevent a Communist takeover without provoking a full-scale U.S. occupation, another "Trujillo" or another "Budapest."[133] The orders that the Joint Chiefs of Staff gave to the commander of the U.S. intervention force sum up Washington's goals for the operation:

> Your announced mission is to save U.S. lives. Your unannounced mission is to prevent the Dominican Republic from going Communist. The President has stated that he will not allow another Cuba—you are to take all necessary measures to accomplish this mission. You will be given sufficient forces to do the job.[134]

JOHNSON SELLS THE OPERATION TO THE AMERICAN PUBLIC

Over the course of a little more than forty-eight hours, President Johnson had escalated the U.S. response to the Dominican crisis from a force of 500 Marines intended to evacuate American nationals and protect the U.S. embassy to a full-scale intervention into an incipient civil war. What is clear is that, in addition to securing the safety of U.S. citizens including the embassy personnel, the entire evolution of the response was predicated on preventing an outcome in the Dominican Republic that was antithetical to U.S. interests.

In a significant departure from Johnson's press release on April 28 that characterized the initial Marine invasion as one to protect American lives, on April 30 he warned that there were "signs that people trained outside the Dominican Republic are seeking to gain control."[135] Then in his May 2 speech, Johnson more specifically focused on the necessity of preventing a Communist takeover:

> Ambassador Bennett urged your president to order an immediate landing. In this situation hesitation and vacillation could mean death for many of our people as well as many of the citizens of other lands. I thought that we could not—and we did not—hesitate. Our forces, American forces, were

ordered in immediately to protect American lives. They have done that. They have attacked no one, and although some of our servicemen gave their lives, not a single American civilian and the civilians of any other nation, as a result of this protection, lost their lives. . . . The revolutionary movement took a tragic turn. Communist leaders, many of them trained in Cuba, seeing a chance to increase disorder, to gain a foothold, joined the revolution. They took increasing control. What began as a popular democratic revolution committed to democracy and social justice very shortly moved and was taken over and really seized and placed into the hands of a band of Communist conspirators. We know that many who are now in revolt do not seek a communist tyranny. We know it's tragic indeed that their high motives have been misused by a small band of conspirators who receive their directions from abroad. . . . Our goal in keeping the principles of the American system is to help prevent another Communist state in this hemisphere, and we would like to do this without bloodshed or without large-scale fighting.[136]

While not very controversial at the time he gave the speech, over the next several weeks a number of analysts and members of Congress began to question the justifications that Johnson used in this talk. The main criticism was that he exaggerated the Communist takeover threat to justify what had turned into a full-scale intervention. For example, journalist Tad Szulc started to openly question the true extent of Communist involvement in the revolt, as what he was witnessing on the ground in Santo Domingo did not fully square with the administration's portrayal of events. One particularly controversial episode occurred on April 29, when the U.S. embassy released a list of fifty-three identified Communists within the Constitutionalist ranks. Secretary of State Rusk backed up these assertions on April 30 during classified congressional hearings when he testified,

We have identified eight well-known Communist leaders who are very active at the present time in leading armed groups. We know there are about 40 to 50 Dominicans in the Dominican Republic who have been trained by Castro.[137]

Yet, contrary to the administration's claims, it was soon reported that some of the persons were double listed, in jail, or out of the country. The list was revised to include only fifty names.[138] As the situation stabilized in Santo Domingo following the U.S. intervention, it became readily apparent to many observers that the Johnson administration would not be able to credibly substantiate its claims about the overwhelming Communist domination of the Constitutionalist movement.

This skepticism of the veracity of the administration's claims began what came to be known as the "credibility gap," something that started with the Dominican intervention and became a much larger problem during the Vietnam conflict.[139] By the end of the first week of May, the *New York Times* wrote its first editorial on the crisis, stating that they would not have been against an intervention had a Communist takeover been imminent. "American troops were used almost as soon as they had landed for political ends on the basis of reports that a few dozen communists were involved in the rebellion and on the fear that they might gain control of it."[140] In short, many observers had no problem with a U.S. intervention to protect American lives, but they were entirely unprepared for an occupation that was taking sides in what appeared to them to be an internal conflict.

In the week following the intervention, the first voices from Capitol Hill began to question the administration's Dominican policy. At this point, the chief critic was Senator Robert Kennedy (D-N.Y.), who, in a May 6 speech on the Senate floor, questioned that "I don't think we addressed ourselves to the implications of what we did in the Dominican Republic." Kennedy went on to urge the United States to avoid a "blanket" condemnation of the Constitutionalist cause because "our objective must surely be not to drive genuine democrats in the Dominican revolution into association with the communists."[141] At the same time, though, there were voices in Congress that unequivocally supported Johnson's moves. Chief among these was Senator Thomas J. Dodd (D-Conn.), who advocated the interpretation that the Communists were in the process of hijacking the Constitutionalist revolt when the United States intervened:

> Extreme leftists took control of Radio Santo Domingo and operated in typical Castro style, parading captured Loyalists before television cameras and haranguing viewers with slogans and denunciations of the "bourgeois reactionaries, imperialists" and so forth. . . . This was the complexion of the rebellion when the original PRD leaders, who had organized the revolt to

restore Bosch, realizing that their movement had been captured by the Castroist and Communist left, took asylum and by this action renounced their by now nominal leadership.

Dodd also connected the United States' willingness to respond in Santo Domingo to the credibility of the United States in Vietnam:

> I hope the Senate will move rapidly to demonstrate that in the case of freedom we are prepared to pay any price. I have said, because I believe it to be true, that the outbreak in the Dominican Republic is directly tied to our struggle in Southeast Asia to defend freedom and independence of the people of Vietnam.[142]

Robert Kennedy's increasingly harsh criticisms did not deter the Johnson administration, as it stuck to the line that the threat warranted the military response, something that continued to be the mantra of the intelligence reports that were being passed to the White House. In comments made on May 4, President Johnson continued to press the Communist threat and danger to American lives:

> We are not the aggressor in the Dominican Republic. Forces came in there and overthrew that government and became aligned with evil persons who had been trained in overthrowing governments and in seizing governments and establishing Communist control, and we have resisted that control and we have sought to protect our citizens against what would have taken place. Our Ambassador reported that they were marching a former policeman down the streets and had threatened to line a hundred up to a wall and turn a machinegun loose on them. With reports of that kind, no President can stand by.[143]

In a telling comment that demonstrated his frustration with the way that the U.S. media were attacking his credibility on the Dominican issue, six weeks after the intervention Johnson told his cabinet members in a meeting,

> If I were called on to review the incidents of the Dominican Republic, beginning Saturday and going up through Wednesday and Sunday, I would take the same action. . . . I would have nothing to apologize for. . . . I am

very proud of what we did. . . . We evacuated 5,500 people. We landed
troops within the hour of our decision. We brought about generally a cease-
fire. . . . Castro is not as of now operating in the Dominican Republic. . . .
I want it clearly understood when any of my ambassadors tell me anyone
is shooting at American embassies and he Ambassadors are hiding under
desks—and we have five or six thousand people who stand a chance to be
murdered—the Ambassadors are going to get some action out of this government. You don't necessarily have to get the editorial approval. We are
going to go and do it.[144]

What is interesting about the Johnson administration's credibility gap
on the Dominican conflict is that, although they certainly were guilty of
inflating the Communist threat, there was far less controversy over the
intervention itself. In other words (and as we will continue to see), the
administration's biggest critics on Capitol Hill and the domestic media did
not have any serious problem with the administration's anti-Communist
justifications for going into the Dominican Republic; rather, they just did
not like the way that the administration publicly overhyped the reasons
for the intervention.

It is crucial to point out that just because the administration's portrayal
of the Communist involvement in the revolt was overstated and turned
out to be exaggerated does not mean that Johnson and his chief advisers
did not perceive a real threat brewing in Santo Domingo. In fact, transcripts of the taped recordings of Johnson's deliberations in the White
House during the Dominican crisis reveal an administration—and in particular a president—terrified by the potential for a Communist takeover
in the Dominican Republic. Once this is taken into consideration, we can
see how the credibility gap was driven by inaccurate and incomplete intelligence reports attempting to describe and predict events in Santo
Domingo. The transcripts and documents also reveal that Johnson was
deeply involved in the decision-making process leading up to, during, and
in the months following the intervention.

As we saw previously, Ambassador Bennett's cables beginning on April
28 left no doubt whatsoever where he believed the Dominican Republic
was headed without U.S. intervention. Influenced tremendously by Bennett's reporting and CIA intelligence reports, by April 30 Johnson's comments to his trusted adviser Abe Fortas show a president convinced that
American action was the only appropriate response:

They're killing our people. . . . They've captured our tanks now and they've taken over the police, and they're marching down the street, and they've got a hundred of them as hostages, and they're saying they're going to shoot them if they don't take over. Now, our CIA says this is a completely led, operated, dominated—they've got men on the inside of it—Castro operation. That it started out as a Bosch operation but he's been moved out of the picture . . . and their people took over. . . .

Since last Saturday, Bosch lasted for a few hours. Then Castro started operating.

We know it's Communist. So I think we ought to get [the CIA] to give us name, address, chapter, and verse . . . and say, "This is a case of Cuba doing this job . . . we ought to have our military forces in sufficient quantity . . . to take that island. And if we can get any other forces to join us, well and good. . . . [They should be] ready to do whatever job they may be called upon, without taking any overt action at this moment toward the invasion. . . . But if all that fails, I'm not going to sit here and say . . ." I can work it out after the Communist government is set up and start issuing orders.[145]

Later that same day, Johnson told Fortas, "I think that the worst domestic political disaster we could suffer would be for Castro to take over."[146] Amazingly, even though the conventional historical record has ultimately condemned Johnson for his decision to intervene on the side of the Loyalist forces, by April 30 Johnson was kicking himself for not having taken more decisive (more than the initial Marine deployment) sooner. "While we were talking yesterday, we ought to have been acting. . . . I think they're going to have that island in another twenty-four hours."[147]

Even more than a week after the initial intervention when criticism for the administration's exaggerations was becoming sharper and more abundant, Johnson clung to his belief that the Communist threat was real. On May 12 during a White House meeting, Secretary of Defense McNamara told the president that he was "dubious" that fifty-eight Communists could "control the revolt" and that he did not "believe that story that Bosch and Caamaño are controlled by the Castroistes." Johnson agreed with McNamara that their involvement was not certain but that "they [the Communists] can sure have a hell of an influence."[148]

What is critical to take into consideration when evaluating the Johnson administration's decisions is that they were based on inadequate, incomplete, and at times mistaken intelligence reporting; yet these intelligence reports defined the White House's "consciousness" on the Dominican crisis. Richard Rovere made this point in a May 1965 article in *The New Yorker*:

> If the CIA hugely exaggerated the strength of anti-Communist sentiment in Cuba at the time of the Bay of Pigs landings four years ago, it may well have exaggerated pro-Communist strength in the Dominican rebellion. But in situations such as the one he faced ten days ago, the President is hardly in a better position to reject the findings of the CIA than he is to challenge the reports of astronauts on conditions in outer space.[149]

THE JOHNSON ADMINISTRATION'S RESPONSE IN HISTORICAL AND GLOBAL CONTEXT

While with the benefit of several decades of hindsight the Johnson administration's preoccupation with the Communist question might seem either pathological or absurd, it is important to keep in mind the stakes that U.S. policymakers believed were in play in these types of Cold War crises. Based on the Cold War logic of containing communism at all costs, any expansion of Soviet or Cuban influence was by definition a threat to Washington.

At the height of the crisis on April 30, Johnson rhetorically asked Secretary of Defense McNamara and Undersecretary of State George Ball, "We have resisted communism all over the world—Vietnam, Lebanon, Greece. What are we doing under our doorstep?" The United States had to act forcefully because "Castro cannot take over."[150] In his memoirs in 1971, Johnson recalled, "The Communist leader in Havana was always alert to any exploitable weakness among his neighbors. He was promoting subversion in many countries in the Western Hemisphere, and we knew he had his eye on the Dominican Republic."[151]

It is also clear that the Johnson administration saw the Dominican crisis in global terms, especially in that a failure or lack of resolve in America's backyard could weaken its credibility around the world. Early on in the crisis, an exasperated Johnson asked himself, "What can we do in Vietnam if we can't clean up the Dominican Republic?"[152] In a White House cabinet meeting six weeks after the intervention began, Dean Rusk put the Dominican intervention in global terms when he said that global Communist propaganda is now concentrating on criticizing us on South Vietnam, the Congo and the Dominican Republic. Because it is quite clear that they had had plans for all three of these places that they have tried to commit to execution. So naturally since we are standing in their way, we are going to become the brunt of their propaganda typhoon. . . . But the Communist world has had plans on all three of these. . . . The Dominican Republic is under control. There will not be a Castro government in the Dominican Republic.[153]

THE ROLE OF THE OAS

From the beginning of the White House's reaction to the events in Santo Domingo, President Johnson knew that the OAS was critical for the operation's international legitimacy even if it was not needed militarily. Given that the United States was one of the chief architects of the structure of the inter-American system beginning in the 1930s and continuing in the post–Cold War period, the OAS's response to the Dominican crisis would be of critical importance if the Johnson administration wanted to be able to claim that it was acting with the OAS's approbation. In other words, Washington wanted to prevent a Communist takeover but was also concerned about hemispheric and global opinion.[154] This point was made well by Johnson adviser Arthur Schlesinger Jr. when he wrote to Bundy on May 2 that

> the problem is to prevent a communist takeover in the DR while doing as little harm as possible to our general position in the hemisphere. . . . It is conceivable that we may have no choice but to accept hemispheric condemnation, damn the torpedoes and go ahead; but clearly we should not pursue a course so risky to our long-term objectives unless we have exhausted all other possibilities.[155]

The United States had worked to create the OAS to resolve hemispheric disputes, and thus the events in Santo Domingo in 1965 would be a firm test of the organization's effectiveness and, more important, the willingness of the United States to work through the OAS as opposed to unilaterally. Yet at the same time, Johnson had almost no confidence in the hemispheric body's ability to effectively stabilize the situation in Santo Domingo, let alone ensure that the Communists did not take power. In a conversation with Senate Majority Leader Mike Mansfield on the morning

of April 30, the day the 82nd Airborne was going into San Isidro and the
OAS was voting on cease-fire resolution, Johnson said that

> The Castro forces are really gaining control. . . . We begged the [OAS] to
> send somebody last night. . . . They're just the damnest fraud I ever saw.
> . . . These international organizations aren't worth a damn, except window
> dressing. . . . It looks to me like I'm in a hell of a shape. . . . They're going
> to eat us up if I let another Cuba come in there. They'll say, "Why did you
> sit on your big fat tail?"[156]

Starting at 10:00 P.M. on April 29 but not finishing their deliberations
until 2:00 A.M. the next morning, the OAS passed its first resolution on
the Dominican situation, calling for an immediate cease-fire and the
establishment of an international security zone in Santo Domingo that
was intended to protect the various embassies in the capital.[157] The vote
was sixteen to zero with four abstentions (Chile, Uruguay, Mexico, and
Venezuela). With the Marines and the 82nd Airborne were already in
operation when the resolution was passed, the timing of the OAS's resolution immediately compromised the Johnson administration's attempt to
portray the intervention as an OAS-sanctioned, multilateral effort. Any
OAS approval of the intervention would be retroactive.[158]

A subsequent vote on May 6 to create the Inter-American Peace Force
(IAPF) to serve as peacekeepers in Santo Domingo received only the minimum fourteen votes (and this included the representative of the just
ousted—and far from legitimate—Dominican government).[159] The U.S.
delegation needed fourteen votes to pass the resolution, but on May 6,
Washington had lined up only twelve supporting nations. Thus, the vote
of José Bonilla Atiles—the Cabral government's delegate to the OAS—was
added to the thirteen existing votes. The governments voting in favor of
the IAPF were overwhelmingly from military regimes such (Brazil or Honduras) or dictatorships (Nicaragua and Paraguay). Costa Rica was the only
democratic government that participated in the IAPF, and it sent only
twenty police officers.[160] The IAPF soon began peacekeeping operations in
Santo Domingo.

While President Johnson was at best dubious of the OAS's ability to
accomplish anything worthwhile in Santo Domingo, in the early days following the intervention his administration nonetheless began to rely on

the OAS to lead the political negotiations. Declassified White House memoranda indicate that there was in fact a concerted effort to use the OAS to
promote a settlement that would restore a political system and a set of
leaders who were in the line of the Alliance for Progress's model of Latin
American social democratic reformers, such as former Venezuelan president Rómulo Betancourt.[161]

Washington's hope for a democratic-left commission with the credibility to resolve the crisis never went operational in Santo Domingo in part
because the Brazilian and Paraguayan foreign ministers objected to this
group, viewing them as too liberal and too partial to the Constitutionalist
side. At the same time, though, the fact that Washington even considered
this commission reveals a key component of U.S. policy following the sta-
bilization of the fighting: Washington made a number of concerted efforts
with the other Latin American countries to promote an outcome that consisted of left-leaning democratic leaders assuming political control.

For the Johnson administration, the only real excluding qualification
was that they could be viewed as Communist or even willing to tolerate
Communist activity in the country. For example, on May 26, the Department of State sent a cable to Bundy (who by then was in Santo Domingo
attempting to negotiate an agreement between the two factions) informing him, "We hope OAS will continue to establish [sic] government of
moderate progressively oriented anti-communist elements representing a
broad spectrum of Dominican opinion. We are making our information
available to the OAS."[162]

WASHINGTON DETERMINES THE OUTCOME IN
SANTO DOMINGO

In the midst of the fighting in Santo Domingo, the Loyalist forces named
air force general Pedro Bartolomé Benoit as president of the newly formed
junta. The junta immediately called for the Constitutionalist forces to surrender, yet this was a demand the Loyalist forces could not enforce seeing
as their forces had just been defeated at the battle of the Duarte Bridge.[163]
Benoit also immediately called on the United States to intervene to maintain order, a request that was rejected by Ambassador Bennett.

By May 7, when the fierce fighting had subsided and U.S. troops had
cut off the Constitutionalist forces from the rest of the city, Benoit stepped
down and was replaced by a Government of National Reconciliation

(GRN) headed by Antonio Imbert, who had been one of Trujillo's assassins. Imbert stated that he had joined the GRN in order to "save the Dominican people from Communist dictatorship."[164] Yet the establishment of the new Loyalist junta did not end the legitimacy problem: on the same day, Colonel Caamaño was sworn in to be the "constitutional president," meaning that there were two competing governments in the capital city.

For the next several days following the creation of the Imbert junta, U.S. diplomats worked with the papal nuncio, Monsignor Emanuele Clarizio, in efforts to get the two sides together. These delicate negotiations were complicated by the fact that Constitutionalist forces were taking advantage of the cease-fires to move snipers into position, and the Loyalists were planning for a major offensive. Indeed, on May 14, Imbert's forces attacked the Constitutionalist-held *Radio Santo Domingo* station from the air. By the end of the second week of May, at least two cease-fires were broken. The situation remained tense and could have easily spilled out of control, another indicator that U.S. intervention might have been the only thing that kept the two sides from outright warfare.

From Washington's perspective, the Imbert junta served as an important political ballast to Caamaño's "government." At the same time, though, and especially after the immediate threat of a Communist takeover had been addressed through the military intervention, U.S. officials were fearful that allowing Imbert to take over permanently would create "another Trujillo." This was certainly true of Johnson, who on May 12 shouted, "I'm not going down in history as the man responsible for putting another Trujillo in power."[165] As we will see, Imbert had more permanent plans for himself than did Washington, a key difference that led to great tension between the two sides over the next several months. In fact, in the fall of 1965, Imbert was a much greater obstacle to the U.S. plans for a democratic election and withdrawal of foreign troops than were the Constitutionalists.

THE GUZMÁN FORMULA

In early May, the White House established the "Bundy committee" to promote a political solution to the standoff in Santo Domingo. The committee members were the key decision makers on the Dominican crisis from the involved agencies and included Thomas Mann, Deputy Secretary of Defense Cyrus Vance, Deputy Director of the U.S. Information Agency

Donald Wilson, and Deputy Director of the CIA Richard Helms. At the same time that the Bundy committee was being organized in Washington, responding to a special request from President Johnson, John Martin, who had been ambassador in Santo Domingo during the Bosch years, met with Bosch in Puerto Rico.

Within two weeks Bundy, Abe Fortas, Cyrus Vance, and Jack Hood Vaughn also went to Puerto Rico to meet with Bosch. The talks finally moved forward once Bosch dropped his call for an immediate withdrawal of U.S. troops. After days of secret talks, Bosch and Bundy agreed on the main components of what came to be called the "Guzmán formula." Bosch and Bundy agreed that PRD leader Silvestre Antonio Guzmán Fernández would be the choice for provisional president.[166] From Washington's perspective, Guzmán was the best among the liberal candidates, as he was viewed as one of the most pro-American. Indeed, an October 1963 National Security Council memorandum described Guzmán as "very pro-U.S." and "not strong PRD."[167]

The Bundy committee's initial support of the "Guzmán formula" indicates that Washington was looking for a solution that would allow for a social democratic government as long as it was squarely anti-Communist. A State Department memo stated that Guzmán "does not seem to us very strong, but we believe his repeated assertion of convinced anti-communism. . . . While discussion shows solid base of your basic policy: Constitution Si, Communism No."[168] Indeed, the major point of contention between Bundy and Guzmán was what to do about Communists in any Guzmán government or even just in the country. On May 16, Fortas returned to Washington, and Bundy and Vance moved on Santo Domingo to continue the negotiations.

As one might expect, Imbert was furious that Bundy was working with Guzmán, who "will be nothing but a puppet of Bosch" and the proposed provisional government "would again open doors to [the] growth of Communist influence and would lead to another blood-bath."[169] Yet the politically liberal Bundy remained committed to producing an outcome that adhered to at least some of the provisions of the 1963 constitution.

In fact, even Bennett, who had been the main advocate for a U.S. intervention, was concerned with Imbert and the potential for Trujillo supporters to get back into positions of political power. In a cable to Bundy on May 20, Bennett wrote that "concerning active Communists and active

Trujillistas it is agreed that they present a problem for democratic government in the Dominican Republic and that effective measures must be taken by the Constitutionalist Government to protect the Dominican people from their subversive activities."[170] He followed up the next day with another cable to Bundy that read,

> [As] regards Imbert, the gangster side of his nature has surged rapidly to the fore as he has felt himself more pressed. He is getting advice from among others, old Trujillo types whom I find unacceptable to U.S. interests as extreme left elements downtown.[171]

Yet as Bundy was continuing to work on the Guzmán formula in Santo Domingo, back in Washington, Johnson was beginning to voice concerns about the U.S. support for Guzmán. All of Johnson's top liberal advisers, such as Abe Fortas and Arthur Schlesinger Jr., believed that Guzmán would be another Bosch but without "Boschismo": all the democratic reform but none of the worry about communism. On the other side were Johnson's more conservative voices, such as Mann, Bennett, and Bruce Palmer, who commanded the U.S. forces in the Dominican Republic. They believed that both Bosch and "Boschismo" (read Guzmán) needed to be prevented at all costs and that Washington should work to get someone such as Balaguer back through democratic elections. This diversity of views that Johnson drew on is noteworthy and shows a laudable commitment to open dialogue and debate.

Transcripts from White House deliberations reveal that Johnson was torn between his liberal and conservative advisers. For example, on the evening of May 14, Abe Fortas—operating under the code name Mr. Davidson—reported to Johnson that progress had been made on negotiations with Bosch in Puerto Rico. Johnson was immediately excited that progress was being made toward a solution, but he also worried that he would be attacked by conservatives for being too soft on the Communist question: "Here's our problem. . . . My right wing . . . won't give me forty cents if I'm not careful. . . . I've got my Ambassador and I've got my general and I've got my CIA people and I got my Navy admiral, and they're just about to revolt on me."[172]

As the days passed, Johnson becomes increasingly unable to comprehend that the U.S. approach—provisional government, democratic elec-

THE DOMINICAN INTERVENTION, 1965

tions, but no communism—was not working. He was also being criticized from the left, which saw the American position as imperialist, and the right, which viewed it as weak on communism. On May 18, Bundy updated the president from Santo Domingo about potential scenarios, and Johnson responded,

> It doesn't look like to me that there is any evil in this—if we get reasonably honest people, if they're anti-communists, if we're going to have a popular referendum in two months on the basics of the machinery—the constitution. . . . Now I don't know what else you could do. We could pick a dictator and just say, "To hell with the constitution!" . . . Looks to me like we're being about as democratic as you can be. . . . I don't know what else we could do if we stayed there a million years.[173]

There is no question that Johnson would have ideally preferred the Guzmán formula. Yet, even though the Constitutionalists were isolated in Santo Domingo, Johnson concluded that Guzmán was not the right man. Johnson also betrayed his growing irritation with liberal U.S. critics of his administration's policies toward the crisis. Referring to his support of Mann and other conservative voices in the administration,

> I'm not going to let . . . a bunch of little yellow pinkos run them out of the government. . . . They're loyal and they work hard. They're not going to get rid of me for four years, and they're not going to get rid of them.[174]

Convinced that he could not risk an outcome that would paint him as hesitant or unwilling to address communism at America's doorstep, Johnson ultimately agreed with his conservative advisers. Johnson instinctively sided with his more straight-talking conservative advisers than the intellectual and elitist liberal ones (almost all holdovers from the Kennedy administration). On May 19 at the White House, Johnson remarked,

> I have more confidence in Mann's judgment that I do Bundy's. . . . Now he is a whipping boy, and he had incurred the displeasure of the Bundy's and the Schlesinger's and the rest of them, because he doesn't agree with each theoretical thing.[175]

On May 26, the Guzmán formula finally ended, and after ten days of furious negotiations in the country, Bundy immediately returned to Washington. Johnson had decided that Guzmán was simply not worth the risk.[176]

THE AD HOC COMMITTEE

By June, the OAS created a new three-person mission known as the Ad Hoc Committee (AHC) with representatives from the United States, Brazil, and El Salvador. The committee ultimately was able to iron out a lasting agreement between the two sides that paved the way for democratic elections the following year. Ellsworth Bunker, who up until this point was still the U.S. ambassador to the OAS, was appointed as the U.S. representative on the committee. The committee began its work in Santo Domingo during the first week of June.[177] Constitutionalist commander Caamaño immediately rejected the AHC, believing that, especially after the breakdown of the Guzmán formula, the OAS was a tool of Washington and that the rebels were better off negotiating through the United Nations.

In fact, UN Secretary-General U Thant sent José Antonio Mayorbe, a Venezuelan from Betancourt's *Acción Democratica* party, as a "special observer." Bunker was concerned that Mayorbe, who was openly critical of the U.S./OAS approach, was getting in the way of the AHC's negotiations and that he might lead the Constitutionalists to believe that a more favorable accord could be reached.[178] In short, Bunker wanted to keep the United Nations out and the OAS in.[179]

By June, the two warring Dominican sides were getting firmer, and a solution appeared farther away than ever. Bunker made it clear to Washington that he would tell it what needed to be done rather than wait for its instructions. Bunker's negotiations were much slower than Bundy's, as he did not believe that a "home-run" solution was possible. Rather, the crisis was now "trench warfare," and a settlement would be more attrition than decisive victory.[180] During its existence, the AHC met with Caamaño forty-eight times and with Imbert or the Loyalist military fifty-three times.[181]

The Constitutionalists had five demands: reinstatement of the 1963 constitution, restoration of the 1963 congress, formation of a democratic government, continuation of Constitutionalist forces in the military, and the immediate withdrawal of the American and OAS troops. By contrast, the GRN argued that it was the sole legitimate government and that it must rule in that capacity during any transitional period. Bunker soon realized that it would be virtually impossible to get the two factions to agree to a settlement and that he needed to reach over their heads and appeal directly to the Dominican people. In a June 10 cable to Dean Rusk, Bunker wrote,

> I have reached the conclusion that about [sic] only way to break present political impasse here and restore a measure of harmony is to let the people decide for themselves through free and open elections supervised by OAS and the formation in the meantime of a provisional government of technicians who, governing under an institutional act with strong OAS support, could take [sic] country to elections.[182]

On June 16 and 17, the AHC's recommendations were published in two documents that took the Dominican population's desire for democracy and attempted to channel it in support for a provisional government.[183]

Unlike the Guzmán formula, which attempted to rely on a complete package solution, the AHC's proposal was a framework and not a settlement. What was needed was for the Dominican people to believe in the process of the proposal; details would be worked out later. The proposals addressed issues such as a general amnesty, a temporary constitution that would guarantee civil liberties, military reform, and elections of local and national leaders to be held six to nine months after the establishment of the provisional government.

GARCÍA GODOY BECOMES PROVISIONAL PRESIDENT

On June 20, Caamaño announced over the radio his intention to negotiate on the basis of the proposals. He added that the IAPF must leave no later than one month after the establishment of the provisional government and that all rebel officers be reinstated at their original mark, among other demands. The GNR indicated its support for the proposals but said that they should also include the deportation of all identified Communists as well as the immediate removal of the IAPF. Knowing that the IAPF's departure would likely lead to more fighting, Bunker did not consider either side's claim. Instead, Bunker identified Dr. Héctor García Godoy, who had served as foreign minister under Bosch and as vice president of Balaguer's Reformist Party, as the candidate for provisional president.

The biggest obstacle to the García Godoy solution was Imbert, who had become quite comfortable in his position as head of the GNR. In one aborted plan, Bunker and Bennett jointly recommended to Washington that Johnson issue a statement awarding Imbert a medal or an invitation for him and his wife to visit the White House. The request was withdrawn, as it was decided that it was too sensitive for Johnson to be seen courting an undemocratic leader.

The pressure on Imbert to step down increased when, after a few weeks of deadlock, the Constitutionalist leadership agreed to the AHC's plan for the provisional government; they also announced that they would not oppose García Godoy as president. Far-left groups such as the 14th of June Movement, however, criticized the Constitutionalists' decision, arguing that García Godoy was a "reactionary" imposed by the OAS. On June 28, Balaguer returned from exile and announced his support for the proposal.

In early August, the AHC distributed what it considered the final settlement proposals. These documents contained the texts of the "Acts of Conciliation," an agreement drafted by the AHC that set out the specifics of the provisional government. They key element of the act was the naming of García Godoy as provisional president, a general amnesty, and measures to release political prisoners. Weeks of jockeying by both sides ensued. During this time, the State Department continued to remind Bunker that Washington's first priority was still preventing a Communist government:

> The objective of preventing communist takeover in the Dominican Republic remains [sic] essential U.S. objective. In view of weakness and division in non-communist ranks it is important that person emerging as single president of [sic] provisional government clearly understand [sic] communist problem and that he be determined to deport or otherwise immobilize leading communist personalities in all three parties and prevent three communist parties from participating in an electoral process.[184]

Weakened even further by his own military's support for the AHC plan, Imbert resigned on August 30, and the next day the Act of Reconciliation was signed by the Constitutionalists and the military, which signed for the Loyalist side. García Godoy took over as head of the provisional government on September 3, and Bunker then assumed the role of "adviser" to the provisional government. From now on, the IAPF no longer maintained its ostensible neutrality between the forces; it was now overtly supporting the provisional government. General elections were to be held in no more than nine months' time.

No puppet of the United States, García Godoy's first critical task was to take care of problematic (i.e., those not cooperating with the U.S.-supported solution) military officers among the Constitutionalist and Loyalist ranks. García Godoy first focused on Wessin, who for many Dominicans had by now become a symbol of antidemocratic forces. Yet Wessin commanded an intensely loyal following and had no desire to leave the country. After a tense standoff—which included IAPF units blocking his forces—Wessin agreed to leave the Dominican Republic for Miami on a U.S. military plane.[185]

A few months later, García Godoy turned his sights to the Constitutionalist side. On January 6, 1966, García Godoy announced on national radio that dozens of Constitutionalist and Loyalist officers—including Camaaño—would have to step down. While there was initial resistance to this decision, including a move from disgruntled Loyalist forces against the provisional government, García Godoy was able to quell this attempt with the reluctant support of the IAPF.

It is important to point out that while the White House was squarely behind the García Godoy government, IAPF commanders Palmer and Alvim still leaned toward the Loyalist/military forces, a departure from U.S. policy that was eventually corrected through stern words from Washington. The Johnson administration had its strategy in place, and it was not about to allow one of its military officers to set his own policy. Several weeks later and with the help of Juan Bosch, who acted as a mediator, Colonel Camaaño agreed to be "reassigned" as a military attaché in London.

Over the course of the fall of 1965, there was continued concern in Washington that García Godoy had appointed leftist leaders to his cabinet, but Bennett argued successfully that giving him a looser rein would demonstrate his independence and bolster his legitimacy. If anything, repeated rightist attempts against García Godoy served to ingratiate him with American diplomats and the White House, as he was increasingly seen as a critical moderate voice between two extremist sides. In one indication of his growing legitimacy, a November 21 right-wing coup attempt against him was put down by the military, not the IAPF.[186]

On September 25, 1965, Bosch returned to the Dominican Republic. In a fit of irony, U.S. soldiers guarded Bosch as he departed the plane to chants of "Yankees no!"[187] But by this point, the Johnson administration was not overly concerned with Bosch returning to the political scene in the Dominican Republic. However, there was still a lingering fear that he would be manipulated or eventually ousted by more hard-line leftist elements.[188]

More than Bosch, it was Bosch's party, the PRD, that Washington had its eye on. Rostow warned about the "political polarization" in the Dominican Republic, which, left unchecked, could allow for the PRD's "radical elements" to move toward the "extreme left" and "make for common cause with the Communists." In a memo, Rostow provided Johnson with three scenarios:

> Let matters take their course and hope for the best. (This is out of the question.)
>
> Encourage the death of the PRD to the point that it becomes an extreme left splinter associated with or allied to the Communists, and thereby discredited. (It is too risky to let the Communists capture the PRD label.)
>
> Try to keep the PRD from moving to the far left and at the same time persuade Balaguer to open up his party. (This is the sensible course we *must* follow.)[189]

FULBRIGHT ATTACKS JOHNSON'S DOMINICAN POLICY

In September 1965, the Johnson administration's Dominican policy—which by this point was looking increasingly successful, as the García Godoy government was in office and presidential elections were slated for the following year—received by far its sharpest critique. It is interesting that Senator Fulbright—who in the early days of the crisis appeared supportive if not uninterested—led the charge. Fulbright's attack centered largely on the administration's credibility; more important, this was a more personal matter against the president, as he "decided to go for it on the Dominican Republic because he felt he was being stonewalled (by Johnson) on Vietnam."[190] Specifically, Fulbright had felt betrayed on the Gulf of Tonkin Resolution (which gave the president greater leeway to escalate the U.S. commitment in Vietnam without Congress's approval) the previous year. Fulbright was even more heated that Johnson had not met with congressional leaders in July before he announced a move to increase troop numbers in Vietnam.[191]

This theme continued in his dramatic September 15 speech on the Senate floor (Fulbright had provided the White House with a copy that morning). The senator focused on Johnson's credibility on the Dominican issue. American policy in the Dominican crisis was "characterized initially by timidity and subsequently by overreaction. Throughout the whole affair, it has also been characterized by a lack of candor." Fulbright conceded that it was "understandable that administration officials should have felt some sense of panic; after all, the Foreign Service officer who had the misfortune to be assigned to the Cuban desk at the time of Castro's rise to power has had his career ruined by congressional committees."[192] Fulbright nevertheless also criticized the administration from straying from the principles of the inter-American system:

The point I am making is not—emphatically not—that there was no communist participation in the Dominican crisis, but simply that the administration acted on the premise that the revolution was controlled by Communists—a premise which it failed to establish at the time and has not established since. . . . The United States had legal recourse when the crisis broke on April 24, 1965. We could have called an urgent session of the Council of the OAS. . . . But we did not do so. The United States thus intervened in the Dominican Republic unilaterally—and illegally. . . . Underlying the bad advice and unwise actions of the United States was the fear of another Cuba. The specter of a second Communist state in the Western Hemisphere—and its probable repercussions within the United States and possible effects on the careers of those who might be held responsible— seems to have been the most important single factor in distorting the judgment of otherwise sensible and competent men. . . . The tragedy of Santo Domingo is that a policy purported to defeat communism in the short run is more likely to have the effect of promoting it in the long run.[193]

As one might expect, Johnson "went nuts" after hearing about Fulbright's speech and never forgave the senator for his perceived betrayal. Johnson quietly barred Fulbright from state ceremonies; a few months later, he denied Fulbright and his staff a jet to use to travel to a conference in New Zealand. As Fulbright's aide Pat Holt recalled, the irony of this move was that it forced Fulbright to take three more days to make the trip, time that "gave him lots of time to read up on Vietnam."[194] While Johnson would not express his outrage publicly, Senator Thomas Dodd had no reservations about accusing Fulbright of suffering from "an indiscriminating [sic] infatuation with revolutions of all kinds." Dodd also implied that Fulbright's speech benefited Fidel Castro. "The [chairman's] speech will be picked up and played heavily by every Communist and crypto-Communist and anti-American leftist who wields a pen in the Latin American press."[195]

While Fulbright's speech has been used by critics as the manifestation of important parts of the U.S. political establishment's turning against Johnson's Dominican policy, once put into context Fulbright's actual criticisms—while certainly valid—lose some of their bite. For example, Fulbright lambasted the administration for acting on the "premise" that the revolution was controlled by Communists. What Fulbright failed to acknowledge is that the administration truly believed that the revolution was controlled—or could soon be controlled—by Communists.

One might ask, What would have been Fulbright's reaction if Johnson had not intervened "unilaterally" and "illegally" and Communists took over? Nor did Fulbright give Johnson credit for orchestrating a "liberal" postintervention solution, one that led to Bosch's return to the Dominican Republic only ten days after he made his Senate speech. The truth of the matter is that, as his initial response to the crisis indicated, Fulbright had no problem with a "unilateral" and "illegal" intervention. Rather, Fulbright "didn't like being lied to (by Johnson)" and thus wanted to expose the imperfections of Johnson's Dominican policy.[196]

THE 1966 ELECTIONS

The Reformist Party's Balaguer won the IAPF-supervised presidential election in June 1966 with 56 percent of the votes; the PRD's Bosch came in second with 39 percent, and Rafael Bonnelly of the National Integration Movement received 35 percent. The pro-Castro 14th of June Movement took less than 1 percent.

Bosch ran a listless campaign; in fact, concerned for his safety, he rarely left Santo Domingo. On the other hand, Balaguer ran an aggressive and well-organized effort, one that went after Bosch's former base of support:

rural farmers and women. There is no doubt that some Dominicans were afraid to vote for Bosch because they feared that, while he was their true choice, his return to the presidency would entail a renewal of violence or political instability. A classified American intelligence report on the elections characterized Dominican voter preference:

> The US is almost certainly viewed as anti-Bosch and committed to the Balaguer candidacy. This will give Bosch the benefit of anti-Yankee prejudice at the polls. At the same time, many Dominicans will recognize that, without US economic aid and its steadying influence exercised through the OAS and the IAPF, no solutions to the country's grave political and economic problems are possible. Many such people will vote for Balaguer despite a possible distaste for the Yankee presence.[197]

We know that the Dominican people voted enthusiastically for Bosch back in 1962, yet his tenure as president was viewed largely as disappointing. This fact helps explain why opinion polls in precrisis 1965 had Balaguer ahead of Bosch. Amazingly, Balaguer's margin of victory over Bosch in 1966 closely mirrored the pre-1965 polling numbers. In other words, it is not unreasonable to conclude that Bosch would have lost a free and fair election to Balaguer even if the United States had not intervened in 1965 or provided secret funds to the Balaguer campaign in 1966.[198]

Declassified documents show that, to help ensure that its preferred candidate won the elections, the Johnson administration organized a covert effort to assist Balaguer's campaign. Interestingly, Washington decided to provide support for Balaguer in part because it concluded that critics would accuse the United States of supporting Balaguer even if it actually remained neutral.[199] As part of this operation, Washington even considered also providing support to Bosch (although in much smaller amounts) to make him seem like a "viable" candidate.[200] The U.S. government organized the 303 Committee to carry out this operation. A secret memo laid out its mission:

> The purpose of the projected operation is to provide essential support to Balaguer's campaign; its implementation must be guided by certain basic considerations. First, it is essential that the operation be carried out in such a way that United States sponsorship cannot be proven in any way.
> Two factors enter here: (a) the U.S. is already believed to favor Balaguer

and will be accused of supporting him regardless of its real actions; (b) the exposure of actual facts of U.S. support would be nonetheless damaging both to the U.S. and to Balaguer. Normal operating conditions in the gold-fish bowl environment of Santo Domingo present difficult security problems. Such problems will be further complicated by the international attention and interest which will be focused to an unprecedented degree on the Dominican elections.

Second, while Balaguer will need financial help as well as assistance in other forms in order to overcome certain handicaps, the amount of assistance given him must be controlled to avoid overweight. His campaign should be lean and hungry and his party organization should exert itself to the utmost in order to achieve the necessary degree of efficiency and at the same time hold to a minimum the inevitable accusations that he is getting help from non-Dominican sources. In addition to money, Balaguer will need help in the form of advice and information.[201]

Opinion polls taken in the fall of 1965 suggested that Balaguer enjoyed a wide lead over Bosch (42 to 28 percent) in a head-to-head presidential contest. (The poll also found that 64 percent of Dominicans viewed the U.S. intervention positively.)[202] Yet, in what adds a layer of complexity to the conclusion about the impact of the U.S. covert assistance, the Johnson administration was alarmed by confidential polls taken in the weeks leading up to the June 1966 election indicating that Bosch was closing the gap on Balaguer.[203] It is likely that covert American funds were used to help Balaguer campaign aggressively during these crucial final weeks, especially in rural areas. Adviser Walt Rostow wrote in a memo to President Johnson, "I underlined again that nothing should be spared which will not be counterproductive to get out the rural vote."[204] It is impossible to know for certain to what extent this secret funding influenced the outcome of the election. Yet the extent of American involvement was very likely far less than outright fraud.

While it was an open secret that Johnson and his key advisers in the White House and State Department desperately wanted Balaguer to win the 1966 election, it is noteworthy that at the same time the U.S. government's most critical intelligence estimate argued that a Bosch presidency might not be as bad as many in Washington feared:

This is not to say that Bosch would set a policy line antithetical to US interests, but simply that he bears a bitterness which cannot readily be erased and would not be likely to cooperate more enthusiastically than he thought necessary. For example, a government headed by Bosch would probably be difficult in dealings with the US on OAS matters, but would probably go along with the US position on most global issues considered by the UN. In general, we believe that he would be likely to follow foreign policy lines acceptable to the US, mainly because of concern that badly-needed US economic aid would not otherwise be continued.[205]

It is unlikely that President Johnson would have agreed with this more encouraging assessment of Bosch, but the fact that the report represented the consensus view of the American intelligence community suggests that there were important elements within the U.S. government that would have been more accepting of a Bosch presidency.

A DEMOCRATIC LEGACY?

Perhaps one way to evaluate the quality of democracy in the Dominican Republic is not to necessarily condemn it because Bosch failed to win the presidency in 1966 but rather to look at the Dominican political system in the years following the intervention. While far from perfect, Dominican democracy was unquestionably stronger than it had been before the U.S. intervention.

Balaguer's tenure in office often tended toward the autocratic and certainly was not a model of democratic practices. Yet at the same time, Balaguer was reelected in 1970—the first time in Dominican history that a president had been democratically elected for two consecutive terms without military intervention or chaos. Interestingly enough, in the years immediately following Balaguer's election, Washington secretly funded non-PRD leftist parties so that the "participation of a responsible opposition also served to make the victory of the PR [Reformist Party] more generally acceptable and had the net effect of strengthening both President Balaguer's image and the democratic process in the Dominican Republic."[206]

A decade later, in 1978, Balaguer lost to Antonio Guzmán, the very same politician of the failed "Guzmán formula." The 1978 election was not perfect, as the military intervened when it was clear that Guzmán was going to win. Yet, under pressure from the Carter administration, Guzmán took office, and a peaceful transition of power from one elected president to another took place.[207]

In 1982, Jorge Blanco, also of the PRD, was elected. Tragically, Guzmán committed suicide before Blanco was inaugurated. Bosch ran unsuccessfully for president in 1966, 1978, 1982, and 1990, indicating that he was never able to regain the popularity he enjoyed when first elected president. Unlike its absolute dominance in the centuries and decades leading up to 1965, the Dominican military has been largely and increasingly out of politics since the intervention.

As we have discussed previously, the conventional critique of the U.S. intervention is that it forestalled a scenario that would have inevitably been progressive and democratic had U.S. Marines and paratroopers not squashed it. Yet we should weigh any damage caused by the 1965 intervention or subsequent meddling in the 1966 elections against the U.S.-orchestrated political settlement that led to relatively free elections and the rapid departure of American forces.

Given the country's tumultuous and violent history, a compelling case can be made that the U.S. intervention prevented an incipient civil war from turning into something much worse. The intervention also helped promote a modern political system that has provided four decades of highly imperfect but uninterrupted democracy after over a century of tumult.

There is no question that democracy in the Dominican Republic after the American intervention did not emerge nearly as quickly or as strongly as was the case after the U.S. interventions in Grenada and Panama. What is interesting about this fact is that the U.S. use of military force in the Dominican crisis was much *less* than the full-scale invasions that took place in Grenada and Panama.

This is not to say that a full-scale invasion in 1965 would necessarily have ensured faster and better democracy in the Dominican Republic. Nevertheless, even raising this question should make us reconsider the still pervasive view that U.S. intervention dashed the country's "glorious" future and replaced it with a much darker chapter in Dominican history.

NOTES

1. Abraham F. Lowenthal makes a similar point in *The Dominican Intervention* (Cambridge, Mass.: Harvard University Press, 1972), 151.
2. Lowenthal, *The Dominican Intervention*, v.
3. Piero Gleijeses, *The Dominican Crisis: The 1965 Constitutionalist Revolt and American Intervention* (Baltimore: Johns Hopkins University Press, 1978), xi.

4. Gleijeses, *The Dominican Crisis*, 287.

5. John Bartlow Martin, *Overtaken by Events: The Dominican Crisis from the Fall of Trujillo to the Civil War* (New York: Doubleday, 1966), 31.

6. Martin, *Overtaken by Events*, 22.

7. Abraham F. Lowenthal, "The United States and the Dominican Republic: Background to Intervention," *Caribbean Studies* 10, no. 2 (July 1970): 31.

8. Martin, *Overtaken by Events*, 22.

9. Quoted in Martin, *Overtaken by Events*, 23.

10. Martin, *Overtaken by Events*, 24.

11. Quoted in Martin, *Overtaken by Events*, 26.

12. Nancy Mitchell, *The Danger of Dreams: German and American Imperialism in Latin America* (Chapel Hill: University of North Carolina Press, 1999), 225–26.

13. G. Pope Atkins and Larman C. Wilson, *The Dominican Republic and the United States: From Imperialism to Transnationalism* (Athens: University of Georgia Press, 1998), 40.

14. Martin, *Overtaken by Events*, 27.

15. Gleijeses, *The Dominican Crisis*, 15.

16. Martin, *Overtaken by Events*, 28.

17. Atkins and Wilson, *The Dominican Republic and the United States*, 45.

18. Gleijeses, *The Dominican Crisis*, 17.

19. See Lowenthal, *The Dominican Intervention*, 9.

20. Martin, *Overtaken by Events*, 29.

21. Martin, *Overtaken by Events*, 29.

22. For this type of interpretation, see Gleijeses, *The Dominican Crisis*, 17–18.

23. Martin, *Overtaken by Events*, 30.

24. Atkins and Wilson, *The Dominican Republic and the United States*, 51–52.

25. Martin, *Overtaken by Events*, 31.

26. Martin, *Overtaken by Events*, 30.

27. Atkins and Wilson, *The Dominican Republic and the United States*, 53.

28. Quoted in Martin, *Overtaken by Events*, 31.

29. Atkins and Wilson, *The Dominican Republic and the United States*, 59.

30. Peter Smith, *Talons of the Eagle: Dynamics of U.S.-Latin American Relations* (Oxford: Oxford University Press, 2000), 61.

31. Atkins and Wilson make a similar point in *The Dominican Republic and the United States*, 61.

32. See Max Boot, *The Savage Wars of Peace Small Wars and the Rise of American Power* (New York: Basic Books, 2002), 180–81.

33. Atkins and Wilson, *The Dominican Republic and the United States*, 59.

34. Quoted in Gleijeses, *The Dominican Crisis*, 21.

35. Vásquez's was originally elected to a four-year term in 1924. After that, he was not allowed to succeed himself.

36. Quoted in Martin, *Overtaken by Events*, 44.

37. Audrey Bracey, *Resolution of the Dominican Crisis, 1965: A Study in Mediation* (Washington, D.C.: Institute for the Study of Diplomacy, Edmund A. Walsh School of Foreign Service, Georgetown University, 1980), xi.

38. Atkins and Wilson, *The Dominican Republic and the United States*, 66.

39. Martin, *Overtaken by Events*, 45.

40. Gleijeses, *The Dominican Crisis*, 23.

41. Atkins and Wilson, *The Dominican Republic and the United States*, 96.

42. The insurgents consisted of fifty-five Dominicans in the first three landings. Six days later, two more landings by boat took place near Estero Hondo and Maimóm, towns on the country's northern coast. See Martin, *Overtaken by Events*, 50.

43. Martin, *Overtaken by Events*, 50.

44. On June 24, 1960, Betancourt was badly burned when a device planted along a parade route exploded near him. Betancourt then asked the OAS to sanction the Trujillo government. See Martin, *Overtaken by Events*, 45. In June 1960, the OAS's Inter-American Peace Committee accused the Dominican government of "flagrant and widespread violations of human rights." This was the first official condemnation of Trujillo's regime. Soon after, in August 1960, the OAS responded at the Sixth Meeting of Consultation of Ministers of Foreign Affairs in San José, Costa Rica. See Larman Wilson, "The Monroe Doctrine, Cold War Anachronism: Cuba and the Dominican Republic," *Journal of Politics* 28, no. 2 (May 1966): 336.

45. For more on U.S. involvement in Trujillo's assassination, see Stephen G. Rabe, *The Most Dangerous Place in the World: John F. Kennedy Confronts Communist Revolution in Latin America* (Chapel Hill: University of North Carolina Press, 1999), 39.

46. See Lowenthal, *The Dominican Intervention*, 26.

47. Bracey, *Resolution of the Dominican Crisis, 1965*, xii.

48. Center for Strategic Studies, *Dominican Action, 1965: Intervention or Cooperation?* (Special Report Series No. 2, Georgetown University, Washington, D.C., July 1966), 2; see also Eric Thomas Chester, *Rag-Tags, Scum, Riff-Raff, and Commies: The U.S. Intervention in the Dominican Republic, 1965–1966* (New York: Monthly Review Press, 2001), 27. Wessin commanded the Armed Forces Training Center at San Isidro. It was an elite group of around 2,000 infantry troops that had tanks and artillery. San Isidro housed a total of 4,000 troops, all the tanks in the armed forces, and almost all of the air force. One observer noted, "Everyone in the Dominican Republic knew that whoever controlled San Isidro controlled the country." See Lawrence A. Yates, *Power Pack: U.S. Intervention in the Dominican Republic, 1965–1966* (Fort Leavenworth, Kans.: Combat Studies Institute, U.S. Army Command and General Staff College, 1988), 22.

49. Quoted in Wilson, "The Monroe Doctrine, Cold War Anachronism," 333.

50. Quoted in Lowenthal, "The United States and the Dominican Republic," 50.

51. Quoted in Rabe, *The Most Dangerous Place in the World*, 41.

52. The PRD was founded in 1939 in Havana by a group of Dominican exiles. In 1961, it enjoyed a membership of around 3,000 exiles and 3,000 Dominicans operating underground. See Gleijeses, *The Dominican Crisis*, 38.

53. Richard Pearson, "Juan Bosch, 92, Dies; Led Dominican Republic," *Washington Post*, November 2, 2001.

54. Atkins and Wilson, *Dominican Republic and the United States*, 129.

55. Jerome Slater, "Democracy vs. Stability: The Recent Latin America Policy of the United States," *Yale Review*, winter 1966, 174; see also Theodore Draper, "The Dominican Crisis," *Commentary* 40, no. 6 (December 1965): 33–68.

56. Martin, *Overtaken by Events*, 347.

57. Lyndon Baines Johnson, *The Vantage Point. A Time of Testing: Crises in the Caribbean* (New York: Holt, Rinehart & Winston, 1971), 189.

58. Quoted in Yates, *Power Pack*, 16.

59. Lowenthal, *The Dominican Intervention*, 31.

60. Quoted in Chester, *Rag-Tags, Scum, Riff-Raff, and Commies*, 39.

61. Quoted in Rabe, *The Most Dangerous Place in the World*, 47.

62. Tad Szulc, *Dominican Diary* (New York: Delacorte Press, 1965), 13.

63. Yates, *Power Pack*, 17.

64. Bracey, *Resolution of the Dominican Crisis, 1965*, xiii.

65. Atkins and Wilson, *Dominican Republic and the United States*, 131.

66. Rabe, *The Most Dangerous Place in the World*, 47.

67. Lowenthal discusses this in *The Dominican Intervention*, 30–37. See also Gleijeses, *The Dominican Crisis*, 97–99.

68. Lowenthal, *The Dominican Intervention*, 38.

69. Ramón Tapia stepped down from the Triumvarite on April 8, 1964, and was replaced by Ramón Cáceres. Manuel Taveres left on June 27, 1964, and was not replaced.

70. Chester, *Rag-Tags, Scum, Riff-Raff, and Commies*, 41–42.

71. Center for Strategic Studies, *Dominican Action, 1965*, 3.

72. Lowenthal, *The Dominican Intervention*, 41.

73. Alan McPherson, *Yankee No!: Anti-Americanism in US-Latin American Relations* (Cambridge, Mass.: Harvard University Press, 2003), 159.

74. Special National Intelligence Estimate SNIE 86.2–64, Washington, D.C., January 17, 1964; Daniel Lawler and Carolyn Yee, eds., and Edward C. Keefer, general ed., *Foreign Relations, 1964–1968: Dominican Republic; Cuba; Haiti; Guyan* (Washington, D.C.: U.S. Government Printing Office, 2005), 1–7.

75. Martin, *Overtaken by Events*, 648.

76. Lowenthal, *The Dominican Intervention*, 54.

77. Yates, *Power Pack*, 24–28.

78. See "Dominican Coup Deposes Regime; Rebels Are Split," *New York Times*, April 26, 1965.

79. Gleijeses, *The Dominican Crisis*, 159.

80. Bruce Palmer, *Intervention in the Caribbean: The Dominican Crisis of 1965* (Lexington: University Press of Kentucky, 1989), 20.

81. Tad Szulc, "US to Evacuate Nationals Today in Dominican Crisis," *New York Times*, April 27, 1965. See also Tad Szulc, "Dominican Revolt Fails after a Day of Savage Battle," *New York Times*, April 28, 1965.

82. Szulc, *Dominican Diary*, 43.

83. Yates, *Power Pack*, 31.

84. Lowenthal, *The Dominican Intervention*, 93.

85. Jerome Slater, *Intervention and Negotiation: The United States and the Dominican Revolution* (New York: Harper and Row, 1970), xv.

86. Center for Strategic Studies, *Dominican Action, 1965*, 29.

87. Molina Ureña left the U.S. embassy building and went to the Colombian embassy, where he requested and received political asylum.

88. Center for Strategic Studies, *Dominican Action, 1965*, 30.

89. Szulc, *Dominican Diary*, 23.

90. Quoted in Yates, *Power Pack*, 31.

91. Slater, *Intervention and Negotiation*, xvi.

92. Yates, *Power Pack*, 47.

93. Lowenthal, *The Dominican Intervention*, 80.

94. Theodore Draper, "A Case of Defamation: U.S. Intelligence versus Juan Bosch," *New Republic*, February 19, 1966, 18.

95. Theodore Draper, "A Case of Defamation: U.S. Intelligence versus Juan Bosch—II," *New Republic*, February 26, 1966, 15–18.

96. Gleijeses, *The Dominican Crisis*, 288.

97. "The Communist Role in the Dominican Rebel Movement, 16–27 May," CIA Intelligence Memorandum, May 27, 1965, *Dominican Republic*, Declassified Documents Reference System (hereafter cited as DDRS) (Farmington Hills, Mich.: Gale Group, 2003).

98. Senate Committee on Foreign Relations, "The Situation in the Dominican Republic," 14 July 1965, *Executive Sessions of the Senate Foreign Relations Committee* 17, 89th Cong., 1965 (declassified in 1990), 788.

99. Senate Committee on Foreign Relations, "The Situation in the Dominican Republic," July 16, 1965, 867.

100. Senate Committee on Foreign Relations, "The Situation in the Dominican Republic," July 16, 1965, 883.

101. Senate Committee on Foreign Relations, "The Situation in the Dominican Republic," July 19, 1965, 915.

102. Palmer, *Intervention in the Caribbean*, 3.

103. Chester, *Rag-Tags, Scum, Riff-Raff, and Commies*, 58.

104. Szulc, *Dominican Diary*, 33.

105. Palmer, *Intervention in the Caribbean*, 25.

106. Szulc, *Dominican Diary*, 33.

107. Quoted Michael Beschloss, *Searching for Glory: Johnson's White House Tapes* (New York: Simon & Schuster, 2001), 284–85.

108. "Department of State Memorandum for McGeorge Bundy," April 26, 1965, DDRS.

109. "CIA Report on Whether the Dominican Republic Will Turn into Another Cuba," April 27, 1965, DDRS. The memo states that it was passed the secretary of state on April 27, 1965.

110. CIA cable, April 29, 1965. This same cable reported that forty-five "extremists" had returned to the Dominican Republic since the previous October and that they had received training in Cuba or elsewhere in the Soviet bloc.

111. Quoted in Michael Beschloss, *Searching for Glory: Johnson's White House Tapes* (New York: Simon & Schuster, 2001), 287.

112. Quoted in Beschloss, *Searching for Glory*, 287.

113. Quoted in Beschloss, *Searching for Glory*, 288.

114. Philip Geyelin, "The Dominican Republic—'Just Like the Alamo,'" in *Lyndon B. Johnson and the World* (New York: Praeger, 1966), 236–58.

115. Herbert G. Schoonmaker, *Military Crisis Management: U.S. Intervention in the Dominican Republic, 1965* (New York: Greenwood Press, 1990).

116. Quoted in Szulc, *Dominican Diary*, 44.

117. For more on this point, see Leonard C. Meeker, "The Dominican Situation in the Perspective of International Law," *Department of State Bulletin* 53, no. 1359 (July 12, 1965): 60.

118. Quoted in Chester, *Rag-Tags, Scum, Riff-Raff, and Commies*, 78.

119. Martin, *Overtaken by Events*, 656. Quotation is from Yates, *Power Pack*, 49.

120. Center for Strategic Studies, *Dominican Action, 1965*, 35.

121. Quoted in Howard J. Wiarda, "The United States and the Dominican Republic: Intervention, Dependency, and Tyrannicide," *Journal of Interamerican Studies and World Affairs* 22, no. 2 (May 1980): 247; see also "Minutes of Meeting with Congressional Leadership on Dominican Republic. The Cabinet Room," April 28, 1965, DDRS.

122. Quoted in H. W. Brands Jr., "Decisions on American Armed Intervention: Lebanon, Dominican Republic, and Grenada," *Political Science Quarterly* 102, no. 4 (winter 1987–1988): 619.

123. Martin, *Overtaken by Events*, 657.

124. Quoted in Yates, *Power Pack*, 55.

125. Szulc, *Dominican Diary*, 34.

126. To be sure, there is no question of where the White House's or the U.S. embassy's sympathies lay before April 29. For example, on Monday, April 26, U.S. military attachés at San Isidro relayed requests to the U.S. embassy for communications equipment for the Loyalist forces.

127. Lowenthal, *The Dominican Intervention*, 95–118.

128. See Max Frankel, "Latins' Aid Asked; Hemisphere Is Urged to Join to Prevent Another Cub," *New York Times*, May 3, 1965.

129. Gleijeses, *The Dominican Crisis*, 258.

130. Szulc, *Dominican Diary*, 80.

131. Chester, *Rag Tags, Scum, Riff-Raff, and Commies*, 103.

132. Slater, *Intervention and Negotiation*, 55.

133. Lowenthal, *The Dominican Intervention*, 119.

134. "43, Editorial Note," in Lawler et al., *Foreign Relations, 1964–1968*, 102.

135. Quoted in "Statement by President Johnson," *Department of State Bulletin* 52, no. 1351 (May 17, 1965): 742.

136. "Text of Johnson's Address on U.S. Moves," *New York Times*, May 3, 1965.

137. "The Situation in the Dominican Republic and Vietnam," U.S. Senate Hearing, Committee on Foreign Relations, Washington, D.C., April 30, 1965, *Executive Sessions of the Senate Foreign Relations Committee, Together with Joint Sessions with the Senate Armed Services Committee* 17, 89th Cong., 1965 (declassified in 1990).

138. See Murray Marder, "Crisis under the Palms," *Washington Post*, June 27, 1965.

139. Beschloss writes that the term "credibility gap" was first used on May 23, 1965, by the *New York Herald Tribune*. See Beschloss, *Searching for Glory*, 310.

140. Quoted in Szulc, *Dominican Diary*, 146.

141. Quoted in Chester, *Rag-Tags, Scum, Riff-Raff, and Commies*, 111; see also John D. Morries, "Kennedy Critical of Johnson Move," *New York Times*, May 8, 1965.

142. Thomas J. Dodd, "Vietnam and the Dominican Republic," *Congressional Record* 4 (May 1965): 9356–57.

143. Senate Foreign Relations Committee, *Background Information Relating to the Dominican Republic*, 89th Cong., 1st sess. (Washington, D.C.: U.S. Government Printing Office), July 1965, 63.

144. Lyndon B. Johnson, "The Cabinet Meeting of June 18, 1965," Executive Office of the President, *Presidential Document Series, Minutes and Documents of the Cabinet*

Meetings of President Johnson (1963–1969), Primary Sources in US Presidential History,
Lexis-Nexis.

145. Quoted in Beschloss, *Searching for Glory*, 297–300.

146. Quoted in Beschloss, *Searching for Glory*, 301.

147. Quoted in Beschloss, *Searching for Glory*, 304.

148. Quoted in Beschloss, *Searching for Glory*, 317.

149. Richard Rovere, "Letter from Washington," *The New Yorker*, May 15, 1965,
204–13.

150. Quoted in Brands, "Decisions on American Armed Intervention," 611.

151. Johnson, *The Vantage Point*, 188.

152. Quoted in Atkins and Wilson, *The Dominican Republic and the United States*,
136.

153. Johnson, "The Cabinet Meeting of June 18, 1965."

154. Lowenthal, *The Dominican Intervention*, 115.

155. Schlesinger to Bundy and Moyers, May 2, 1965, DDRS.

156. Quoted in Beschloss, *Searching for Glory*, 297.

157. Palmer, *Intervention in the Caribbean*, 28–29. On the morning of April 28, the
U.S. delegation asked at the regular meeting of the OAS for more discussion of the
Dominican crisis. No request was made to authorize an intervention, as U.S. officials
did not believe it would be necessary. On Thursday, April 29, a special session of the
council of the OAS met in Washington and decided that it would be necessary to
invoke the Rio Treaty or call a consultation of foreign ministers under the OAS charter. The foreign ministers' meeting took place at 10:00 P.M. on April 30 and lasted until
2:00 A.M. the next day.

158. Center for Strategic Studies, *Dominican Action, 1965*, 43.

159. Gleijeses, *The Dominican Crisis*, 261.

160. Atkins and Wilson, *The Dominican Republic and the United States*, 138–39. An
OAS resolution on May 10 created a unified command for the IAPF, and then on May
22 the OAS authorized that Brazil would command the force and that the United
States would serve as the deputy commander. Thus, General Hugo Panasco Alvim was
named commanding general and General Bruce Palmer, the former U.S. commander,
his deputy. The U.S. military began withdrawing troops after the Latin American
forces began arriving. Still, during the summer of 1965, the Latin American forces were
largely token compared to the size of the U.S. presence. As of July 1965, the IAPF
consisted of 1,735 military personnel from six Latin American countries: 1,115 from
Brazil, twenty policemen from Costa Rica, three officers from El Salvador, 250 troops
from Honduras, 164 troops from Nicaragua, and 183 troops from Paraguay. During
the fighting, Loyalist forces lost roughly 825 persons (500 armed forces and 325 police
officers), while the Constitutionalist forces suffered 600 killed. Total civilian and military casualties were around 6,000. The U.S. forces lost forty-four persons (twenty-
seven killed in action) and 172 wounded. The IAPF had six Brazilians and five Para-
guayans wounded. See Atkins and Wilson, *The Dominican Republic and the United
States*, 147.

161. "White House Memorandum from Gordan Chase to McGeorge Bundy," May
6, 1965, DDRS.

162. "Department of State Cable. Outline of Bundy Mission to the Dominican
Republic," DDRS.

163. Chester, *Rag-Tags, Scum, Riff-Raff, and Commies*, 75.

164. Quoted in Szulc, *Dominican Diary*, 155.

165. Quoted in Yates, *Power Pack*, 115.

166. The first scenario considered was that Guzmán would serve out the remainder of Bosch's term. Bundy then received orders that this idea should be dropped and that Guzmán would instead serve as a provisional president until new elections could be held.

167. Quoted in Chester, *Rag-Tags, Scum, Riff-Raff, and Commies*, 138.

168. "Department of State Memorandum," May 16, 1965, DDRS.

169. Quoted in Chester, *Rag-Tags, Scum, Riff-Raff, and Commies*, 159.

170. "Cable to McGeorge Bundy, Department of State," May 20, 1965, DDRS.

171. "White House Cable from Ambassador Bennett," May 21, 1965, DDRS. On the same day that Bundy arrived in Santo Domingo, Imbert launched *operación limpieza* (operation cleanup) against the Constitutionalist forces. Imbert continued to push U.S. commanders to allow him to cross over the line of control and finish off the Constitutionalist forces for good.

172. Quoted in Beschloss, *Searching for Glory*, 325.

173. Quoted in Beschloss, *Searching for Glory*, 331.

174. Quoted in Beschloss. *Searching for Glory*, 327.

175. Quoted in Beschloss, *Searching for Glory*, 332–33.

176. Memorandum for the Record, Cabinet Room, White House, Notes from Richard Helms, Deputy Director of the CIA, June 2, 1965, in Lawler et al., *Foreign Relations, 1964–1968*, 254.

177. Bunker had previously been ambassador to Argentina and was the successful mediator of the Dutch–Indonesian crisis in 1962.

178. Atkins and Wilson, *The Dominican Republic and the United States*, 139.

179. On May 3 at the United Nations, the Soviet Union accused the United States of having "flagrantly violated" the UN Charter with its "criminal intervention" in the Dominican Republic. The U.S. ambassador to the United Nations, Adlai Stevenson, responded by saying that the Soviet Union was "attempting to exploit the anarchy in the Dominican Republic for its own ends." See Senate Foreign Relations Committee, *Background Information Relating to the Dominican Republic*.

180. Gleijeses, *The Dominican Crisis*, 273.

181. For a thorough analysis of the AHC, see Bracey, *Resolution of the Dominican Crisis, 1965*, 1–30.

182. "Department of State Telegram to the Secretary of State from Ellsworth Bunker," June 10, 1965, DDRS.

183. The proposals were called the "Declaration to the Dominican People" and "Proposals for a Solution to the Dominican Crisis."

184. "Outline of Objectives in Restructuring Dominican Government. Department of State Memo for Bunker," June 26, 1965, DDRS.

185. Slater, *Intervention and Negotiation*, 143.

186. One episode was particularly controversial. On December 19, 1965, 30 Loyalist troops attacked Colonel Camaaño and a group of 100 former Constitutionalist forces who had just attended a memorial service outside the provincial city of Santiago. The fighting continued until IAPF forces arrived, but the OAS-sanctioned force was criti-

cized for its delay in arriving, something that critics believed was intended to assist the Loyalist forces. See Gleijeses, *The Dominican Crisis*, 277–78.

187. McPherson, *Yankee No!*, 160.

188. For Johnson's views on Bosch, see Johnson. *The Vantage Point*, 180–205; see also Kurt Wagenheim, "Talking with Juan Bosch," *The New Leader*, February 28, 1966, 7–10.

189. "White House Memo from Walt Rostow," November 18, 1966, DDRS (underline in the original).

190. Author phone interview from Duck, North Carolina, with Seth Tillman, Fulbright Staff Member on the Senate Foreign Relations Committee, July 17, 2003.

191. The Senate Foreign Relations Committee began an investigation into the U.S. intervention in July 1965. These hearings culminated in Fulbright's September speech. What was clear from these combative hearings was that Fulbright was much more concerned about the veracity of the administration's claims than the intervention itself. See "The Situation in the Dominican Republic," *Executive Sessions of the Senate Foreign Relations Committee, Together with Joint Sessions with the Senate Armed Services Committee 17*, 89th Cong., July 15, 1965.

192. "The Situation in the Dominican Republic," *Congressional Record—Senate*, September 15, 1965, 23855–65. For Thomas Mann's comments on these points, see Thomas C. Mann, "The Dominican Crisis: Correcting Some Misconceptions," *Department of State Bulletin 53*, November 8, 1965, 730–38. See also "U.S. Policy toward Communist Activities in Latin America: Pro and Con." *Congressional Digest*, November 19, 1965, 260; "The Dominican Crisis: The Hemispheric Acts," United States Department of State, 1965.

193. "The Situation in the Dominican Republic," *Congressional Record-Senate*, September 15, 1965, 23855–65.

194. Author interview with Pat Holt, staff member on the Senate Foreign Relations Committee, Arlington, Virginia, July 18, 2003.

195. Quoted in Peter G. Felten, "The Path to Dissent: Johnson, Fulbright, and the 1965 Intervention in the Dominican Republic," *Presidential Studies Quarterly* 26, no. 4 (fall 1996): 1014.

196. Author phone interview with Seth Tillman.

197. National Intelligence Estimate, April 28, 1966; Lawler et al., *Foreign Relations, 1964–1968*, 398.

198. Memorandum from the Assistant Secretary of State for Economic Affairs (Solomon) to President Johnson, 17 June 1966; Lawler et al., *Foreign Relations 1964–1968*, 420.

199. Memorandum Prepared for the 303 Committee, January 11, 1966; Lawler et al., *Foreign Relations 1964–1968*, 368–70.

200. Lawler et al., *Foreign Relations 1964–1968*, 357–61.

201. Lawler et al., *Foreign Relations 1964–1968*, 357–61.

202. Letter from the Ambassador to the Dominican Republic (Bennett) to the Undersecretary of State for Economic Affairs (Mann), November 20, 1965. Lawler et al., *Foreign Relations 1964–1968*, 346–47.

203. Memorandum from the President's Special Assistant (Rostow) to the President, May 10, 1966; Lawler et al., *Foreign Relations 1964–1968*, 411.

204. Memorandum from the President's Special Assistant (Rostow) to the President, May 10, 1966; Lawler et al., *Foreign Relations 1964–1968*, 411.

205. National Intelligence Estimate, April 28, 1966; Lawler et al., *Foreign Relations 1964–1968*, 400.

206. Memorandum Prepared for the 303 Committee, June 28, 1968; Lawler et al., *Foreign Relations 1964–1968*, 520.

207. James Nash, "What Hath Intervention Wrought? Reflections on the Dominican Republic," *Caribbean Review* 14, no. 4 (1985): 9.

3

The Invasion of Grenada, 1983

The Reagan administration's decision to invade Grenada in October 1983 is best viewed in the context of the changing global environment in the 1970s and early 1980s. Unlike the Dominican invasion that occurred before the "credibility gap" and before the politically divisive and militarily dubious war in Vietnam, the Grenada invasion took place at a time when many Americans were questioning America's morality and resolve in the world.

The Iranian hostage crisis that began in 1979 and the Soviet invasion of Afghanistan the same year exacerbated the post-Vietnam and post-Watergate malaise in the country. Furthermore, the economic stagnation of the late 1970s and early 1980s did nothing to bolster confidence in America's position in the world.[1] Indeed, by the end of Jimmy Carter's term in early 1981, a growing number observers—especially conservatives—began to believe that the United States was on the defensive in the international arena, especially vis-à-vis the Soviet Union.

The Marxist Sandinista guerrilla insurgency's consolidation power in Nicaragua after the more broad-based overthrow of dictator Anastasio Somoza—and the prospect that the same thing was going to happen in El Salvador—led many U.S. policymakers to believe that the United States was also losing the war against communism right in its own backyard. After taking office in 1981, the Republican administration under Ronald Reagan started to ratchet up its rhetoric against the Sandinistas and leftist guerrillas attempting to seize power in nearby El Salvador. The Reagan administration firmly believed that the Soviets and Cubans were implementing a phased strategy to turn Central America into a series of Communist satellites. To prevent this perceived doomsday scenario, the Reagan administration adopted a "zero-tolerance" policy against Communist expansion in the region in addition to supporting efforts to militarily overthrow the Sandinistas.

Reagan made no apologies about his belief that the United States needed to check and even roll back perceived Communist gains in Central America and throughout the world. Reagan believed he was elected in large part to restore America's prestige and self-confidence. Thus, Reagan interpreted the invasion of Grenada and its subsequent approbation from the American people as the triumph, validation, and viability of the anti-Communist, hawkish interpretation of the Cold War. In the words of one of Reagan's senior foreign policy advisers, Grenada was a "small but crucial piece of a very large geopolitical jigsaw puzzle."[2]

Early on, the Reagan administration identified the Grenadian regime as a threat to security as well as an extension of the Soviet/Cuban axis into the Western Hemisphere. Then in 1983, when it was perceived that American lives were being threatened, Reagan did not hesitate to order U.S. troops onto the island to secure the safety of the American citizens and enact what was later called "regime change" in one of the "Evil Empire's" Caribbean outposts. The Reagan administration viewed its battle with communism as one pitting good versus evil, and Grenada was too close geographically and too easy militarily to pass up.

Critics denounced the invasion for many of the same reasons that conservatives had embraced it. While conservatives celebrated the use of U.S. military force to protect Americans, oust a murderous regime, and install a democracy, many academics and liberals saw the invasion as one more example of U.S. imperialism in the Caribbean.[3] In particular, opponents of the invasion also strongly objected to Reagan's rhetorical justification for the invasion. Comments such as Reagan's famous quip "We got there just in time" infuriated observers who believed that Reagan was resorting to this moralistic rhetoric in order to cover the more nefarious and calculating means of the United States.

To be sure, in the post-Vietnam era, many conservatives and increasing numbers of ordinary Americans wanted "victories," and Reagan provided them with Grenada. Grenada was undoubtedly a case of rolling-back communism that could not lose. Yet the case of Grenada goes well beyond this widely held interpretation. The intelligence reports that the White House had received in the years preceding the invasion indicated that the country was indeed being readied to serve as a base for Cuban operations in the region.

Like the case of intelligence regarding the Constitutionalist revolt in Santo Domingo, the critical question is not whether this intelligence was correct but whether U.S. policymakers perceived it to be correct. The Reagan administration also received intelligence reports that concluded that the safety of the American medical students could not be guaranteed and that a "Tehran-like" hostage situation was not out of the question.

Thus, no matter how inflated Reagan's rhetoric justifying the invasion might have seemed to critics, there were several legitimate reasons why a regime change option was preferable to, say, an economic embargo against Grenada or simply doing nothing. There is no denying that the timing of the Grenada crisis was extremely critical to the Reagan administration's decision to invade. In addition to the looming nightmare of another hostage situation, the more immediate tragedy of a terrorist attack in Beirut that killed 241 Marines only a few days before the invasion weighed heavily on the minds of White House officials.

What many critics of the Grenada operation did not anticipate was the American public's widely supportive response to it. Liberal Democratic congressmen immediately jumped on the invasion as evidence that Reagan was a warmongering "cowboy" who had unleashed naked American aggression and could not be trusted with foreign policy lest he act too rashly and get the United States involved in an unnecessary war with the Soviets. Governments throughout the world were outraged at the seemingly unprovoked U.S. military adventure in the Caribbean; some focused on the abstract idea of an "invasion," arguing that the violation of another state's sovereignty was always wrong.[4] Still others were quick to draw a moral equivalency between the U.S. invasion of Grenada and the Soviet invasion of Afghanistan a few years earlier.

Based on polls conducted shortly after the invasion, one can infer that many Americans believed Reagan when he told them that Grenada was being readied as a military base.[5] They believed him when he told them that American lives were in danger and that the United States needed to act promptly in order to prevent a bad situation from becoming much worse. They believed him when he said that the United States would leave behind a free and democratic Grenada. A solid majority of the American people saw little if any equivalency with Soviet actions in Afghanistan. As we will see, this unprecedented level of support for Reagan's moral, muscular, and unapologetic foreign policy left many of his political opponents breathless; in fact, many initial congressional critics quickly came around to supporting the president's action.

A common perception following the Vietnam debacle was that the American public was unwilling to support sending its young men to other countries in order to fight ill-defined wars against ill-defined enemies. And, indeed, had the Dominican crisis come after Vietnam, there is little doubt that there would have been many more critics to the Johnson administration's decision to intervene in that civil war.[6]

The fact that almost all of Grenada's island neighbors were squarely behind the invasion weakened the critics' argument that this was a unilateral action and that it was unpopular regionally. In fact, from the beginning of the crisis, the Caribbean nations were out well ahead of the United States in their belief that a U.S.-led invasion was both desirable and necessary.

It certainly did not hurt that Grenada was "close, convenient, and small" (whereas Vietnam was "far, inconvenient, and jungly") and that the American public received the news of the invasion as a fait accompli.[7] With its population of around 100,000 and size of 142 square kilometers, Grenada might have not been very representative of the sacrifice and effort normally needed to roll back Communist regimes and install democracy around the globe. (A joke that circulated at the time went something like, "Why didn't Reagan invade Rhode Island instead?" Answer: "Too big!") Nonetheless, Grenada was a feather in the cap for the "Reagan Doctrine": a new type of post-Vietnam foreign policy.[8]

Given the public's post-Vietnam hostility toward large-scale U.S. military interventions abroad, President Reagan knew very well that regime change through military invasion in Cuba or even Nicaragua was out of the question. So in terms of his anticommunism strategy, Grenada offered a great deal: it made Americans feel good about themselves and sent a message of resolve to the rest of the world. In this sense, the Reagan administration achieved an extraordinary "bang for its buck" in Grenada as it simultaneously demonstrated America's willingness to use force to back up its policies, rally Americans around the flag, address a perceived threat to Americans, and overthrow a repressive, hated regime and replace it with a democratic one.

The invasion of Grenada relegitimized the use of military force as a means of effecting political and strategic change in areas of the world where the United States had an interest.[9] The invasion of Panama in 1989 to remove Manuel Noriega's regime from power was the next example of regime change and democracy by force. Yet had there been no successful and popular Grenada invasion, it is highly unlikely that the George H. W. Bush administration would have ordered the invasion of Panama.

In this sense, the Grenada and Panama invasions can be seen as precursors to the military operations in Kosovo in 1999 and Operation Iraqi Freedom in 2003. Grenada was undoubtedly a creation of the unique climate of the Cold War and its singular focus on preventing Communist expansion, yet its lessons outlived the Cold War and continue to influence U.S. foreign policy.

It is also important to evaluate the Grenada invasion in terms of what the United States left behind after its military troops left the island. In a prescient article soon after the invasion, *The Economist* magazine laid out the appropriate criteria for evaluating the invasion:

> If, as the Americans have promised, the invasion enables the Grenadians to restore their democratic institutions and freely choose who shall govern them, that will provide a stronger justification than is likely to be found in any other quarter. It may also make some of this week's shouting sound far too shrill.[10]

GRENADA UNTIL 1983

In 1833, Grenada became part of the British Windward Islands administration, which meant that the governor of the Windward Islands ruled Grenada until the end of colonial rule in 1974. The country's modern history began in the early 1950s, when young Grenadian-born black labor activist Eric Gairy returned to his country and began to organize against the colonial government and Grenada's mulatto elite. Gairy was a former teacher, sugarcane cutter, and oil refinery worker. He first gained notoriety when he won compensation for tenant farmers who were from a rural estate. One of the first Grenadians to activate the politics of the majority

Grenada

★ National Capital
--- Parish Boundary
--- Road
···· Rivers

0   4   8 Kilometers
0   4   10 Miles

**Saint Vincent
And The
Grenadines**

Mayreau

Tobago Cays

Union
Island
Ashton

Prune Island
(Palm Island)

Martinique Channel

Petit Saint Vincent
Island

Petit
Martinique

GRENADINES

Hillsborough

Grand Bay

Carriacou

Saline Island

Frigate Island

Large Island

C a r i b b e a n   S e a

Diamond
Island

Les
Tantes

Ronde
Island

Caille Island

London Bridge

Green Island

Sandy Island

Bird
Island

Sauteurs

Victoria

Tivoli

Gouyave

Grand Roy

Grenville

Marquis

Grenada

St.George's

Saint
Davids

Belmont

Calivigny

Point
Salines

Pt. Salines
Intl. Airport

Glover
Island

black working class, in 1950 Gairy registered a labor union whose creation led to a general strike in February 1951. The colonial authorities responded by declaring a state of emergency, and British troops arrested Gairy.

Gairy was first elected to the Legislative Council in the British colonial administration in 1951. In 1961, Gairy became chief minister, but only a year later the British suspended the constitution and dismissed Gairy and his administration for the misuse of public funds. Undeterred, Gairy returned to power in 1967, when his political party, Grenada United Labour Party (GULP), won the elections and placed Gairy as prime minister.[11] As prime minister, Gairy used his charisma to rail against the bureaucracy and political and economic elites and champion the plight of rural agricultural workers. Gairy also maintained cordial relations with Washington, although Grenada's low geopolitical standing meant that there was never much of a strategic relationship.

Quickly, however, Gairy consolidated his increasingly autocratic rule and, in the spirit of the Dominican Republic's Trujillo, conferred on himself "some thirty honors, decorations, degrees, and titles."[12] While he did not kill or torture as many people as Trujillo did, Gairy did establish a police state—including the notorious militia group the "Mongoose Gang"—filled with informers and security agents. Fear was widespread. Gairy was also one of the world's most bizarre political figures. For example, Gairy asked the UN General Assembly to declare 1978 "the year of the UFO." Gairy also believed that his rule was a direct command from God and claimed that he could send out "love waves" to his enemies that prevented them from sleeping or eating.[13]

Historian Gordon Lewis has described Gairy's ideas as a "curious mix of God, Marx, and the British Empire" and "bogus radicalism."[14] In addition to his heavy-handed rule, Gairy's inept economic management further increased resentment against his regime. In 1976, his government enacted a law that required banks to place 5 percent of their deposits in the treasury; this increased to 10 percent two years later and then was increased to 20 percent.[15]

By the early 1970s, there was growing opposition to Gairy's increasingly unpredictable and authoritarian rule. Many middle-class Grenadians who had been studying in the United States returned to oppose a repressive political system; Gairy responded to this incipient political opposition by further strengthening the state's repressive apparatus. The New Jewel Movement (NJM) was founded on March 11, 1973, and was a combination of three opposition movements that were united against Gairy and his GULP Party.[16]

The NJM was a formation of middle-class intellectuals who met in small private groups in the late 1960s and early 1970s to discuss political issues. Similar groups had been active in Trinidad and Jamaica in the 1940s and 1950s.[17] The NJM was especially influenced by events such as the Cuban revolution and the black power and civil rights movements in the United States. Many of its leaders had studied outside Grenada, including Maurice Bishop, who had studied in London, and Bernard Coard, who had studied at Brandeis University in Massachusetts.

The NJM initially represented a diverse cross section of the anti-Gairy movement; it included groups from militant labor unions all the way to the Lions Club. Yet as the 1970s wore on and opposition to Gairy's rule galvanized, the NJM continued to move away from its black power orientation and toward "scientific socialism" and the "Leninization" of the party, a shift that continued to split the party right up until the U.S. intervention in 1983. In a manifestation of the breadth of the opposition against Gairy, in 1976 the NJM united with two conservative groups—the Grenada National Party and the United People's Party—to form the Popular Alliance coalition.

THE 1979 COUP AND THE NJM IN POWER

Gairy's answer to the rise of the NJM was to "meet steel with steel." For example, in 1973 Gairy ordered his henchmen to beat up NJM leaders, and soon after he repressed a general strike.[18] Throughout the late 1970s, Gairy used his Mongoose Gang to target political and labor opponents. Yet Gairy's heavy-handed tactics served only to swell the ranks of his detractors.

On March 13, 1979, roughly fifty men took part in a coup attempt to overthrow Gairy's regime. Within twelve hours, the thirty-four-year-old Bishop routed Gairy's cabinet ministers out of their sleep, arrested them, and immediately burned the police headquarters and the barracks of the 500-member Grenada Defence Force. The coup ended in success as the army and police surrendered without firing a shot. Only three people were killed. The coup plotters claimed that the effort was a "seizure of state

Honduran soldiers, first troops of Inter-American peace force, arrive to assume peace-keeping in the revolt-torn country, January 1, 1965. Photo by Jack Lartz. Courtesy of the Department of Defense.

American GIs engaged in a firefight, push child under jeep for protection, Santo Domingo, May 5, 1965. Photograph by Jack Lartz. Courtesy of the Department of Defense.

GIs playing baseball with Dominican children. Santo Domingo, May 5, 1965. Photograph by Jack Lartz. Courtesy of the Department of Defense.

Food distribution in front of a "Yankees come back" sign, Santo Domingo, May 9, 1965. Photograph by Jack Lartz. Courtesy of the Department of Defense.

President Reagan and Prime Minister Eugenia Charles of Dominica at a White House press conference announcing the invasion of Grenada, October 25, 1983. Courtesy of the Ronald Reagan Library.

Cuban prisoners stand in line along a runway as they prepare for their departure from Grenada, October 25, 1983. Courtesy of the Department of Defense.

Flight deck crewmen hose down a UH-60 Blackhawk helicopter upon its landing aboard the amphibious assault ship USS Guam during Operation Urgent Fury. The helicopter's engine was hit by anti-aircraft fire on the island of Grenada. Courtesy of the Department of Defense.

A U.S. Air Force cameraman videotapes the activities of 82nd Airborne Division troops during the multiservice, multinational Operation Urgent Fury. The soldiers are stationed near the Port Salines airfield, where a C-141 Starlifter aircraft is preparing to take off, October 28, 1983. Photograph by Mike Creen. Courtesy of the Department of Defense.

Troops from the 82nd Airborne Division at a checkpoint shortly after the invasion of Grenada. Courtesy of Chick Harrity for U.S. News & World Report.

An American soldier with the 82nd Airborne Division poses with students from the St. George's University Medical School on Grenada a few days into the invasion. AP/Wide World.

President H. W. Bush on a conference call right before the invasion of Panama, accompanied by National Security Advisor Brent Scowcroft and Chief of Staff John Sununu. Courtesy of the George H. W. Bush Presidential Library.

An M-113 armored personnel carrier from 4th Battalion, 6th Infantry, 5th Infantry Division, drives down the highway in front of the base to help control a demonstration being held outside the gate by supporters of General Manuel Noriega, November 18, 1989. Photograph by J. Elliott. Courtesy of the Department of Defense.

American soldier checks displaced persons at Balboa High School shortly after the invasion of Panama. From the Collection of Burt Mead.

power by the Grenadian people," but is clear that it was done by a small group and that the Grenadian people did not know about it until afterward.[19]

The same day of the coup, Bishop went on the air at Radio Free Grenada (they had already changed the name from Radio Grenada) to inform his fellow Grenadians, "People of Grenada, this revolution is for work, for food, for decent housing and health services, and a bright future for our children and great grandchildren."[20] A week later, Bishop announced that the revolution was irreversible.

While it suspended the Gairy-era postcolonial 1974 constitution, the new government decided to remain a constitutional monarchy, which meant that the British Queen was still head of state and was represented on the island by Governor General Sir Paul Scoon, who had been appointed in 1978 on Gairy's recommendation. The PRG ruled using a sixteen-member Central Committee. Day-to-day decisions were made by an inner circle of eight members called the Political Bureau.

Bishop, appointed as prime minister, had the role of approving most of the decisions of the political bureau. The NJM inherited a stagnant economy mired with high unemployment, inflation, and a large balance-of-payments deficit. Indeed, for the next several years the PRG was forced to balance idealism with pragmatism, and this often was related to the economic realm. Of particular note, Deputy Prime Minister Bernard Coard advocated an orthodox Leninist approach, while the more moderate and pragmatic Bishop wanted something more mixed.[21]

While the economy continued to suffer, Bishop enjoyed the strong levels of popular support that Gairy had initially enjoyed when he assumed office in the 1960s. Bishop was the NJM's charismatic, more pragmatic leader, while Coard acted as the party's "chief theoretician."[22] Following the coup, Bishop, Coard, and other leaders announced the formation of the Provisional Revolutionary Government, which was later named the People's Revolutionary Government (PRG). Hudson Austin was named general of the armed forces and chairman of the Revolutionary Military Council (RMC).

On taking office, the NJM received support from Cuba as well as East Germany, Bulgaria, and North Korea. Over the next few years, Grenada signed a number of trade agreements with the Soviet Union. The PRG remained in the regional multilateral organizations Caricom (the Caribbean economic community) and the Organization for Eastern Caribbean States (OECS). Jamaica, Barbados, and Guyana recognized the PRG within ten days of its creation, but most OECS countries (OECS members are Antigua and Barbuda, St. Kitts-Nevis, St. Lucia, Montserrat, St. Vincent, Dominica, and Grenada) remained more hostile.

Using social programs, political propaganda and mobilization, and the creation of a "vanguard" political movement, the PRG attempted to turn Grenada into a Marxist–Leninist society. With the Cuban revolution as a model, the government enacted free milk and lunch programs for elementary schools, eliminated secondary school fees, and built medical clinics across the island. In addition, like Cuba, Bishop did not hold elections after the coup even though he would have certainly won them. When Fidel Castro visited Nicaragua in July 1980, he stated that, "There is only one road to liberation: that of Cuba, that of Grenada, that of Nicaragua. There is no other formula."[23]

Starting in 1979, Cuba became Grenada's main supplier of military hardware and training. In late 1981, the PRG and the Cuban government signed a protocol of military collaboration that established a twenty-seven-man Cuban military mission in Grenada, a group given the task of training the newly formed People's Revolutionary Army (PRA).[24] The Cuban government subsequently supplied thousands of rifles, machine guns, and rocket launchers up until the U.S. invasion in October 1983. Grenada also signed military assistance agreements with the Soviet Union and North Korea, paving the way for weapons shipments from both countries. According to then prime minister of Barbados, Tom Adams, Grenada was "one of the perhaps dozen most militarized states in the world in terms of population under arms."[25]

THE CARTER AND REAGAN ADMINISTRATIONS RESPOND TO THE NJM

Just a few days after the coup, Bishop met with U.S. Ambassador Frank Ortiz, who warned him that the United States would not look kindly on the NJM if it developed closer ties with Cuba. Bishop responded by delivering a strongly worded speech three days afterward, declaring, "We are not in anybody's backyard."[26] It is interesting that Ortiz reported on the meeting back to Washington that Bishop was "pleased" with Washington's "speedy recognition" of the new government and that he appeared to want to have "friendly relations," allow the Peace Corps to remain in the country, and assure the protection of U.S. citizens and property on the island.[27]

Although few shed any tears for Gairy's overthrow, the Carter administration reacted to the Bishop government with a considerable amount of concern. In fact, on the basis of the intelligence reports that they were receiving, President Carter's top advisers on Latin America recommended that the United States make a concerted effort to ensure that Washington not "lose" Grenada to the Communist camp.

Just two days after the coup, National Security Adviser Zbigniew Brzezinski wrote a memo to Carter pointing out that he believed the NJM was "sensitive to the international reaction to their coup" and "eager to gain international legitimacy." But he also warned that if Washington was not "sensitive" to their overtures, they could turn toward "social revolution or towards alliance with the Cubans." Brzezinski recommended that the United States make "concrete inducements" to ensure that the NJM remained "directed to a more stable and democratic future."[28]

While the initial reaction to the NJM government was one of caution, there remained a hope that a warm relationship could be established between the two governments. Within a month, however, President Carter's top advisers were beginning to sour on the new government in Grenada, above all concerned about perceived growing Cuban involvement. Part of the Carter administration's alarm regarding Grenada came as a result of the recent discovery of a Soviet combat brigade station in Cuba, a revelation that soured relations between Washington and Havana. In response to the growing security concerns in the Caribbean, in 1979 Carter announced the establishment of a permanent Caribbean Joint Task Force Headquarters and the expansion of military exercises.[29]

On April 14, White House aide Robert Pastor wrote a memo to Brzezinski titled "New Direction in Grenada: The Cubans Arrive." In it, he wrote that

the Cubans are now directly involved in trying to help "consolidate" Bishop's revolution. Eight Cubans arrived covertly yesterday. A large shipment of arms was flown from Cuban to Guyana where it was transshipped to Grenada. . . . While telling us (and Canada and UK) of his interest in obtaining military support, he was already receiving covert military support from Cuba. A Cuban merchant ship (Viet Nam Heroico) with 200 cadets on board is apparently on its way to Grenada.

Pastor added that he believed that Bishop had "lost interest in free elections" and that "it looks as if he might try to create a one-party state. It is conceivable he could have his closest ties with the Cubans. Grenada could become a training camp for young radicals from other islands." Pastor recommended a new strategy for U.S. policy whereby Washington should demonstrate to the new government that it was "serious" but that the United States should work in a "supportive role" behind Trinidad and Barbados and "in concert" with the Canadians and the British. He urged that Washington send "a clear message to the Cubans to stay out." Pastor also considered using a recent volcanic eruption on St. Vincent as a cover for sending "a number of vessels" to the region as a show of force. A few days later, Pastor wrote another memo in which he stated that "while recognizing the 'mouse that roared' dimensions of Grenada," it would be "an error to underestimate the domestic, political and geo-political importance of Grenada's shift to the left and towards Cuba."[30]

Over the course of the next several months, memoranda from Carter's advisers began to be enacted into policy. In January 1980, Hurricane Allen destroyed agricultural crops on Grenada, St. Vincent and the Grenadines, St. Lucia, and Dominica. The United States granted aid to all these countries except Grenada. President Carter also instructed his new ambassador, Sally Shelton, not to pay a courtesy farewell to Grenada (the United States conducted its relations with Grenada through its ambassador in Barbados who was also accredited as ambassador to the nearby island nations) even though Bishop invited her.[31]

THE REAGAN YEARS

As one might suspect, the tilt toward Cuba and Marxist–Leninism won Bishop and the PRG few friends in the Reagan administration after it took office in January 1981. Between 1981 and 1983, the Reagan administration continuously attempted to pressure the PRG. Secretary of State Alexander Haig directed the State Department's Bureau of Inter-American Affairs to ensure that Grenada did not receive "one penny" from any international financial institution.[32] For the next two years, U.S. officials repeatedly attempted to exclude Grenada from receiving international assistance, although these efforts were met with mixed results, as other countries often were unwilling to go along with Washington's wishes.

In June 1983, Bishop made a widely publicized trip to the United States. He hoped to meet with Reagan, but this request was denied, so he instead met with senior administration officials such as National Security Adviser William Clark and Deputy Secretary of State Kenneth Dam as well as congressional leaders. Above all, Bishop needed money for his faltering revolution. In a memo that Dam wrote to President Reagan on June 7, he summarized the meeting as "straightforward but amicable" and that he relayed the fact that normalization of relations would depend on Grenada's actions in "key areas" such as improving civil liberties, cutting Soviet/Cuban presence, and "toning down" anti-American rhetoric. Dam also reported that Bishop "demurred" on his government's relations with Cuba and the Soviet Union and had "nothing to say" on human rights.[33]

Reagan continued his rhetorical war on Grenada through a series of speeches on the topic. In February 1982, Reagan told representatives of the Organization of American States (OAS) that Grenada was in the "tightening grip of the totalitarian left," and a few months later he told OECS leaders in Barbados that Grenada had the "Soviet Cuban trade mark."[34] Reflecting that by 1983 his advisers were in strong agreement about the nature of the PRG, on March 25, 1983, Reagan told the American people on national television that

> Grenada, that tiny little island—with Cuba at the west end of the Caribbean, Grenada at the east end—that tiny little island is building now, or having built for it, on its soil and shores, a naval base, a superior naval base, storage bases and facilities for the storage of munitions, barracks, and training ground for the military. I'm sure all of that is simply to encourage the export of nutmeg. People who make these arguments haven't taken a good look at a map lately or followed the extraordinary buildup of Soviet and Cuban military power in the region or read the Soviet's discussions about why the region is important to them and how they intend to use it. It isn't nutmeg that is at stake in the Caribbean and Central America. It is the United States' national security.[35]

Many critics viewed Reagan's public condemnations of the PRG as another manifestation of his administration's hyperbole and paranoia when it came to leftist socially oriented regimes in the Third World. The belief was that Reagan had confused a progressive leftist government with a pro-Soviet, pro-Cuba totalitarian state. Classified intelligence reports, however, repeatedly highlighted growing Cuban involvement. In other words, contrary to what many people then believed about what was coming out of the White House, Reagan's heated rhetoric was based on hard intelligence.

For example, in January 1983 a CIA intelligence report indicated that "the scale of military collaboration between Cuban and Grenada contradicts claims by Havana that it has no strategic interest in Grenada."[36] It added that a new military camp would enable Cubans and Grenadians to "train leftists from other English-speaking islands, or possible [sic] to stockpile weapons for transshipment to revolutionary regimes in the region." Another CIA memo estimated that Cuban economic aid had reached a "conservative estimate" of $66 million and that the Cubans are "hoping that Grenada will feel so indebted to Cuba that they will give the Cubans a free hand in the island's future."[37]

The PRG's motives appeared even more dangerous with the 1980 construction of a new runway at Point Salines. The new runway was ostensibly intended to replace the older "Pearls" strip located in the northeastern end of the island at the end of a long and poorly maintained road. Grenadians often had to spend a day in Trinidad or Barbados waiting for a connecting flight to the island. The old runway was 5,520 feet long, and the new one that had been under construction in some form or another for over a decade was proposed to be more than 9,000 feet long, a length that would put it right in line with that of its neighbors. While financing for the runway came from a variety of sources, including some in the United States, there is no question that Cuban aid was critical for the construction. By October 1983, Cuban assistance for the airport had reached an estimated $60 million, and hundreds of Cubans were working on the project.

The intended use of the runway remains a controversial question. Reagan's critics argued that the runway was the key to Grenada's economic well-being and cited reports that American medical students lived within a mile of the strip and used it as a jogging track. Reagan's supporters highlighted the arms caches that were discovered near the airport, the fact that no hotels were being built, and that the Cuban workforce had jumped from 150 in 1979 to 650 in 1983.[38] According to a senior Reagan administration official, "You could tell it was for military purposes. . . . We had the satellite intelligence. There was no question in my mind."[39]

Whatever the case might have been, there is no question that the runway could have easily been used for either purpose, a fact that observers on both sides tended to overlook. What is more certain, however, is that U.S. intelligence services mirrored Reagan's conclusions about the intentions for the airport.

In May 1983, a U.S. intelligence memo indicated that "Cuba's prominent role in the airport project suggests that Havana sees some potential strategic benefits from the airport."[40] Another report posited that the airport, "which may be complete by mid-1983, could provide a refueling and transit route for Cuban transport bound for other points in the Western Hemisphere or for Africa."[41] American officials also believed that Soviet long-range TU-95 Bear bombers and reconnaissance aircraft would be able to use the strip. These planes had been flying from the northern Soviet base of Olenogorsk to Havana, and extending the route to Grenada would have increased Moscow's strategic position in key oil-shipping lanes between Venezuela and the Gulf of Mexico.[42]

Both Reagan and his advisers clearly believed that the airport could have easily been used for military purposes. It is also clear that Reagan was "deeply interested in the airport issue" and that he was briefed on it "all the time."[43] This reality added a "new and serious dimension" to America's security concerns in the region.[44] During his March 23, 1983, address to the nation, President Reagan showed aerial reconnaissance photographs of Grenada and explained that "the Cubans with Soviet financing and backing are in the process of building an airfield with a 10,000 foot runway. Grenada doesn't even have an air force. Whom is it intended for?"[45]

To keep up the pressure against a regime that it perceived was firmly in Cuba's camp, between 1981 and 1983 the United States held its largest naval operations since World War II. Called Ocean Venture, the operations involved 120,000 troops, 250 warships, and 1,000 aircraft. Part of the exercise was labeled "Amber and the Amberdines," a thinly veiled reference to Grenada and the Grenadines. The exercise took place on the Puerto Rican island of Vieques and simulated an invasion and occupation of a small island.[46] By early 1983, Grenada was undoubtedly a concern to the Reagan administration, but it would take a series of events in the fall of that year to lead to the decision to launch a full-scale invasion.

THE MURDER OF BISHOP

Both publicly and privately, the Reagan administration continued its pressure on the PRG well into 1983. Yet it was internal divisions and an anemic economy, not American pressure, that by the middle of 1982 were causing deep divisions within the NJM's leadership. In July 1982, Coard resigned from the Political Bureau and Central Committee in disgust over Bishop's putative moderate policies. Yet this change was not enough to alleviate the tension between Coard and Bishop. Throughout September 1983, the Coard faction argued that the party was imploding and that the population's ideological development needed to be the priority. They said that Bishop had become a "right wing opportunist" and was not moving the party toward pure Marxist–Leninism.[47]

Then, on September 25, 1983, right before departing on a trip to Czechoslovakia and Hungary, Bishop agreed with Coard on a power-sharing system. After stopping off in Havana on his return from eastern Europe, Bishop arrived in Grenada on October 8. In an ominous sign, none of the Central Committee members showed up at the airport to greet him.[48] On the eve of the Political Bureau meeting slated for October 12, Coard's faction told members of the army that they should no longer take orders from Bishop, only from the Central Committee. Following the meeting the next day, Bishop was forced to go on national radio to dispel a rumor that he had started a rumor that Coard planned to assassinate him.

On October 12, Bishop was again called to a NJM meeting at which he was accused of plotting against his fellow central committee members. A few days later, the Central Committee proceeded to place Bishop under house arrest, a move that sparked widespread protests in St. George's against Coard and for Bishop. During Bishop's six days of house arrest, General Austin, who was supporting Coard, declared,

> Sisters and brothers, over the past four and a half years, the Central Committee has struggled very hard to win Comrade Bishop to a position of collective leadership. Comrade Bishop was hoping to use the masses' love for him and violate the principled stand by the Central Committee of the

party. . . . Even with all the love and admiration that exists within our party for Comrade Maurice, the entire membership, except for a tiny minority, fully support the position of the Central Committee. . . . Comrade Bishop is at home and he is quite safe.[49]

A week later, on October 19, known as Bloody Wednesday, the pro-Bishop protests swelled to over 10,000 people who gathered in St. George's central square chanting, "We want Maurice."[50] Coard's faction clearly underestimated the extent of support for Bishop. Then between 3,000 and 4,000 Bishop supporters broke away from the protest and headed up the steep steps to Bishop's house. There they forcibly entered and rescued Bishop and his pregnant mistress and education minister Jacqueline Creft.

The newly liberated Bishop went to the central square and told his supporters that he wanted to go over to Fort Rupert to use the army transmitter to address the nation. In his communiqué, Bishop announced that General Austin was no longer head of the PRA. Bishop and a few dozen supporters remained at the fort for several hours until dozens of PRA troops led by Major Leon Cornwall arrived in a convoy of three Soviet BTR-60 armored personnel carriers.[51] Some of Bishop's loyalists believed that Cornwall might have been arriving to join Bishop.

That hope was immediately dispelled when shots rang out and Bishop's supporters realized that they were surrounded. Under orders from Coard, Bishop was executed by a hastily organized firing squad in front of a mural of Ché Guevara along with seven close supporters, including his mistress Jacqueline Creft.[52] The day after Bishop's assassination, Austin announced the establishment of the sixteen-man RMC, which comprised sixteen politically active members of the PRA. Coard was not named, but he remained one of the new regime's key figures. The RMC immediately imposed a twenty-four-hour shoot-to-kill curfew.

It is no exaggeration to say that Bishop's murder is the critical episode that led to the U.S. invasion just a few days later. The Reagan administration had been concerned enough about Grenada to include it in the president's March 1983 address to the nation; it also held massive military exercises in the region that simulated an invasion of the island. Yet with no apparent threat to American lives and perceiving Grenada's role as a lily pad for Communist expansion still just a future threat, there was no compelling reason for the Reagan administration to go beyond its saber rattling to a full-scale invasion. For them, Grenada was just too small and still not an imminent threat to U.S. interests to justify an invasion. There is no indication that Washington was planning an imminent invasion before October 19.

THE REAGAN ADMINISTRATION RESPONDS

In the weeks following the invasion, critics began to make a number of arguments that placed the administration's justifications in doubt.[53] The most cutting criticism was that the American students' lives were not in any real danger and that, at the very least, they could have been evacuated. Observers disputed the administration's claims that the Pearls airport had been closed, citing evidence that charter flights had been taking off and landing until right before the invasion. Robert Pastor, who in 1979 as Carter's national security adviser for Latin America had recommended a hawkish policy toward Bishop's new government, testified in front of Congress that "we know that airplanes went in and out through the weekend (October 21–23). Four to five airplanes left on Monday."[54]

While an evacuation was one of the first options considered (they even considered using a nearby *Cunard* cruise liner to which they could evacuate the students), it was ultimately discarded, as officials believed that they could not rely on the regime (or the Cubans for that matter) to cooperate.[55] On October 20, Secretary of State George Shultz and Chairman of the Joint Chiefs of Staff John W. Vessey Jr. told the Special Situation Group chaired by Vice President George Bush that the Grenadian junta "might resist" a U.S. evacuation attempt and that "armed Cuban construction workers might intervene."[56]

Critics of the invasion have also cited the fact that the RMC attempted on a number of occasions to convince U.S. government officials that American lives were not in any danger. And there is absolutely no doubt that U.S. officials received oral and written messages from the RMC to this extent. In fact, later on, the White House admitted that two days before the invasion, the RMC offered the U.S. government an opportunity to evacuate its nationals but that the administration doubted the veracity of the offer.

For better or worse, the Reagan administration decided to ignore the RMC's assurances, believing that the RMC could not be trusted to keep its word. For example, in an effort to stave off any type of military response from the United States, in the days after Bloody Wednesday the RMC broadcast announcements every fifteen to thirty minutes on Radio Free Grenada stating that no American citizens or foreign nationals had been harmed as a result of the curfew.

Nonetheless, on October 21, the U.S. embassy in Bridgetown sent a cable to the White House reporting that the RMC broadcasts must be "taken with a grain of salt" and that it was "obvious" that the RMC was "talking a very well defined party line of psy-ops in an attempt to obviate the need for foreign intervention. It is also very evident that there are in fact life-threatening situations in Grenada."[57] In a memo strikingly similar to what Ambassador Bennett was sending from Santo Domingo in 1965, on October 19 Ambassador Milan Bish sent an urgent cable to Washington that warned that an invasion of Grenada might be necessary:

> There appears to be imminent danger to U.S. citizens resident in Grenada due to the current deteriorating situation, which includes reports of rioting, personnel casualties (possibly deaths), automatic weapons being discharged, Soviet-built armored personnel carriers in the Grenadian streets, and some loss of water and electricity on the island. . . . AmEmbassy Bridgetown recommends that the United States should now be prepared to conduct an emergency invasion of U.S. citizens residing in Grenada.[58]

A strong counterfactual case can be made that had there been no invasion, the RMC still would have never threatened Americans on the island since it would have undoubtedly provoked an American military reaction. In fact, the RMC offered vehicles to shuttle the students between the two medical school campuses. The RMC also apparently knew that a Marine task force 350 miles out of Norfolk en route to the Mediterranean had just been diverted to the Caribbean.[59]

On October 20, a State Department cable reported that American diplomats had two "lengthy conversations" with Charles Modica, who was the chancellor of the St. George's medical school on the island that had over 500 Americans living on its two campuses.[60] The cable reported that Modica said that "on balance" the RMC would not harm Americans so as to avoid using the incident as a "pretext for invasion." But Modica also warned that the shoot-to-kill curfew made an evacuation more complex and that an incomplete evacuation could trigger attacks against those Americans left behind.[61]

On the night of Sunday, October 23, medical school administrators met with the students and found out that about 10 percent wanted to leave. Some parents of the students met in New York City and sent a telegram to President Reagan urging him not to take provocative actions in Grenada.[62]

Yet the Reagan administration was in no mood to take this chance. This tiny island nation governed by a gang of thugs was a perfect case for regime change by force. The administration feared that had it not acted, it "might have had some dead students on its hands."[63] Indeed, it would have taken nothing at all for the RMC to seize the students in a matter of minutes. In his memoirs, Secretary of State Shultz recounted the medical student dilemma:

> We [Assistant Secretary of State Tony Motley and Shultz] both had the searing memory of Tehran and the sixty-six Americans seized from our embassy on November 4, 1979, and held hostage for well over a year. We both knew what Ronald Reagan's reaction would be to such a development in Grenada. He would not stand still while American hostages were held for 444 days. In fact he probably wouldn't stand still for a week. With as many as 1,000 students scattered between two campuses, the town, and the countryside, much blood would be shed if our forces had to go in to rescue students or other American citizens taken hostage or held in some sort of forcible detention. We had to avoid such a situation.[64]

The invasion of Grenada was a choice, and its success was never guaranteed, but for the Reagan administration it was a relatively easy one.

THE OECS INVITATION

On October 19, Washington began serious planning for a "nonpermissive" evacuation that would have extracted the students without resorting to a full-scale invasion.[65] Interagency meetings chaired by Assistant Secretary of State Motley had met before while Bishop was under house arrest, but U.S. concern increased only after Bloody Wednesday. In fact, that same day U.S. diplomats in Barbados attempted to travel to Grenada to assess the situation but had to turn back because the Pearls airport was closed. Then, on October 22, two diplomats arrived on a charter flight. The next day, one of them met with RMC leaders who assured them that an evacuation was not necessary.[66]

In the days following Bloody Wednesday, the Reagan administration considered an evacuation of the American medical students in order to prevent a Tehran-like hostage crisis. It was actually the leaders of the OECS who strongly urged the United States to invade Grenada. In fact, even as late as October 21, top American officials were still hesitant about an American-led invasion. For example, Shultz sent a memo to the U.S. embassy in Kingston, Jamaica, that indicated that "the preferable approach would be for Grenada's democratic neighbors to act to resolve the Grenada problem. . . . The U.S. might consider supporting others in an effort to restore freedom to the Grenadian people; but our support should be clearly secondary."[67]

The United States received its first "urgent approach" from the OECS on October 15, four days before Bishop was murdered.[68] But at this point, the only response that the U.S. officials provided was the possibility that Washington would provide a military force to go in and free Bishop. (In October 1983, the OECS chairperson was Dominica's prime minister, Eugenia Charles. Caricom consisted of thirteen Caribbean members—all the OECS countries plus Barbados, the Bahamas, Belize, Guyana, Jamaica, and Trinidad and Tobago.[69])

Prime Minister Tom Adams of Barbados spearheaded a response to the Grenada crisis through the OECS rather than Caricom because he believed that Guyana's leftist government would never approve any aggressive actions. Instead, even though Barbados was not a member, Adams nonetheless relied on strong OECS support at a meeting on October 21; he then brought Jamaica's Edward Seaga on board, a move that solidified widespread Caribbean support for an invasion.

Some Caricom countries proposed a fact-finding mission and other diplomatic initiatives, but the OECS countries would not budge. On October 22, the OECS invoked article 8 of its Treaty of Association, which allowed it to "take action for collective defense and preservation of peace and security against external aggression."[70] The OECS imposed a number of economic and political sanctions on Grenada.

Taken by surprise by the rapidity and aggressiveness of the Caribbean leaders' moves, the Reagan administration worked furiously to keep pace with the OECS requests. On October 21, a State Department cable reported that Seaga had proposed a naval blockade as an alternative to an invasion. The report also indicated that Seaga expressed his "deep concern" over the "Soviet/Cuban menace in Grenada" and that he believed that the "successful consolidation of Cuban control in Grenada would promptly destabilize St. Vincent and perhaps other adjacent islands."[71]

The next day, the White House received a cable from Ambassador Bish in Bridgetown indicating that Adams and Charles—the leaders of Barbados and Dominica, respectively—had said that within the OECS there were "no reservations whatsoever" about an invasion. Bish continued on that the OECS had formally resolved to form a "multinational Caribbean force" to "depose the outlaw regime" in Grenada by "any means." Bish also reported that even Seaga had now moved "beyond the question of a blockade alone." The ambassador concluded his cable by stating that "they cannot do it alone. The prospect of help from the U.S. (although we told them no repeat no decision had been taken) sustains the active spirit of these leaders. If we falter, so will their effort."[72]

After receiving the informal request from the OECS, on October 22 Reagan requested preparations for a broader mission, one that included a full-scale invasion. In the meantime, Reagan, Shultz, and newly appointed National Security Adviser Robert McFarlane traveled to Augusta, Georgia, for a golf outing scheduled for the weekend of October 21–23. At 2:45 A.M. on Saturday, Schultz was awakened and told that the OECS, after consulting with Bish and veteran U.S. diplomat Charles Gillespie (who had arrived in Barbados to assist with the crisis), had verbally requested U.S. participation in a full-scale invasion of Grenada.[73] The formal OECS request arrived on Sunday evening.[74]

Shultz and McFarlane (who had replaced William Clark) discussed the news with Vice President Bush.[75] They were most concerned about another Tehran-like situation and were dismayed that their decision to redirect the Marine task force to the Caribbean had been leaked to the press. At 5:15 A.M., President Reagan was awakened to be briefed on the OECS request and possible U.S. reactions. Reagan and Shultz decided to remain in Augusta in order not to arouse suspicion of any imminent military response. It is clear that by this point Shultz was increasingly in favor of a full-scale invasion and that he had the president's ear. According to one official who was involved in the deliberations, "In Augusta, Shultz had Reagan to himself, far away from the generals."[76] While the official order would come two days later, Reagan effectively ordered the invasion of Grenada while at Augusta, one day before the Beirut attack.

It is worth mentioning that at this point in the crisis, the Pentagon remained hesitant about a full-scale invasion, believing that the mission was still ill defined (rescue or regime change?) and that Grenada was of little importance. The Joint Chiefs of Staff were shocked by what happened in Beirut that morning and were not at all eager to get into another situation that would involve additional casualties. At one point in the planning of a response to the crisis, one of the members of the Joint Chiefs told senior State Department officials that, with respect to a full-scale invasion, "you guys are out of your minds."[77]

Reagan was once again pulled out of bed, this time at 2:37 A.M., on Sunday morning, to be notified about the terrorist attack against the Marines barracks in Beirut. Reagan spent most of the day discussing the Beirut tragedy; it was only later in the day that their conversations turned to Grenada. With the deaths of hundreds of Marines on his mind and the potential for U.S. hostages in Grenada, Reagan appeared tired and dispirited; he is believed to have lamented, "I'm no better than Jimmy Carter."[78]

On Sunday evening, McFarlane drew up the national security directive that Reagan needed to sign for the invasion to go ahead; Reagan signed it that same evening. Unlike the Joint Chiefs of Staff, Shultz urged the president to take military action and to "strike while the iron is hot."[79] According to McFarlane, Reagan uttered only one word when he approved the largest U.S. military operation since Vietnam: "Go." The full-scale invasion preparation had been under way for only four days, and Reagan signed the directive only thirty-six hours before the main assault force was to go in. He had twenty-four hours to abort the operation.[80] From this point on, the Pentagon was fully on board with the invasion.

PLANNING THE INVASION

The speed at which events were unfolding and the international political context must also be taken into consideration when evaluating the Reagan administration's response to the crisis in Grenada. Like Johnson during the Dominican crisis, in October 1983 the White House's understanding of the situation rapidly unfolding in Grenada was only as good as the intelligence it was receiving. And that intelligence was reporting that the situation was chaotic and that American lives could easily come into danger.

After Reagan gave the final approval for the full-scale invasion on Sunday night, he spent a Monday afternoon revising invasion plans during a meeting with Secretary of Defense Caspar Weinberger and the Joint Chiefs of Staff.[81] Atlantic Fleet headquarters had proposed a plan that called for Navy and Marine units to stage a big landing at the Grand Anse beach to be followed by a quick dash across the peninsula to cut off the Salines airport from St. George's.[82]

The thinking behind this plan was that it would isolate the Cubans stationed at the airport. It was overruled by the Joint Chiefs of Staff, who wanted all four services to be involved in the operation.[83] It is also worth mentioning that during a critical operation planning meeting in Norfolk, Virginia, some of the involved generals told State Department officials that they still needed "weeks, maybe months," to put together an effective invasion operation.[84] But administration officials knew that they did not have that much time: the invasion would have to be planned from start to finish in four days.

Many of the U.S. military commanders assigned to the Grenada operation had served in Vietnam, and there is no doubt that the experiences made them highly cautious when it came time to deploy U.S. troops abroad. At one point during the operation, Joint Chiefs chairman Vessey requested that the State Department provide him with a detailed time line of when the U.S. troops would be withdrawn from Grenada.[85]

During the series of interagency meetings leading up to Reagan's decision to launch a full-scale invasion, planners in the Pentagon had encouraged an "Entebbe-style" invasion that would insert elite troops onto the island to rescue students in one stealth swoop. There is no doubt, though, that political considerations are part of what led Reagan to go for an overwhelming invasion force. Reagan knew well that Jimmy Carter's Entebbe-style rescue attempt in Iran ended up as a military and political debacle. In addition, some of Reagan's advisers believed that a decisive move in Grenada would send a strong message to leftist governments, such as the Sandinistas in Nicaragua, to be careful.

Yet at the same time, the push toward a full-scale invasion was in fact led by more "dovish" State Department officials, ones who at times were privately critical of Reagan administration policies in Nicaragua. According to one official, "I was the first to oppose U.S. military intervention in Central America. I was also the first to urge a full-scale invasion in Grenada."[86]

The invasion plan that was agreed on was called Urgent Fury and was based on the Ocean Venture operations held in the region the previous

two years. Thus, while the specific invasion plans were drawn up in a matter of just a few days, the U.S. military had been planning for an invasion
of an island like Grenada for several years. This full-scale invasion operation had been drawn up over the past several days in addition to a number
of other options. Vice Admiral Joseph Metcalf III, who was already in
place on the amphibious ship USS *Guam*, assumed command of the newly
formed joint task force (JTF-120). His deputy was Army Major General
H. Norman Schwarzkopf, the future commander of American forces during the Gulf War in 1991.[87]

Critics have argued that the Reagan administration cynically concocted
the Grenada invasion in order to "wag the dog" by distracting the American public from the tragedy in Beirut. However, the invasion plan had
been in the works before the Beirut bombings on Sunday. In fact, when
warned by his advisers that the timing of the Grenada invasion might
bring about that very criticism, Reagan said privately that "if this [inva-
sion] was right yesterday, it's right today and we shouldn't let the act of a
couple of terrorists dissuade us from going ahead."[88]

The Joint Chiefs divided the island in half, with the north end allocated
to the Navy and Marines and the south to the Army and Air Force. The
first objective was to secure the students and the evacuation route, an
effort complicated by the fact that it was not apparent to some of the military planners (and certainly not the invading troops) that the medical
school actually had three campuses.[89] In addition, in something that hin-
dered its ability to know exactly what was transpiring on the island, the
U.S. government had no covert intelligence operatives in Grenada leading
up to the invasion.[90]

The invasion plan had three main goals: rescue the students, restore a
democratic government, and eliminate and prevent further Cuban intervention on the island.[91] Reagan clearly wanted to present the invasion to
the American people as a fait accompli: that the United States went in,
rescued, cleaned up, and went home. This would not be another Vietnam.

The administration's thinking in the planning stage is well summarized
by the words of an unnamed official close to the president who said that

the overriding principle was not to allow something to happen worse than
what we were proposing to do. The purpose was to deny the Russians/

Cubans a feeling of potency in grabbing small vulnerable states in the region. It had to be nipped in the bud before it developed into another Cuba.[92]

On Monday evening, White House Chief of Staff James Baker contacted congressional leadership to invite them to a confidential meeting. Baker told Speaker of the House Thomas "Tip" O'Neill (D-Mass.), Senate Majority leader Howard Baker (R-Tenn.), House Majority Leader James Wright (D-Tex.), and Senate Minority leader Robert Byrd (D-W.Va.) that the meeting was so secret that they could not even contact their wives to tell them that they would be late for dinner. During the two-hour meeting that was also attended by Shultz, Weinberger, McFarlane, and Attorney General Edwin Meese, Reagan (who had been told by Weinberger that elite Navy SEALs were already in operation in Grenada) informed the congressional leaders that he had approved a plan to invade Grenada. He noted the OECS request, the danger to the medical students, and the RMC's shoot-to-kill curfew. Reagan concluded the meeting by saying, "I feel we have absolutely no alternative but to comply with this request. I think the risks of not moving are far greater than the risks of taking the action we have planned."[93]

The congressmen's reactions were mixed. O'Neill was uncertain, even though after the briefing he said, "God bless you, Mr. President." In the immediate aftermath of the invasion, O'Neill lamented that "we can't go the way of gunboat diplomacy. His policy is wrong. His policy is frightening."[94] James Wright was largely supportive, and Byrd strongly opposed the action.

Reagan then called British Prime Minister Margaret Thatcher and informed her of the impending invasion. Thatcher was surprised by the late notification and told Reagan in the "strongest language" to call off the operation. She reminded Reagan that Grenada was still part of the British Commonwealth and that the United States "had no business interfering in its affairs." Unmoved by the curt words from his special ally in London, Reagan stuck to his decision. Reagan administration officials were also taken back by Thatcher's vituperative response, as Washington had gone to enormous lengths to support the British effort during the Falkland Islands crisis the year earlier.[95]

THE INVASION

The recent media reports about the diverted U.S. warships had eliminated the element of surprise and forced the operation to be speeded up considerably.[96] Military planners were now worried that this revelation would prompt the Grenadians and Cubans to seize the medical students as hostages. Operation Urgent Fury called for a Marine amphibious unit assault at daybreak on October 25 at the older Pearls airport and nearby locations. These forces were then supposed to secure the northern half of the island. Army Rangers from the 75th Ranger Regiment were to simultaneously parachute into the incomplete Point Salines airfield, which would allow an Air Force C-141 troop transport to land, carrying a brigade from the 82nd Airborne Division, the same division that landed outside Santo Domingo in 1965. These troops would then rescue the medical students at the nearby "True Blue" medical campus and move on St. George's. Navy SEALs and other elite forces were to be inserted to capture General Hudson Austin and rescue Governor General Scoon as well as capture the main radio station and free political prisoners from Richmond Prison.[97]

The Navy cordoned off the island using ships and aircraft. All told, approximately 8,000 American soldiers and 353 troops from Caribbean forces participated in the operation. The Grenadian forces were estimated to be 1,200 men strong, with an additional 2,000 to 5,000 militia and 300 to 400 armed police. The Cuban presence was set at thirty to fifty advisers and 600 construction workers. While a small force, the extent of Cuban resistance turned out to be a "tactical surprise."[98]

The invasion began inauspiciously when on October 24 (a day before the invasion was to begin in force) four members of a SEAL team "vanished in rough seas" during a reconnaissance mission to place infrared beacons on the runway at Point Salines.[99] The SEALs had parachuted into the ocean during the mission and had become trapped in their own parachutes. The surviving SEALs continued on with the mission, but their Boston Whaler boats quickly became flooded after they cut the engines to avoid detection by a Grenadian patrol boat. The following night, poor weather conditions prevented the SEAL mission at the airport. Consequently, the Rangers were forced to land "blind."[100]

DAY 1: TUESDAY, OCTOBER 25

A twenty-two-man SEAL mission was the first to go ashore on October 25. Its mission to rescue Governor General Scoon almost ended in disaster. The force made its way to the Government House, where Scoon was being held. The plan was to deliver Scoon to a safehouse until he could be evacuated at a later time. After the SEALs had entered the house, nearby Grenadian forces counterattacked and advanced toward the house in armored troop carriers. The U.S. force called in an AC-130 transport, which destroyed three armored personnel carriers. Yet both the commandos and Scoon were now trapped inside of the house. Two Marine AH-1 Cobra helicopters were also scrambled to assist the operation, and one quickly went down from fire. The other Cobra was downed in St. George's harbor while it was flying on a mission to rescue the pilot from the first downed helicopter.[101]

After the two Cobras went down, Metcalf ordered a full-scale attack on the St. George's defense. These strikes took out some anti-aircraft position, but they also hit the adjacent Fort Matthew, which had been converted into a mental hospital. Dozens of patients were killed. Metcalf then ordered SEALs to make another landing on the October 26; the heavily armed force moved on the Government House and rescued the occupants while encountering little resistance. The governor general and his family and staff were evacuated to the *Guam*. The next day, the U.S. military made public a letter dated October 24 that Scoon had written to Tom Adams requesting military assistance.[102]

A unit of the elite Delta Force carried out a ground attack on the Richmond Hill Prison. There was concern that the PRA would execute the political prisoners before the American forces arrived. The Delta Force team was supported by helicopters from the 101st Airborne Division. The initial helicopter attack was met with heavy resistance—one Black Hawk helicopter was shot down—and the attack was abandoned.[103] The Army attempted to take the fort the next day and also failed. In an embarrassing episode, on the third day some journalists walked into the prison and declared it captured.[104]

The Rangers' assault on Point Salines was delayed for thirty-five minutes because of the loss of a navigation system in the lead C-130 that had left Savannah, Georgia, for Grenada. One company was slated to parachute in and the rest would come in on C-130 transports. A number of these came under heavy anti-aircraft fire near the airport, forcing some of the troops to jump from an altitude of only 500 feet, something that had not been done since World War II. Since only 5,000 feet of the runway was usable, more of the Rangers had to parachute than was originally planned. The saving grace was that Grenadian anti-aircraft guns were aimed at an altitude of 1,200 feet, so the Rangers literally parachuted in "under the radar." Amazingly, the operation to drop 500 soldiers took around ninety minutes, an inexcusable amount of time in such a delicate and time-sensitive operation. Two Special Forces members died in parachute failures.

By 6:30 A.M., the runway was clear, and two battalions of the Second Brigade of the 82nd Airborne came in over a four-hour span, along with troops from the Caribbean Peacekeeping Forces. The 82nd troopers had been assigned the duty of securing the island after the Rangers and Marines had completed their missions. The Salines airport was given a new name, the MCAS Douglas (Marines Corps Air Station Douglass), in honor of 8th Marines Sergeant Major F. B. Douglas, who was killed in the Beirut bombing.[105]

Within a few hours, though, the U.S. forces had secured a perimeter around the airport. Five Rangers were killed while clearing the airport. The Rangers then departed the airport and two hours later reached the True Blue medical school campus, where they found 130 students who were scared but safe. This is when the Rangers learned that there was a larger campus with several hundred more students at Grande Anse, located halfway to St. George's. In fact, more than 200 students ended up waiting over a day before being evacuated, an egregious delay that could have easily opened them up to being taken hostage, one of the very concerns that the invasion was supposed to eliminate.[106]

The Marine helicopter assaults began early on October 25. AH-1 gunships from the USS *Guam* led a number of CH-46 Sea Knight helicopters that were carrying troops from the 2nd Battalion's E Company toward Pearls airport. The Marines landed near the airport and took it without much resistance and then quickly captured the nearby town of Grenville.[107] The Marine operation on the northern half of the island went so well that quickly the Marines had very little to do. This situation led Metcalf to order an amphibious force of 250 Marines to sail around the island and land north of St. George's to assist in the more difficult operations there.[108] These Marines ended up participating in the rescue of the governor general.

DAYS 2 AND 3

The second day of the attack mainly consisted of the Rangers' assault on the Grande Anse campus. Up until this point, the American forces' contact with the students there had been through shortwave radio. American commanders decided to launch a helicopter assault because that way they could use the same helicopters to evacuate the students. A fifteen-minute barrage of the adjoining area by A-6 and A-7 attack aircraft preceded the helicopter mission.[109] At 4:30 P.M., a student at the campus looked outside and saw "something right out of Apocalypse Now": a line of helicopters was heading in from the bay. Anti-aircraft fire took down one Marine CH-46 helicopter, but the Rangers were still able to land just short of the beach. After a firefight of close to thirty minutes, the Rangers stormed the dormitories, and the students were led outside in groups of forty and loaded onto the helicopters.[110] With the loss of the one CH-46, the rescue force was now short twelve seats for the evacuation, so a dozen Rangers volunteered to stay behind. After the rescue force departed, the remaining Rangers evaded PRA forces, stole a fishing boat, and headed out to sea, where a U.S. destroyer picked them up.[111] During the assault on Grande Anse, the Rangers learned that there was yet another medical school campus located on a peninsula near St. George's.[112]

By days 2 and 3, many of the Cubans and PRA soldiers were discarding their uniforms and attempting to blend in with the civilian populations. Grenadian civilians greeted U.S. troops with cheers, food, and water. One remaining concern was the Calivigny Barracks, which was a PRA installation guarded by Cuban and PRA soldiers and anti-aircraft guns.[113] Two Black Hawk helicopters were shot down in the attempt to seize the garrison, killing three Americans and injuring twelve more. The remaining four Black Hawks landed safely, and Rangers secured the camp in fifteen minutes. This was a difficult and even embarrassing operation from the U.S. military's perspective, seeing as how there turned out to be only thirty defenders and only two of the Black Hawks escaped damage. An escorting OH-58 helicopter was badly shot up, and another helicopter crashed while trying to recover a downed Army aircraft.

The military operation took three days. By October 31, all Marines were back aboard their ships, and 82nd Airborne and OECS troops conducted cleanup operations. All told, 599 American citizens and 121 foreign nationals were evacuated. An estimated 100 to 200 Grenadians, 50 to 100

Cubans, and 18 Americans (11 soldiers, 3 Marines, and 4 SEALs) were killed; 116 American troops were wounded. The Pentagon awarded 8,633 medals out of the 7,000 U.S. military participants in the invasion. This is compared to the 679 medals that the British military awarded out of the 28,000 participants in the Falklands War a year earlier.[114]

There were several logistical and tactical failures that complicated the execution of what was expected to be an easy victory. The U.S. military did not know about the main medical campus at Grande Anse, troops lacked detailed maps of the island (the map of the task force's Grenada file was of Guyana, and many of the maps that troops used had to be glued together as they disintegrated in the rain), U.S. forces bombed their own positions on several occasions, and a relatively high ratio of aircraft was either shot down or collided with one another.[115] Of the roughly 100 helicopters committed to the operation, 9 were destroyed and many more damaged. Aside from their eventual rescue at the Government House, all Special Forces missions ended in failure or tragedy.

While Chairman of the Joint Chiefs of Staff Vessey bragged that "we blew them away," he also admitted that "we got a lot more resistance than we expected."[116] In fact, at one point in the operation, Vessey called the commander of the 82nd Airborne and said, "We have two companies of Marines running all over the island and thousands of Army troops doing nothing. What the hell is going on?"[117] Immediately after the mission, critics questioned why it took two Ranger battalions, a brigade of the 82nd Airborne, a Marine amphibious unit, an aircraft carrier, and Air Force transports to defeat fewer than 700 Cubans and a Grenadian army that barely provided any resistance.[118] In addition, all the medical students were not accounted for until three days after the invasion.[119] Part of these embarrassing failures was due to the fact that the operation was thrown together in only four days and that up until the last minute the Pentagon had not supported (nor did it believe there would be) an invasion.

CUBAN RESISTANCE
In a development that helped legitimize the invasion, probably the biggest intelligence failure was in underestimating the number of Cuban personnel on the island who put up a stiff resistance. For example, American forces had little understanding of the extent of Cuban anti-aircraft capa-

bilities, something that might have averted the surprisingly high number of helicopter losses. Of the almost 7,800 Cubans in Grenada at the time of the invasion, around 636 were construction workers (who had also received military training), and the rest were members of the armed forces.

The Pentagon decided to label the captured Cubans as "personnel under protective custody" rather than "prisoners of war" so that there would be no indication that the United States was "at war" with Cuba. In addition, in something that foreshadowed the Guantanamo Bay controversy following the 2001 military operation in Afghanistan, U.S. military officers were concerned that the prisoner-of-war status would give the Cubans certain rights under the Geneva Convention.[120]

Cuba had generously provided military assistance to Grenada since Bishop took power in 1979. Castro had called the NJM's coup a "big revolution in a small country," and the two governments enjoyed warm relations right up until Bishop's murder. In fact, Castro gave Coard and the RMC a cold shoulder after they assumed power, in part because of Castro's affinity for Bishop but also because Castro knew that these types of antics drastically increased the likelihood of a U.S. invasion.

The Cuban military officer who led Cuba's military mission from 1981 until May 1983 returned to Grenada less than twenty-four hours before the invasion began. He was to command the Cuban resistance and had been instructed by Castro to "fight to the death," although other reports have indicated that Castro instructed him to neither surrender nor oppose the occupation of the island.[121] Whatever Castro's instructions really were, the Cubans no doubt put up a fight, one much fiercer than the Pentagon's military planners had anticipated.

Following the invasion, Admiral Wesley L. McDonald, commander in chief of the U.S. forces in the Atlantic, said that Cuban military documents discovered in Grenada indicated that Cuba had intended to send to Grenada an additional 341 additional military officers and 4,000 reservists. McDonald also claimed that there were more than 1,100 Cubans on the island, but by October 30, U.S. officials did not dispute the estimate that there were a little less than 800 Cubans on the islands.[122] His forces defeated, Castro nonetheless lashed out at the United States for launching the invasion:

The invasion of Grenada was a treacherous surprise attack . . . presented to the U.S. people as a great victory for Reagan's foreign policy against the socialist camp and the revolutionary movements [and] linked to the resurgence of the United States as an influential power on the world scene. A dirty, dishonest appeal was made to U.S. patriotism, to national pride, to the grandeur and glory of the nation. . . . The deplorable, truly dangerous fact is that, when world opinion unanimously denounced the warmongering, aggressive, unjustifiable action that violated a people's sovereignty and all international norms and principles, most of the people of the United States—manipulated, disinformed, and deceived—supported the monstrous crime committed by their government.[123]

THE REAGAN ADMINISTRATION DEFENDS THE INVASION

At 9:00 A.M. on October 25, the first day of the invasion and before the medical students had been evacuated, President Reagan announced at a press briefing that the invasion had been "forced" on the United States by an event that had "no precedent in the eastern Caribbean and no place in any civilized society." American objectives, he indicated, in the invasion were to "protect innocent lives, including up to a thousand Americans, whose personal safety is, of course my paramount concern." Reagan also stated that the "multinational effort" was a demonstration of "collective actions" intended to "forestall further chaos" and to "assist in the restoration of conditions of law and order and of governmental institutions to the island of Grenada."[124] Reagan also explained that he had received a call from the OECS nations to assist in a joint effort and that he had accepted their request to form part of the multilateral force.

Critics made much of the fact that Reagan did not mention anything about Cuban or Soviet involvement on the island. They believed that this proved that the administration invented the Cuban threat only after the decision to invade was made in order to cover up the fact that the threat to the students was overblown. But while Reagan did not mention Cuba in his first press briefing, he had already made a great deal about Cuba's involvement in Grenada on prior occasions, such as his March 1983 national television address.

Over the course of the next several days, the administration's public reasons for the invasion shifted toward Grenada's geopolitical significance, specifically the threat that the island would turn into another Cuba. On

October 27, President Reagan made a thirty-minute address to the nation that focused on the Beirut bombing and Grenada invasion:

> The events in Lebanon and Grenada, though oceans apart, are closely related. Not only has Moscow assisted and encouraged the violence in both countries, but it provides direct support through a network of surrogates and terrorists. It is no coincidence that when the thugs tried to wrest control of Grenada, there were 30 Soviet advisors and hundreds of Cuban military and paramilitary forces on the island.

He continued,

> We have discovered a complete base with weapons and communications equipment which makes it clear a Cuban occupation of the island had been planned. . . . Grenada, we were told, was a friendly island paradise for tourism. Well, it wasn't. It was a Soviet-Cuban colony, being readied as a major military bastion to export terror and undermine democracy. We got there just in time.

He concluded the speech with

> I will not ask you to pray for the dead because they are safe in God's loving arms and beyond need of our prayers. I would like to ask you all, wherever you may be in this blessed land, to pray for those wounded young men and to pray for the bereaved families of those who gave their lives for our freedom. God bless you and God bless America.[125]

Reagan did not stand alone when he justified the invasion to the American people and the world. Instead, Prime Minister Charles of Dominica quickly emerged as an articulate and strong-willed advocate of the invasion, and her tough words reinforced the administration's claim that the OECS had freely requested U.S. assistance. At one point, Charles justified her decision to call on President Reagan by stating that

> Within the last three years, we were a bit concerned about the building up of arms in Grenada. We knew that there were colossal amounts of arms, far in excess of what any country could require in this area. And we were concerned about that. We were also concerned because we knew that the dissi-

dent forces in our islands, in each of the islands, had a little grouping . . .
[the killings in Grenada on October 19] made us realize that if we did not
take steps now we will all be under the control of a small group of thugs in
Grenada. And this we did not want in our country. And therefore we had
no compunction deciding that we must go in and make sure that the Grenadian people got what they wanted and make sure that we didn't get what
we didn't want in our country. We looked down and looked at the fact that
we did not have the means to do what we wanted to do. . . . Quite frankly
I can tell you that if the circumstances arose exactly the same again, I would
take exactly the same action, in spite of the fact that many people in this
room have blamed us for doing it. We are sure that we were right in what
we did.[126]

The American public responded overwhelmingly positively to Reagan's
explanation of the invasion. While critics screamed hyperbole, a strong
majority of the American people believed Reagan when he told them that
the United States had arrived just in time. An *ABC News* poll found that
64 percent of Americans had favored the invasion before Reagan's October 27 speech and that 86 percent favored it afterward. Seventy-four percent of Americans agreed with the statement "I feel good about Grenada
because it showed that America can use its power to protect our own
interests."[127] Inquiries at Marine recruiting stations surged to two to three
times their normal rate. One hopeful volunteer was a seventy-one-year-
old woman.[128] A *USA Today* poll showed that Reagan's lead over potential
Democratic presidential candidate Walter Mondale increased from nine
to twenty-seven points.

The widespread public support for the invasion did not mean that the
Reagan administration avoided criticism. Philip Geyelin's opinion editorial in the *Washington Post* was indicative of many of the criticisms that
came from the left:

Nor can the precedent set by a U.S. government which denounced as
"aggression" the Soviet Union's efforts to "restore" communist institutions
in Afghanistan. There is the propaganda windfall for Latin America's case-
hardened communists. There is also a setback to legitimate forces—political
leaders, intellectuals, and student movements—which actually do set some
store by the democratic values and rule of law to which the U.S. government so regularly professes strict adherence.[129]

The *Boston Globe* wrote in an editorial that

> pretending that this unilateral move was a "joint maneuver" insults the
> intelligence of Americans. Pretending that the United States has suddenly
> developed a lively interest in the democracy that it has ignored in the rest
> of Latin America insults the rest of the world.[130]

Conservatives, on the other hand, were holding up the Grenada case as a
symbol of American resolve and a much overdue response to Soviet/
Cuban expansion in the region. A *Wall Street Journal* editorial wrote that

> The lesson of Grenada is not, as it will be widely argued this weekend, that
> the U.S. is going to the mattress to make war on its enemies. The lesson is
> that it's once again known that the U.S. is *willing* to use its military as an
> instrument of policy. One would think that to be an unstated assumption
> of anyone's foreign policy. Up until this week, that assumption about the
> U.S. military was doubted throughout the world. The world will now
> assume otherwise, and will be better for it.[131]

The American public's support for Reagan's position was bolstered by
the responses of many of the medical students following their rescue. The
students' accounts also made it harder for critics to claim that they had
never been in danger. Rescued students made comments such as the following:

> "We thought we could be potential hostages. We just wanted to get out, if
> we could."
>   "I've been a dove my whole life. And I just can't believe how well those
> Rangers came down and saved us. I don't want anyone to say anything bad
> about the American military."[132] "I fully support President Reagan's
> move. . . . He really did save our lives."[133]

Bolstering the students' views was the development that medical school
chancellor Charles Modica, who initially stated that Reagan had taken
some "very unnecessary risks," now offered a different opinion when he
addressed evacuated medical students on October 26:

> Now that I have a fuller assessment of the situation that existed in Grenada
> over the past week—that control of the military council was not as I had

thought . . . that the military authorities were in fact making it virtually impossible for me to accomplish getting aircraft on the island to get you off safely . . . there is no question, in conclusion, that your safety could not be guaranteed and the action of the President did have a sound basis regarding that issue.[134]

Some have written that the students' subsequent enthusiasm for the invasion was less a result of the fact that they were in serious danger before the invasion occurred and more that they were relieved that the battles had ended safely. While there is certainly an element of truth in this conclusion, it does not change the fact that the overwhelming majority of medical students ended up supporting the invasion. In turn, this result made it infinitely harder for critics to lambaste the president for predicating his decision to invade on the safety of American lives when these lives were not in any danger.

THE UNITED NATIONS

While the American public was firmly behind President Reagan's decision, the UN General Assembly voted 108 to 9 to condemn the U.S. invasion as a "violation of international law," a majority that was even larger that the one that condemned the Soviet invasion of Afghanistan.[135] Jeane Kirkpatrick, the U.S. ambassador to the United Nations, struck back by stating that the Grenadian "terrorists [had] murder[ed] the leading citizenry and leadership of the country" and that collective action was necessary to restore democracy. In comments that turned out to be quite prescient given the type of democracy that Grenada became after the invasion, Kirkpatrick's statement to the Security Council on October 27 struck out against any sort of moral equivalency with the Soviet invasion of Afghanistan and defended the American action in terms of the long-term outcome in Grenada:

But all governments in our time claim to be democratic. They all say they are going to leave as soon as law is restored. What will there be to support the claim that the new government of Grenada will be any more an authentic expression of the will of the people of Grenada than was the gang of thugs from whom Grenada has just been delivered? Again, the answer is easy. There is a simple test. It will be clear that self-government has been restored in Grenada because freedom and the institutions through which free peoples express themselves will be clearly in evidence—a free press, free trade unions, free elections, representatives, responsible government."[136]

Kirkpatrick also pointed out that between 1980 and 1982, five secret military agreements were signed between Grenada, Cuba, North Korea, and the Soviet Union. In her words, these pacts provided for "delivery, free of charge, of millions in military supplies."[137]

When asked about what he felt about the UN General Assembly's vote, Reagan responded, "One hundred nations in the United Nations have not agreed with us on just about everything that's come up before them where we're involved, and [their condemnatory resolution] didn't upset my breakfast at all."[138] Reagan was also asked about the moral equivalency with Afghanistan, and he replied, "I know your frequent use of the word invasion. This was a rescue mission."[139]

The United Nations was not the only location where there was a strong reaction against the invasion. A State Department memo for Secretary of State Shultz reported on anti-U.S. demonstrations throughout Latin America, including the ransacking of the U.S. consular agency in Cochabamba, Bolivia; an attack on a U.S. courthouse in San Juan, Puerto Rico, by persons using a light antitank weapon; and minor damage to the consulate general in Guayaquil, Ecuador.[140]

While the Latin American "street" was outraged by the U.S. action, some Latin American leaders quietly supported the invasion. The *Christian Science Monitor* reported that one Latin American president said that "it had to be done. The growing presence of Cuban troops and arms, the utter chaos of the island's government, and the whole threat to the peace demanded action." A Latin American foreign minister stated,

> We have to protect. If we did not we would not be true to non-intervention. . . . Still, this one is understandable. And I cannot overlook the fact that the Caribbean nations not only joined the intervention but asked the U.S. for it.[141]

At the annual meeting of the OAS that took place right after the invasion, ten nations spoke in favor of the action, seven spoke against it, and ten either remained neutral or did not mention it.[142]

America's European allies remained largely quiet on the matter, not wanting to provoke the United States over an action that had already taken place. French President François Mitterand viewed it as "a surprising action in relation to international law," and West German Chancellor Helmut Kohl said that "if we had been consulted, we would have advised against it."[143]

By far the most delicate reaction, though, came from Thatcher, who was still fuming well after the invasion for being "brushed aside" by the White House after it informed her after the initial operation was under way. Labour Party spokesman Denis Healy labeled the U.S. treatment of the British government a "humiliation" for the United Kingdom.[144] In short, the Reagan administration was willing to allow its strongest ally in Europe to suffer a share of embarrassment in order to maintain the secrecy surrounding its national security goals in the Caribbean.[145]

THE REACTION FROM CONGRESS

During and immediately after the invasion, some of the Reagan administration's harshest attacks came from congressional Democrats. For example, on October 25, Representative Don Bonker (D-Wash.) stated that "committing U.S. troops in Grenada is shocking and flies in the face of the President's condemnation of Soviet interference in other countries." Senator Patrick Moynihan claimed that the United States did not have the right to promote democracy "at the point of a bayonet" and that the invasion was "an act of war" that the United States "does not have the right" to do.[146] Representative James Leach (R-Iowa) quipped that "it may be easy for foreign troops to land in Grenada, but it could prove very difficult for them to leave."[147] Representative Theodore S. Weiss (D-N.Y.) introduced a resolution calling for Reagan's impeachment for "the high crime or misdemeanor of ordering the invasion of Grenada."[148]

While Democrats such as Moynihan criticized Reagan for attempting to bring democracy at the point of a bayonet, Reagan painted the issue as centering on geopolitics and America's national security. He clearly won the political battle. With domestic opinion strongly behind the president, reports that over 90 percent of Grenadians welcomed the invasion, and troves of documents being discovered in Grenada that indicated substantial Cuban and Soviet involvement on the island, politically it was virtually impossible for all but the most liberal Democrats to continue criticizing the president.

On October 26, President Reagan sent a letter to O'Neill stating that his informing Congress of the military actions in Grenada was "consistent" with the 1973 War Powers Resolution. It is interesting to note that the letter did not say that the administration was "complying" with the War Powers Resolution.[149] Squarely in its post-Vietnam mode that made Congress reflexively skeptical of presidents who took unilateral military action, on October 27 members of the House Foreign Affairs Committee approved a bill that declared the Grenada operation under 1973 War Powers Resolution.[150]

The next day, the Senate adopted, 64 to 20, an amendment to a debt-limit bill that also declared that the War Powers Resolution applied to the fighting in Grenada. The debt-ceiling bill did not pass the Senate or the House. Even as a joint resolution, the legislation would have become law only if the president signed it or it was passed over his veto by a two-thirds vote of the House and Senate—an unlikely prospect.[151]

Many Democrats were initially eager to enforce their congressional prerogative that they believed had been usurped by the "imperial presidency" before and during the Vietnam War years. They also wanted to act carefully and forcefully lest they allow another Gulf of Tonkin–like resolution to pass. In any case, the War Powers issue became a moot point, as it soon became clear that U.S. forces had achieved an overwhelming victory and that they would soon be returning home.

In early November, a congressional delegation traveled to Grenada to assess the situation. Scenes of cheering Grenadians and stockpiles of weapons and ammunition led many members of Congress to make public statements in support of the invasion. Elwood H. Hillis's (R-Ind.) comments stated that he viewed "the largest grouping of light arms and ammunition I have ever seen in my lifetime. We saw 5.5 million pounds of light automatic weapon ammunition, estimated to be enough to shoot everybody in the whole Caribbean twice."[152] Michael D. Barnes (D-Md.) stated that "I came down here very skeptical, but I've reluctantly come to the conclusion that the invasion was justified." Delegation leader Representative Thomas Foley (D-Wash.) said that some "Americans here who were, to say the least, not supportive of the President of many issues, said that they felt their lives were in danger."[153] While not all the congressional delegates were convinced, even liberal Ron Dellums (D-Calif.) revealed in his sarcastic remarks that there was some merit to the invasion:

I hope that people understand that Grenada was clearly a unique situation.
Where could the President of the United States find an island where you
could liberate white middle class students, capture some "bad blacks," beat
up some Cubans, humiliate some Soviets, rid the island of communism,
and have the majority of black people on the island say, "Thank you, Uncle
Sam." Only on the island of Grenada.[154]

After the fact-finding mission returned to Washington, Tip O'Neill, who
initially labeled the invasion "gunboat diplomacy," now called the American action "justified."[155]

THE MEDIA CONTROVERSY

In the days and weeks following the invasion, a number of journalists
began to complain that the media had been prevented from reporting on
the invasion. The first indication that the Reagan administration
attempted to control the media occurred before the invasion when White
House spokesman Larry Speakes answered a question about a possible
invasion as being "preposterous." Speakes was apparently "furious" when
he subsequently learned that he had been left out of the loop on the invasion plans.[156] What became even more controversial was that the Pentagon
did not allow journalists to arrive on the island until the third day of the
invasion; even then, only 15 "pool" reporters (selected from around 400
assembled in Bridgetown) were allowed in, and they were not permitted
to leave the Point Salines airport. The American people were soon provided with pictures of cheering Grenadian children, warehouses full of
weapons, and some bedraggled Cuban prisoners of war.

Strong tensions quickly developed between the press and military. The
military thought that the press was out to undermine its mission, and the
press believed that the military was overly secretive and suspicious. The
Pentagon was concerned that the perceived antimilitary, anti-American
bent among the press corps would ensure a negative portrayal of the invasion. The U.S. military was convinced that military operations had suffered in Vietnam because of a dubious press; it had favorably viewed the
British military's strict management of the press in the Falklands War.
Furthermore, the Pentagon was also concerned about the "Tehran effect,"
when there was endless media coverage of the American hostages and Iranian demonstrators.

Publicly, though, the military claimed that the restrictions were intended to protect the reporters' safety, an assertion that was refuted by some in the media who pointed out that American reporters had waded ashore at Normandy and Iwo Jima. The tensions came to a head when seven journalists attempted to land in Grenada on chartered boats and were warned away by U.S. Navy aircraft. While never confirmed, some of the journalists claimed that they heard shots fired over their heads as they approached the island.[157]

Under intense pressure from Congress, a week after the invasion the Pentagon allowed journalists to take any one of three daily flights that were now linking Grenada with Barbados. Yet this was not enough to prevent the media from continuing to question the administration's veracity and U.S. military characterizations of the war. The *New York Times* labeled Grenada the "off the record war," and the *Washington Post* wrote that this "secret war, like a secret government is antithetical to open society. It is absolutely outrageous."[158] Like Johnson, it appeared that Reagan was going to have a "credibility gap" question on the invasion.

However, like the questions about the true danger that the students faced, any real controversy over the media restrictions was overwhelmed by the images of liberation and joy that the very same press was sending back to the United States. In addition, a poll indicated that 90 percent of the American public agreed with the U.S. military's decision to bar the press from covering the war. In November 1983, Caspar Weinberger appointed a fourteen-member Pentagon Press Commission to set down guidelines for future missions. The report concluded that "mutual antagonism and distrust are not in the best interests of the media, the military or the American people" and that the role of the media should be "neither that of a lapdog, nor an attack dog, but rather, a watchdog."[159]

The military's discovery of weapons and secret documents served as important tools in the administration's public relations effort. The administration highlighted the documents that indicated, for example, that in the previous four years Grenada had signed at least five secret military agreements with the Soviet Union, Cuba, and North Korea; by 1986, Grenada was scheduled to receive 15,000 rifles and machine guns, millions of rounds of ammunition, and 15,000 hand grenades. The following April, over a million rounds of ammunition were discovered under a false floor in the abandoned Cuban embassy.[160]

American troops seized seventeen tons of documents and subsequently published many of the most incriminating ones. Former ambassador Sally Shelton was correct when she called the documents a "public relations bonanza for the U.S. government."[161] Commenting on footage of North Korean officials fleeing to Havana, Kenneth Dam quipped that "they weren't there for tourism."[162] While some journalists questioned the extent to which Grenada was the "armed camp" that the administration had said it was—some of the weapons that U.S. military officials displayed were apparently from the nineteenth century—the documents and weaponry reinforced Reagan's public claim that the United States had arrived "just in time."

THE AFTERMATH OF THE INVASION

In the immediate days after the fighting, there was some looting on the island, but it quickly dissipated. Electricity was restored within a week. American combat troops were relieved and replaced by troops from the Caribbean Peacekeeping Force. After the quagmire of Vietnam, Americans were not accustomed to the notion that a local population that had just been invaded by the U.S. military would be so joyful and appreciative. Grenada was not Vietnam. A *CBS News* poll found that 91 percent of Grenadians were "glad the United States troops came to Grenada," and 81 percent said that American troops were "courteous and considerate." Another 67 percent said that they thought Cuba wanted to take control of the government, and 65 percent said that they believed the airport was being readied for Cuban and Soviet military purposes.[163] In fact, many Grenadians took issue with the term "invasion," preferring "rescue operation." In the words of Grenadian journalist Alister Hughes,

> The one thing I want to say and say very strongly is that I am very pleased with the action the Americans took to come in, because if it hadn't happened, if this rescue operation had not been undertaken, we would have been in a very sorry state. I regard this as a rescue operation, and I have not heard any Grenadian who has expressed any other view.[164]

The orthodox academic interpretation of the Grenada operation posits that the Reagan administration exaggerated the threat Grenada posed in order to conduct an unnecessary "can't-lose" invasion that would rally the

American people around the flag at a time when America was questioning its role in the world. This conclusion is complicated, however, by the fact that the intelligence reports following the invasion actually reinforced the notion that the Soviets and Cubans had greater intentions for Grenada.

For example, on October 29 Admiral Jonathan T. Howe sent a memo to Secretary of State Shultz telling him that "we now have evidence that the Soviet Union and its allies were turning Grenada into a fortified base that would threaten those oil lanes and countries in the area." He added, "It is clear the island was being turned into a fortress, a pro-Soviet military facility anchoring the southern end of the Caribbean as Cuba anchors the northern end."[165] Kenneth Dam wrote to Reagan that "the overall picture presented by the evidence is that by October 1983 the USSR and Cuba had made real progress toward turning Grenada into a center for further subversion for the region." Dam concluded that "Cuban control" had started in earnest in April 1983 and that the Cubans had shipped in arms and advisers by "a number of surreptitious means."[166]

CLEANING UP AND GOING HOME

Contrary to what many critics predicted, once U.S. combat troops left, the challenge quickly turned to preparing Grenada to become a democracy. One internal government memo stated that the chief U.S. objective in postinvasion Grenada was to "create a climate in which democratic government can be restored in Grenada."[167] Indeed, the Reagan administration sent millions of dollars in emergency food and economic reconstruction assistance to the new government. In 1984, Grenada received $48.4 million in aid, a sum that on a per capita basis was exceeded only by Israel. Aid dropped to $11.3 million in 1985 and to zero in 1986, an indication that the United States was most content to allow Grenada to move back to a small, unimportant (but democratic) Caribbean island.

American forces also rooted out traces of the PRA and expelled all Soviet-bloc citizens. New elections were held in 1984, and political moderate Herbert Blaize was elected prime minister.[168] On December 4, 1986, a jury convicted eighteen members of the RMC for the crimes of October 1983; fourteen Grenadians (including Hudson Austin and Bernard Coard) were tried and convicted. Grenada was now more free and democratic than at any point in recent memory, and it has remained this way for the past twenty years. Unlike the "militarized camp" that was Grenada in 1983, today the country does not have a military.

The Grenada invasion continued to influence American foreign policy well after the three-day operation had finished. The 1984 platform at the Republican National Convention stated that "Grenada is small and its people few; but we believe the principle established there—that freedom is worth defending—is of monumental importance. It challenges the Brezhnev doctrine. It is an example to the world." Vice President Bush told the delegates, "Because President Reagan stood firm in defense of freedom [in Grenada], America has regained respect throughout the world."[169]

On February 20, 1986, President Reagan told an audience of around 90,000 Grenadians (roughly the entire population) in St. George's, "I will never be sorry that I made the decision to help you."[170] Urgent Fury ended up costing $134.4 million, or $224,000 per rescued student. Columnist George Will wrote, "U.S. Soldiers' boot prints on Grenada's soil will do more than the MX [a tactical nuclear missile] to make American power credible."[171] On the one-year anniversary of the invasion, George Shultz said, "Our response should go beyond passive defense to consider means of active prevention, preemption, and retaliation."[172] The case for preemptive war was given a significant boost within America's conservative foreign policy circles.

The invasion of Grenada was the first foreign policy episode that started to get Americans to stop thinking so much about Vietnam, the hostages in Iran, and the tragically failed mission to rescue those hostages. It now appeared that interventions in the post-Vietnam era did not have to be quagmires. The operation signaled a new era in American foreign policy, one where the use of overwhelming military force was back on the table.

NOTES

1. See Reynold Burrowes, *Revolution and Rescue in Grenada: An Account of the US-Caribbean Invasion* (Westport, Conn.: Greenwood Press, 1988), 127–29.

2. Author phone interview with Kenneth Dam, July 18, 2004.

3. For example, see Ivan Musicant, *The Banana Wars: A History of United States Military Intervention in Latin America from the Spanish American War to the Invasion of Panama* (New York: Macmillan, 1990), 371.

4. For example, after the invasion, Representative Howard Wolpe (D-Mich.) stated, "So, when we engage in an action that in fact does violence both to interna-

tional law and to American professed principles, we play directly into the hands of those in Central American within our western hemisphere who want to portray the United States as an imperialistic power unwilling to countenance the right of people to be self-determining and unwilling to really abide by the principle of nonintervention." Quoted in *Grenada War Powers: Full Compliance Reporting and Implementation*, H.J. Res. 402, 98th Cong., 1st sess., October 27, 1983, 6.

5. "Approval of President Surges," *New York Times*, December 15, 1983.

6. For more on this point, see James Berry Motley, "Grenada: Low-Intensity Conflict and the Use of U.S. Power," *World Affairs* 146, no. 3 (winter 1983–1984): 221–38; see also John Norton Moore, "Grenada and the International Double Standard," *American Journal of International Law*, January 1984, 145; Wiltraud Quiese Morrales, "US Intervention and the New World Order: Lessons from Cold War and Post-Cold War Cases," *Third World Quarterly* 15, no. 1 (March 1994): 1–16.

7. Quoted in "Licensed to Kill?," *The Economist*, November 5, 1983, 13. See also Richard Halloran, "U.S. Command Is Divided in Grenada, Senator Asserts," *New York Times*, November 3, 1983; "Cuban Asserts Reagan Told 'Several Lies' about Grenada," *New York Times*, October 28, 1983; Stuart Taylor Jr., "Treatment of Prisoners Is Defended," *New York Times*, October 28, 1983; "The Priming of the Grenada Grenade," *The Economist*, October 29, 1983, 17; "Power Needs Clear Eyes," *The Economist*, October 29, 1983, 9; "Why the Sledgehammer Hit the Nutmeg," *The Economist*, October 29, 1983, 41.

8. Named after President Reagan's secretary of defense, Caspar Weinberger, the "Weinberger Doctrine" was the conservatives' post-Vietnam doctrine for when and how U.S. military force should be used. It mandated that the United States should engage only in war that it can win quickly, ensure minimum risk to American lives, promote support from the American public, and avoid gradualism. See Caspar Weinberger, "The Uses of Military Power," address at the National Press Club, Washington, D.C., November 28, 1984; see also Caspar W. Weinberger, "U.S. Defence Strategy," *Foreign Affairs* (summer 1986): 684–86.

9. For some critiques of the invasion, see Wendell Bell, "The Invasion of Grenada: A Note on False Prophecy," *Yale Review* 75 (October 1986): 564–88; Eldon Kenworthy, "Grenada as Theater," *World Policy Journal* 1, no. 3 (spring 1984): 635–51.

10. "Ask the Grenadians," *The Economist*, October 29, 1983, 13. For more on the Reagan Doctrine, see William R. Blade, "The Reagan Doctrine," *Strategic Review* 14, no. 1 (winter 1986): 21–29.

11. Courtney Glass, "The Setting," in *American Intervention in Grenada: The Implications of "Urgent Fury,"* ed. Peter M. Dunn and Bruce Watson (Boulder, Colo.: Westview Press, 1985), 4–6.

12. Quoted in Mark Adkin, *Urgent Fury: The Battle for Grenada* (Lexington, Mass.: Lexington Books, 1989), 5.

13. "Grenada: The Love Waves Stopped Working," *The Economist*, March 17, 1979, 66.

14. Quoted in Gordon K. Lewis, *Grenada: The Jewel Despoiled* (Baltimore: Johns Hopkins University Press, 1987), 12, 25.

15. Adkin, *Urgent Fury*, 5.

16. In March 1972, Unison Whiteman, a thirty-two-year-old economist, and Selwyn Strachan, a young sugar factory clerk, organized a movement known as the Joint

Endeavour for Welfare, Education, and Liberation (Jewel). Soon after, the twenty-five-year-old Bishop, who had just returned from seven years in England, and Kendrick Radix founded the Movement for Assemblies of the People. In March 1973, these two groups merged with one more to form the New Jewel Movement.

17. Lewis, *Grenada*, 16.

18. Quoted in Lewis, *Grenada*, 16. In late January 1974, Bishop's father was killed during a clash with police.

19. Lewis, *Grenada*, 21.

20. Quoted in Vijay Tiwathia, *The Grenada War: Anatomy of a Low-Intensity Conflict* (New Delhi: Lancer International, 1987), 33.

21. Peter M. Dunn and Bruce Watson, eds., *American Intervention in Grenada: The Implications of "Urgent Fury"* (Boulder, Colo.: Westview Press, 1985), 4.

22. Robert Beck, *The Grenada Invasion: Politics, Law, and Foreign Policy Decisionmaking* (Boulder, Colo.: Westview Press, 1993), 12.

23. Quoted in Anthony Payne, Paul Sutton, and Tony Thorndike, *Grenada: Revolution and Invasion* (New York: St. Martin's Press, 1984), 79.

24. Adkin, *Urgent Fury*, 22.

25. Quoted in Adkin, *Urgent Fury*, 21.

26. Quoted in Burrowes, *Revolution and Rescue in Grenada*, 32.

27. Robert Pastor, "Update on Grenada," National Security Council Memorandum; Memorandum for Zbigniew Brzezinski, March 27, 1979, Declassified Documents Reference System (hereafter cited as DDRS) (Farmington Hills, Mich.: Gale Group, 2003).

28. Brzezinski, National Security Council Memorandum; Memorandum for the President regarding SCC Meeting on Grenada, March 15, 1979, DDRS.

29. William C. Gilmore, *Grenada Intervention: Analysis and Documentation* (New York: Facts on File, 1984), 28.

30. Pastor, "Update on Grenada," National Security Council Memorandum; Memorandum for Zbigniew Brzezinski, March 14, 1979, DDRS.

31. Payne et al., *Grenada*, 50; see also Burrowes, *Revolution and Rescue in Grenada*, 130. The Carter administration allowed Sally Shelton to visit Grenada only twice. The Reagan administration replaced her with Milan D. Bish, but it refrained from seeking to have him accredited for Grenada. See John M. Goschko, "Invasion Caps 4 years of Tension between Ministate and the U.S.," *Washington Post*, October 26, 1983.

32. Beck, *The Grenada Invasion*, 27. In spite of Haig's words, Grenada did receive some financial assistance for international financial institutions. For example, in August 1983 Grenada obtained a three-year Extended Agreement from the International Monetary Fund (IMF) valued at $14 million. The U.S. State Department was willing to support the request, but the U.S. Treasury opposed it. The IMF went ahead with the loan in any case. See Gary Williams, "Prelude to an Intervention: Grenada 1983," *Journal of Latin American Studies* 29, no. 1 (February 1997): 131–69.

33. Kenneth Dam, Memorandum to President Reagan, June 7, 1983, DDRS; author phone interview with Kenneth Dam, July 18, 2004.

34. Quoted in Tiwathia, *The Grenada War*, 49. See also *Public Papers of the Presidents of the United States, January 1 to July 2, 1982* (Washington, D.C.: U.S. Government Printing Office,1984), 213.

35. Quoted in Beck, *The Grenada Invasion*, 29.

36. Document almost entirely blacked out, January 1983, DDRS.

37. It is interesting that the report also indicated that Soviet economic assistance had been "minimal" compared to that of the Cubans. CIA memo (mostly blacked out), DDRS.

38. Tiwathia, *The Grenada War*, 51.

39. Author interview with Tony Motley, assistant secretary of state for inter-American affairs, Washington, D.C., October 5, 2004.

40. Status of Airport Project, May 1983, DDRS.

41. Title of memo blacked out, regarding Cuban–Grenada military cooperation, January 1983, DDRS.

42. Peter Huchthausen, *America's Splendid Little Wars: A Short History of U.S. Military Engagements, 1975–2000* (New York: Viking, 2003), 66.

43. Author phone interview with Kenneth Dam; author interview with Langhorne Motley, assistant secretary of state for inter-American affairs, October 5, 2004.

44. This comment was made by Stephen W. Bosworth, principal deputy assistant secretary of state for inter-American affairs, to the House Committee on Foreign Affairs, *United States Policy toward Grenada*, 97th Cong., 2nd sess., June 15, 1982, 29.

45. Quoted in Beck, *The Grenada Invasion*, 30.

46. Beck, *The Grenada Invasion*, 28.

47. Dunn and Watson, *American Intervention in Grenada*, 10.

48. Lewis, *Grenada*, 48.

49. Quoted in Departments of State and Defense, *Grenada: A Preliminary Report*, December 16, 1983, 35.

50. Beck, *The Grenada Invasion*, 15.

51. Huchthausen, *America's Splendid Little Wars*, 72.

52. A lucid account of Bloody Wednesday can be found in Payne et al., *Grenada*, 129–36.

53. For example, see Daniel Southerland, "Nagging Questions about Grenada," *Christian Science Monitor*, November 1, 1983; Philip Taubman, "Senators Suggest Administration Exaggerated Its Cuba Assessment," *New York Times*, October 30, 1983.

54. Robert Pastor to House Committee on Foreign Affairs, Subcommittee on International Security and Scientific Affairs and on Western Hemisphere Affairs, *U.S. Military Actions in Grenada: Implications for U.S. Policy in the Eastern Caribbean*, 98th Cong., 1st sess., November 2, 3, and 16, 1983, 73.

55. Assistant Secretary of State Tony Motley even attempted to lease two Pan American Airlines jets in Miami to be used to evacuate the students. Author interview with Tony Motley.

56. Quoted in Ronald H. Cole, *Operation Urgent Fury: The Planning and Execution of Joint Operations in Grenada* (Washington, D.C.: Office of the Chairman of the Joint Chiefs of Staff, Joint History Office, 1997), 2.

57. U.S. Embassy Bridgetown to White House Situation Room, cable regarding Radio Free Grenada, October 21, 1983, DDRS.

58. Quoted in Langhorne A. Motley, "The Decision to Assist Grenada," *Current Policy*, vol. 541 (Washington, D.C.: U.S. Department of State, Bureau of Public Affairs, January 24, 1984), 2.

59. The task force consisted of the amphibious assault shop USS *Guam* with four support vessels. The *Guam* held the 22nd Marine Amphibious Unit with 1,900

Marines. See Adkin, *Urgent Fury,* 117–20. The USS *Independence* battle group was also diverted from the Mediterranean to the Caribbean.

60. The medical school was founded in 1976 by the American entrepreneur Charles R. Modica, who was also the school's chancellor. The school had around 650 students and charged $6,000 in annual tuition. The school was divided into two campus: the Grande Anse campus, near the Grande Anse Beach, and the True Blue campus, located four kilometers to the south near the new airport. See Tiwathia, *The Grenada War,* 53.

61. Cable regarding the attitudes of the Grenada medical school personnel, Department of State, October 20, 1983, DDRS.

62. John Felton, "Congress Reels under Impact of Marine Deaths in Beirut, Invasion of Grenada," *Congressional Quarterly Weekly,* October 29, 1983, 2215.

63. Author phone interview with Kenneth Dam.

64. George P. Shultz, *Turmoil and Triumph: My Years as Secretary of State* (New York: Charles Scribner's Sons, 1993), 328.

65. Motley, "The Decision to Assist Grenada," 2.

66. Departments of State and Defense, *Grenada.*

67. Secretary of State George Schultz, cable on Grenada, Department of State, October 21, 1983, DDRS.

68. Patrick E. Tyler, "The Invasion of Grenada; State Department Denies Report That U.S. Sought Pretext for Invasion," *Washington Post,* October 28, 1983.

69. Burrowes, *Revolution and Rescue in Grenada,* 66.

70. Quoted in Adkin, *Urgent Fury,* 98–99.

71. Cable regarding Joint Caribbean Action and Naval Blockade, Department of State, October 21, 1983, DDRS.

72. U.S. Embassy at Bridgetown to White House Situation Room, cable regarding OECS, Department of State, October 22, 1983, DDRS.

73. Author interview with Tony Gillespie, deputy assistant secretary of state for inter-American affairs, Washington, D.C., November 17, 2004; Williams, "Prelude to an Intervention," 131–69.

74. Bureau of Public Affairs of the Department of State, "The Larger Importance of Grenada," *Current Policy* 526, no. 4 (November 1983): 1–3.

75. Hugh O'Shaughnessy, *Grenada: Revolution, Invasion, and Aftermath* (London: Hamish Hamilton, 1984), 158–59.

76. Author interview with Craig Johnstone, deputy assistant secretary of state for the Caribbean, July 2, 2004.

77. Author interview with Craig Johnstone.

78. Quoted in "Say Something, If Only Goodbye," *The Economist,* March 10, 1984, 31.

79. Michael Rubner, "The Reagan Administration, the 1973 War Powers Resolution, and the Invasion of Grenada," *Political Science Quarterly* 100, no. 4 (winter 1985–1986): 636.

80. Adkin, *Urgent Fury,* 106.

81. Rubner, "The Reagan Administration, the 1973 War Powers Resolution, and the Invasion of Grenada," 632.

82. For a comprehensive history of the military planning of the invasion, see Cole, *Operation Urgent Fury.*

83. William S. Lind, *Report to the Congressional Military Caucus: The Grenada Operation* (Washington, D.C.: Military Reform Institute, April 5, 1984).

84. Author interview with Craig Johnstone.

85. Author interview with Tony Motley, assistant secretary of state for inter-American affairs, October 5, 2004.

86. Author interview with Craig Johnstone.

87. Russell Lee and M. Albert Mendez, "The 'New Jewel' Movement," in *Grenada 1983, Men at Arms Series, 159* (London: Osprey Publishing, 1985), 10.

88. Quoted in Adkin, *Urgent Fury*, 121.

89. Lee and Mendez, "The 'New Jewel' Movement," 11.

90. Author interview with Tony Gillespie, executive to the assistant secretary of state for Caribbean affairs, November 17, 2004.

91. Adkin, *Urgent Fury*, 120.

92. Quoted in "Say Something, If Only Goodbye," 31.

93. Quoted in Beck, *The Grenada Invasion*, 163.

94. Quoted in Burrowes, *Revolution and Rescue in Grenada*, 74.

95. Author interview with Tony Motley, assistant secretary of state for inter-American affairs, October 5, 2004.

96. Cole, *Operation Urgent Fury*, 5.

97. Frank Uhlig Jr., "Amphibious Aspects of the Grenada Episode," in Dunn and Watson, *American Intervention in Grenada*, 91.

98. Quoted in Cole, *Operation Urgent Fury*, 41.

99. Cole, *Operation Urgent Fury*, 35.

100. Huchthausen, *America's Splendid Little Wars*, 79.

101. Lee and Mendez, "The 'New Jewel' Movement," 19.

102. Payne et al., *Grenada*, 157. Some critics have contended that the letter had been backdated.

103. Lee and Mendez, "The 'New Jewel' Movement," 22.

104. G. F. Illingworth, "Grenada in Retrospect," in Dunn and Watson, *American Intervention in Grenada*, 141.

105. Lee and Mendez, "The 'New Jewel' Movement," 24.

106. Adkin, *Urgent Fury*, 23.

107. Huchthausen, *America's Splendid Little Wars*, 79.

108. Cole, *Operation Urgent Fury*, 45.

109. Tiwathia, *The Grenada War*, 93.

110. Cole, *Operation Urgent Fury*, 49.

111. Lee and Mendez, "The 'New Jewel' Movement," 23.

112. Cole, *Operation Urgent Fury*, 57.

113. Richard Harwood, "Tidy War Ends: 'We Blew Them Away,'" *Washington Post*, November 6, 1983.

114. Thomas Carothers, *In the Name of Democracy: US Policy toward Central America during the Reagan Years* (Berkeley: University of California Press, 1991), 274.

115. Dunn and Watson, *American Intervention in Grenada*, 142.

116. Quoted in Gerald Hopple and Cynthia Gilley, "Policy without Intelligence," in Dunn and Watson, *American Intervention in Grenada*, 56.

117. Quoted in Lind, *Report to the Congressional Military Reform Caucus*, 3.

118. See Daniel P. Bolger, "Operation Urgent Fury and Its Critics," *Military Review*,

July 1986, 57–69. See also Drummand Ayres, "Grenada Invasion: A Series of Surprises," *New York Times*, November 14, 1983; Abram Chayes, "Grenada Was Illegally Invaded," *New York Times*, November 15, 1983; Eugene V. Rostow, "Law Is Not a Suicide Pact," *New York Times*, November 15, 1983; David H. Lloyd, "Grenada Invasion: A Legitimate Rescue Mission," *New York Times*, November 17, 1983; Don Oberdorfer, "Applying Pressure in Central America," *Washington Post*, November 23, 1983.

119. Two hundred and two U.S. medical students at the "third campus" on the Lance aux Epines peninsula near St. George's were rescued on October 28. See Cole. *Operation Urgent Fury*, 57.

120. Cole, *Operation Urgent Fury*, 57.

121. Quoted in Departments of State and Defense, *Grenada*.

122. Patrick E. Tyler, "The Making of an Invasion: The Chronology of the Planning," *Washington Post*, October 30, 1983.

123. Quoted in Tony Thorndike, *Grenada: Politics, Economics, and Society* (London: Frances Pinter, 1985), 13.

124. Quoted in Beck, *The Grenada Invasion*, 55.

125. Ronald Reagan, "America's Commitment to Peace," Address to the Nation, October 27, 1983; *Department of State Bulletin* 83, no. 2081 (December 1983): 1–5; quoted in Isaak I. Dore, "The U.S. Invasion of Grenada: Resurrection of the 'Johnson Doctrine'?," *Stanford Journal of International Law* 20 (spring 1984): 176.

126. Quoted in Colin Legum, "Grenada: Linkage and Impact on the Third World," in *Grenada and Soviet/Cuban Policy: Internal Crisis and US/OECS Intervention*, ed. Jiri Valenta and Herbert J. Ellison (Boulder, Colo.: Westview Press, 1986), 156.

127. Frank Gregorsky, "The Liberation of Grenada: The Enslavement of Democrats," *Congressional Record*, November 16, 1983, 33221–22.

128. Walter Isaacson, "Weighing the Proper Role," *Time*, November 7, 1983, 42–62.

129. Philip Geyelin, ". . . And the Pursuit of Short-Term Profit," *Washington Post*, November 1, 1983.

130. "Reagan's Credibility," *Boston Globe*, October 27, 1983; quoted in Kai Schoenhals et al., *Revolution and Intervention in Grenada, the New Jewel Movement, the United States, and the Caribbean* (Boulder, Colo.: Westview Press, 1985), 160.

131. "The Lesson of Grenada," *Wall Street Journal*, October 28, 1980; see also "Lawyers Invade Grenada," *Wall Street Journal*, November 1, 1983; Albert Xavier, "Plotting That Had the Eastern Caribbean on Edge," *Wall Street Journal*, November 1, 1983; Theodore Eliot, "Grenada Doesn't Equal Afghanistan," *Wall Street Journal*, November 7, 1983.

132. The first two quotations are from Frank Gregorsky, "The Liberation of Grenada: The Enslavement of Democrats," *Congressional Record*, November 16, 1983, Extension of Remarks, 33221.

133. Departments of State and Defense, *Grenada*.

134. Quoted in Motley, "The Decision to Assist Grenada," 2.

135. Beck, *The Grenada Invasion*, 2.

136. "Grenada: Collective Actions by the Caribbean Peace Force," *Department of State Bulletin* 83, no. 2081 (December 1983): 75; see also "Grenada; More Light," *The Economist*, November 5, 1983, 39; Jeane J. Kirkpatrick, "The U.N. and Grenada: A Speech Never Delivered," *Strategic Review* 12 (winter 1984): 11–18.

137. Quoted in Beck, *The Grenada Invasion*, 62.

138. Quoted in Beck, *The Grenada Invasion*, 49.

139. Quoted in "Grenada," *Department of State Bulletin*, 78.

140. Memorandum to Secretary of State George Shultz regarding increase in anti-American terrorism in Latin America, Department of State memo, November 3, 1983, DDRS.

141. Quoted in James Nelson Goodsell, "Latin America's Quiet Support for US Intervention in Grenada," *Christian Science Monitor*, November 1, 1983.

142. D. Brent Hardt, "Grenada Reconsidered," *Fletcher Forum* 11 (summer 1987): 307.

143. Quoted in Burrowes, *Revolution and Rescue in Grenada*, 90.

144. Peter Osnos, "Thatcher Says She Attempted to Dissuade Reagan," *Washington Post*, October 26, 1983.

145. O'Shaughnessy, *Grenada*, 170.

146. Quoted in Dan Balz and Thomas B. Edsall, "The Invasion of Grenada: GOP Rallies around Reagan; Democrats Divided on Grenada," *Washington Post*, October 26, 1983.

147. Quoted in Lawrence S. Germain, "A Chronology of Events concerning Grenada," in Dunn and Watson, *American Intervention in Grenada*, 168.

148. Rubner, "The Reagan Administration, the 1973 War Powers Resolution, and the Invasion of Grenada," 642.

149. *Communication from the President of the United States Transmitting a Report on the Deployment of United States Armed Forces to Grenada*, October 26, 1983, 98th Cong., 1st sess., 1983, H. Doc. 98-125. For more on the War Powers Resolution's application to the Grenada case, see House Committee on Foreign Affairs, Subcommittee on International Security and Scientific Affairs, *The War Powers Resolution: Relevant Documents, Correspondence, Reports*, prepared by the Committee on Foreign Affairs, 98th Cong., 1st sess. H.J. Res. 542 is known as the War Powers Resolution.

150. The War Powers Resolution was enacted ten years earlier in 1973, and it required the president to notify Congress within forty-eight hours whenever U.S. troops are engaged in hostilities. Troops must be removed within sixty days from the date of that notification or ninety days if the president requests an extension. Congress can authorize a continued presence.

151. Richard Whittle, "Objectives Achieved, Reagan Says: Congress Examines Causes, Costs of Grenada Operation," *Congressional Quarterly Weekly*, November 5, 1983, 2292.

152. "Reports from the Honorable Samuel S. Stratton, the Honorable Elwood H. (Bud) Hillis, and the Honorable Ronald V. Dellums, on their November 5–6, 1983, visit to Grenada with Speaker's Fact-Finding Mission," hearing before the Committee on Armed Services, House of Representatives, 98th Cong., 1st sess., November 15, 1983.

153. Quoted in Germain, "A Chronology of Events concerning Grenada," 169.

154. "Reports from the Honorable Samuel S. Stratton, the Honorable Elwood H. (Bud) Hillis, and the Honorable Ronald V. Dellums, on their November 5–6, 1983, visit to Grenada with Speakers Fact-Finding Mission."

155. Hedrick Smith, "O'Neill Now Calls Grenada Invasion 'Justified' Action," *New York Times*, November 9, 1983.

156. Lou Cannon and David Hoffman, "Speakes Complained in Memo; Invasion Secrecy Creating a Furor," *Washington Post*, October 27, 1983.

157. George Quester, "Grenada and the News Media," in Dunn and Watson, *American Intervention in Grenada*, 109–27; see also Marcia Block and Geoff Mungham, "The Military, the Media, and the Invasion of Grenada," *Contemporary Crises* 13 (June 1989): 91–127.

158. Quoted in Tiwathia, *The Grenada War*, 155–56.

159. Quoted in Tiwathia, *The Grenada War*, 159.

160. Shultz, *Turmoil and Triumph*, 341.

161. Quoted in Peter Shearman, "The Soviet Union and Grenada under the New Jewel Movement," *International Affairs* 61, no. 4 (autumn 1985): 661.

162. Author phone interview with Kenneth Dam.

163. Adam Clymer, "Grenadians Welcomed Invasion, a Poll Finds," *New York Times*, November 6, 1983.

164. Quoted in Comments of Rep. Henry Hyde (R-Ill.), House Committee, *U.S. Military Actions in Grenada: Implications for U.S. Policy in the Eastern Caribbean*, 117.

165. Jonathan T. Howe, memorandum to Secretary of State George Shultz regarding the strategic importance of Cuban activities on the island, Department of State, October 29, 1983, DDRS. Howe also described how Grenada was close to one of the busiest sea-lanes in the hemisphere as well as to the oil fields in Venezuela and Trinidad.

166. Kenneth Dam, memorandum to the president from Department of State, December 13, 1983, DDRS.

167. Memo titled "Next Steps," date unknown, DDRS.

168. Carothers, *In the Name of Democracy*, 112.

169. Quoted in Michael Clough, "Comments," in Valenta and Ellison, *Grenada and Soviet/Cuban Policy*, 163.

170. Quoted in Beck, *The Grenada Invasion*, 23.

171. George F. Will, "The Price of Power," *Newsweek*, November 7, 1983.

172. George Shultz, "Terrorism in the Modern World," *Survival* 27, no. 1 (January/February 1985): 33; quoted in Tiwathia, *The Grenada War*, 33.

4

The Invasion of Panama, 1989

On the morning of December 20, 1989, 24,000 U.S. troops descended on Panama in order to decimate the country's notorious military dictatorship and apprehend its even more notorious leader, Manuel Antonio Noriega. The invasion of Panama was the largest U.S. military operation since the Vietnam War. It was also the first invasion of a country after the fall of the Berlin Wall in 1989.

The decision to launch such a massive invasion against such a relative "banana republic" resulted from the failure of Washington's foreign policy in Panama during the 1980s. Indeed, the invasion was a "can't-lose" response to Washington's previous inability to remove Noriega from the political scene in Panama.[1] During the 1970s and 1980s, successive U.S. administrations viewed Noriega as an unsavory but critical and efficient provider of intelligence.[2] He was "our man in Panama." But by the mid-1980s, Noriega's increasingly vicious behavior, above all his involvement in the international narcotics trade, made him a liability to the United States, especially at a time when the American public's concern about illegal drugs was reaching its peak.

By 1988, our convenient "ally" had become America's "drug enemy number one."[3] He had to go. Yet two years of economic sanctions and other covert pressures only strengthened Noriega's hermetic grip on Panamanian society. It was at this point—where all previous noninvasion attempts to remove him from power had failed—that the United States decided to launch this massive use of force. The invasion caught Noriega completely by surprise. Noriega took Washington's previous ineffective policies and internal divisions as a sign that the United States would never launch a full-scale invasion. The price in American body bags would not be worth his head, Noriega surmised.

Many scholars have often painted the U.S. invasion as yet another demonstration of U.S. hegemony in Central America and the Caribbean. One observer noted immediately after the invasion that "the invasion of Panama felt like the last gasp in an old, old method of bringing about change in Central America that had been tried more than 60 times before by the United States and that has never really worked."[4] A seminal work on the history of U.S.–Panama relations concluded that the invasion "proved that the American urge to dominate was as strong as ever."[5]

It is easy to see why scholars have come to this conclusion. The United States is a hegemonic power when compared to its Central American and Caribbean neighbors. It can determine outcomes. And, as discussed previously, Washington's legacy of intervention in Central America and the Caribbean is undeniable, and American officials have at times been less than forthright in their justifications. Thus, we often automatically conclude that a mission such as the invasion of Panama could be only for cynical reasons. Moreover, this critical perspective likely led observers to discount President George H. W. Bush's stated motivations for the U.S. invasion: protecting American lives and the security of the canal, arresting Noriega, and promoting democracy in Panama.

Another lasting criticism was that the invasion and apprehension of a foreign leader was a violation of Panama's sovereignty and, thus, of international law. Numerous academic articles have been written that scrupulously detail the invasion in light of international law, arguing convincingly that the invasion was technically illegal. The general conclusions were that the invasion was "the latest in a series of U.S. armed interventions in the Caribbean and Central America that have violated U.S. treaty commitments and the very tenets of international law the United States itself was instrumental in introducing."[6]

Others have suggested that Bush's decision to invade Panama was a way of casting off the impression that he was a "whimp," an impression that had dogged him ever since his time as Ronald Reagan's vice president.[7] But while the successful invasion undoubtedly enhanced Bush's image as a forceful leader, it is important to keep in mind that Bush's decision to launch a full-scale invasion posed the risk of American soldiers coming home in body bags a few days before Christmas.

While all these criticisms have some merit, what is most apparent is that the U.S. action actually represented the continuation of America's traditional "Big Stick" but in a new post–Cold War era, one where national sovereignty was becoming less of a concern. Indeed, the Panama operation was followed by interventions in Haiti, Bosnia, Kosovo, and Somalia.

While there are of course significant differences between the Panama case and these others, in some respects Panama can be seen as a precursor to these actions that dominated the international arena in the 1990s and into the twenty-first century. In fact, like Grenada, Panama demonstrated that the United States—and in particular the president—could exercise the use of force as part of its foreign policy repertoire and gain the support of the American people.[8]

To be sure, there are valid criticisms of the Bush administration's invasion of Panama. Is the United States justified in using overwhelming military force to remove a "two-bit thug"? And, to be sure, Noriega would never have needed to be removed through a massive invasion had Washington not spent millions of dollars supporting his spy network over a span of over fifteen years. However, it should be pointed out that, to many in Washington, Noriega's utility was worth the price paid in morality, especially since successive U.S. policymakers believed that they were pitted in a life-and-death struggle against global communism.

But the legality, morality, or necessity of invading Panama must be evaluated in the context of the overall historical record. For example, officials in the Reagan and Bush administrations received reports documenting hundreds of incidents of violence committed by Noriega's forces against American citizens. By late 1989, U.S. policymakers fully believed that Noriega's regime posed an imminent threat to American installations and citizens. Like Grenada, a Tehran-like hostage crisis was a real concern. In fact, Noriega loyalists apprehended several Americans during the invasion. The number could have easily been much higher.

It is not the purpose of this book to argue that the Bush administration did not have any options available other than a full-scale invasion. For example, the Bush administration could have ordered a massive show of military force inside the Canal Zone to let Noriega know that the United

States would not be intimidated. It could have continued with the economic sanctions that it levied in early 1988. It could have attempted a
commando-style raid to nab Noriega. Some critics have even argued that
Washington should not have done anything at all, that he would have
eventually been overthrown by the Panamanian people.

Yet, while these questions are worth considering, it is by no means clear
that they would have necessarily led to more stable and positive outcomes.
Each scenario has its own costs and benefits. For example, the economic
sanctions approach had been attempted for over a year but if anything
had strengthened Noriega's grip on power. What we do know for certain
is that the invasion of Panama was a response to the Bush administration's
view that a credible and imminent threat existed in Panama.

THE UNITED STATES, PANAMA, AND THE CANAL:
THE EARLY YEARS

Perhaps more so than any other foreign country, Panama's history as a
nation is inextricably linked to the United States. Indeed, Panama received
its independence from Colombia in 1903 only because the United States
was looking for a convenient partner with which to conclude a treaty per-
mitting U.S. access to and control of an interoceanic canal.

For most of the previous eighty years since its break with Spain, Panama remained part of Colombia. Thus, from the 1840s through the early
twentieth century, in its longtime interest and jockeying for canal access,
Washington spent almost all its time negotiating with Bogotá, not Panama
City. The first manifestation of the U.S. interest in the Panama region as
a strategic asset with regard to canal access occurred with the signing of
the Bidlack-Mallarino Treaty in 1846. This committed the United States
to a crossing at Panama and it also granted permission for the United
States to intervene in order to protect transit facilities. Ironically, the
treaty implied that the United States would not allow Panama to secede
from Colombia. Overnight Washington had gained a strategic interest and
foothold in Panama.[9]

On invitation from Colombia, during the next fifty-six years the United
States intervened thirteen times in Panama. Most of the interventions
revolved around protecting infrastructure that was ferrying increasing
numbers of travelers and goods from one ocean to the other. The discovery of gold in California in 1849 was one episode in particular that sparked
increased (in this case, westward) traffic across Panama.[10]

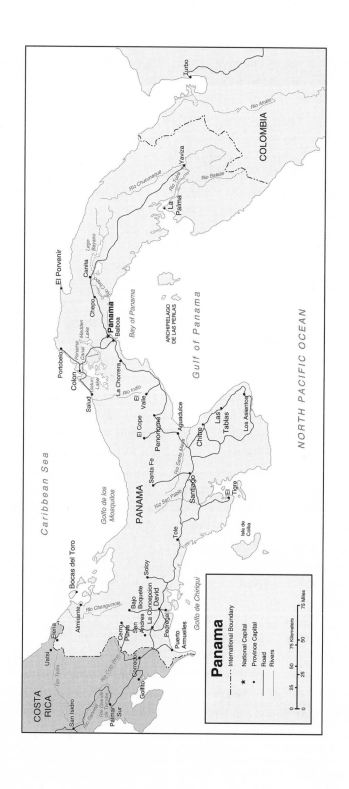

Panama
- - - International Boundary
★ National Capital
• Province Capital
—— Road
—— Rivers

COSTA RICA

COLOMBIA

PANAMA

Caribbean Sea

NORTH PACIFIC OCEAN

Gulf of Panama

Bay of Panama

Golfo de los Mosquitos

Golfo de Chiriqui

ARCHIPIELAGO DE LAS PERLAS

Turbo

Yaviza

La Palma

Río Atrato

Río Chucunaque

Río Tuira

Río Balsas

El Porvenir

Canita

Chepo

Panama

Balboa

Portobelo

Colon

Salud

La Chorrera

El Valle

Aguadulce

Las Tablas

Los Asientos

Chitre

El Tigre

Penonome

El Cope

Santa Fe

Santiago

Tole

Soloy

Bajo Boquete

La Concepcion David

Pedregal

Puerto Armuelles

San Andres

Cerro Punta

Corredor

Golfito

Palmar Sur

San Isidro

Uatsi

Eleria

Almirante

Bocas del Toro

Río Changuinola

Río Teira

Río Coto Brus

Río Caldera

Río Grande de Terraba

Río Indio

Río Santa Maria

Río San Pablo

Lago Bayano

Madden Lake

Gatun Lake

Panama Canal

Isla de Coiba

One of the seminal moments in the U.S. quest for a canal took place in 1898 during the war with Spain when its most powerful battleship, the *Oregon*, had to go around the tip of South America to make it to the theater in Cuba, a journey of sixty-eight days.[11] Pro-canal factions within the American political establishment used this episode as proof positive of the strategic imperative of a canal through Central America, one of course built and exclusively operated by Washington.[12]

The first step toward the unilateral appropriation of canal rights took place in 1901 when Washington signed the Hay-Pauncefote Treaty with Great Britain, which gave the United States the implicit right to construct and operate a canal. What the treaty did not clear up, however, was where the canal would be built. A route through Nicaragua was actually the more appealing option for most of the late part of the nineteenth century. Two U.S. canal commissions had supported the Nicaragua option, and in 1901 a bill for the Nicaragua route passed the House of Representatives 308 to 2. In contrast, Panama was seen as a disease-ridden swamp.

But all was not lost. As generations of U.S. high school students are taught, the indefatigable Frenchman (with a vested interest in the Panama route) Philippe Bunau-Varilla lobbied prominent Republicans in Congress to reconsider their position. After hearing how a volcanic eruption on the island of Martinique killing 30,000 people was followed by an eruption of a volcano in Nicaragua, Bunau-Varilla is reported to have sent a Nicaraguan stamp showing a smoking mountain to senators three days before a crucial vote on the canal route. Panama won the vote forty-two to thirty-four, and the Spooner Act authorized a canal to be built through Panama "within a reasonable time," or else the prize would go to Nicaragua.[13]

Now that it had congressional approval for the Panama option, the next step for Washington was to get approval from Bogotá. In addition to the security necessity, President Theodore Roosevelt wanted the treaty for "posterity and reelection."[14] This effort culminated with the Hay-Herrán Treaty, signed in January 1903 by U.S. Secretary of State John Hay and his counterpart Tomás Herrán. The Hay-Herrán Treaty provided for a 100-year renewable lease that would grant the United States a six-mile-wide zone that would cover the entire length of the canal. Jurisdiction over the canal was to be shared, and Washington would provide Colombia with a $250,000 annuity.[15] The Senate ratified the treaty in March by a vote of seventy-three to five, but the Colombian assembly was much less enthusi-astic, rejecting it unanimously.

The rejection of the treaty forced Roosevelt to reconsider his canal pol-icy. He knew that he could continue negotiations with the Colombians, attempt a project through Nicaragua, and let Congress decide the matter, or he could negotiate a new treaty with a secessionist Panamanian state.[16] It is clear that he had absolutely no desire to continue dealing with the "foolish and homicidal corruptionists in Bogotá," stating, "You could no more make an agreement with them than you could nail currant jelly to a wall."[17] Roosevelt was also incensed because apparently some members of the Colombian legislature wanted bribes in return for favorable votes on the treaty.[18] The stage was set: Roosevelt would help ensure the success of the "notorious little revolution" in Panama that would lead to a new treaty.[19] While Roosevelt had every desire to see Panama break free from Colombia, it is also important to keep in mind that many Panamanians also wanted independence. Washington would just provide the muscle to ensure that the process went smoothly and that the outcome was never in doubt.

In early November 1903, Panamanian rebels declared their indepen-dence from Colombia. While some Colombian soldiers were still able to land, the majority of the forces sent by Bogotá were deterred by the pres-ence of U.S. gunboats off Panama's key coastal areas. In just a matter of a few days, Washington had recognized the new government in Panama. Not surprisingly, efforts to sign a canal treaty followed almost immediately afterward. On November 15, now acting as Panama's temporary represen-tative to the United States, Bunau-Varilla—one of "the great hero-rogues of the imperialist era, the equal of the almost mythical Cecil Rhodes and Conrad's all-too-lifelike Mr. Kurtz"—began negotiations with Hay over a new treaty.[20]

The wording of the treaty was almost identical to the Hay-Herrán doc-ument signed ten months earlier. But, amazingly, Bunau-Varilla feared that the wording was almost too favorable to Panama and that the Senate might reject it and opt for a Nicaraguan route. The accord, known as the Hay–Bunau-Varrilla Treaty, expanded the canal zone from six miles to ten, added several offshore islands to U.S. control, allowed for the con-struction of U.S. military bases, and changed the concession from 100 years to "in perpetuity." Panama had no right to levy taxes in the zone or to fix toll rates on the canal. Rent on the zone was also fixed by the treaty, something that would be greatly reduced by inflation over the years. Hay remarked that the treaty was "very satisfactory, fully advantageous to the United States, and, we must confess, not so advantageous to Panama."[21] The Canal Zone was now an exclusive U.S. territory.

Many Panamanians were outraged at the new terms, but they had little choice but to accept the document. They knew full well that their precarious independence was only as good as Washington's willingness to keep Colombian reinforcements at bay. In addition, there was talk that Bogotá was considering presenting Washington with a new, more generous treaty if it would turn against Panama's independence.[22] On December 2, the same day that the boat carrying the actual treaty arrived in the Caribbean port city of Colón, Panama ratified the treaty unanimously and without modification. The U.S. Senate ratified the treaty twelve weeks later; three days after that, Bunau-Varilla resigned as Panama's minister in Washington.

All Americans did not approve Roosevelt's victory, however. A 1903 *New York Times* editorial said that the canal was "stolen property" and that the administration's partners in Panama were "a group of canal promoters and speculators and lobbyists who came into their money through the rebellion we encouraged, made safe, and effectuated." Roosevelt characteristically dismissed his detractors as a "small body of shrill eunuchs."[23]

U.S.–PANAMA RELATIONS, 1904–1968

The Panama Canal, one of the world's most remarkable feats of engineering, opened on August 15, 1914, when the steamship *Ancon*, used to ferry rock during the construction, passed through it. For the next half century, the canal was America's strategic and economic pearl in the region. During several military conflicts—including two world wars—the canal was an indispensable conduit of American troops and armaments between the two oceans.[24]

The Panama Canal was also a critical component of America's national security identity, something that helps explain why the United States hung onto the canal when it had forfeited most of its other overseas possessions, such as the Philippines. Starting in the 1930s, however, there were growing Panamanian demands for modifications to the treaty. During the height of Franklin Roosevelt's "Good Neighbor Policy," a supplementary treaty (signed in 1936 and ratified in 1939) limited the right of the United States to maintain order in Colón and Panama City, and it clarified that the Canal Zone was "the territory of the Republic of Panama under jurisdiction to the United States."[25] This treaty also started a pattern whereby the State Department would support amendments to the treaty while the War Department (now Defense) opposed them.

During the early years of the U.S. presence in the Canal Zone—and even before the canal was completed—U.S. presidents sent troops or marshals into Panama, often to supervise elections or disperse protests.[26] But even as late as the 1989 invasion, the United States did not intervene on any large scale in Panama. One good reason for this, of course, was that it simply did not have to "intervene," as the Canal Zone was effectively U.S. sovereign territory.

While the United States would have certainly been willing to maintain its command over the canal based on the 1903 treaty, by the 1950s many Panamanians were becoming even more vocal in their belief that changes needed to be made. The incipient revolutionary climate in the 1950s—for example, the social reforms in Guatemala under Jacobo Arbenz, the 1952 revolution in Bolivia, and the 1959 revolution in Cuba—helped foster growing nationalist sentiment in Panama, a feeling that was inextricably tied up with Panama's relationship to the United States and the Canal Zone. A 1955 treaty between the two countries marked an improvement from the 1936 agreement, but for most Panamanians in the throes of the concepts of national liberation, revolution, and heightened self-awareness, this accord was still not enough.[27]

One key Panamanian criticism revolved around the intended use of the American military bases. The treaty allowed for U.S. forces to be stationed in order to defend the canal but not for other activities. But by the 1950s and 1960s, it was apparent to everyone involved that the U.S. bases were much more about Washington's hemispheric security concerns—ones that had been greatly heightened because of the growing Communist threat in the region—than canal defense.[28]

In May 1958, Panamanian university students infiltrated the zone to plant dozens of Panamanian flags as an act of political protest. They returned in November 1959, but this time U.S. authorities barred them from the zone, a move that sparked a march on the U.S. embassy in Panama City. More rioting continued later that month. All told, over 100 Pan-

amanian students were killed, 9 by U.S. forces. In 1960, President Eisenhower responded to the controversy by ordering the Panamanian flag to
be flown in parts of the Canal Zone.[29]

Anti-U.S. sentiment peaked in early 1964 during the infamous "flag
riots." Since Eisenhower's concession several years earlier, high schools
inside the Canal Zone had been exempted from flying the Panamanian
flag alongside the American. On January 9, just two months after President Kennedy's assassination, a few hundred students from the Instituto
Nacional, a Panamanian high school located near the Canal Zone,
marched to Balboa High School inside the zone and attempted to raise
the Panamanian flag. American students and police attempted to stop the
Panamanians, a melee broke out, and supposedly the Panamanian flag was
ripped during the dispute.

Rumors about the incident quickly spread throughout Panama City,
and within hours tens of thousands of Panamanians had taken to the
streets.[30] They proceeded to march down the 4th of July Avenue, which
marked the boundary with the Canal Zone. American troops defended the
zone by using live ammunition; Panamanian snipers took shots at the
American soldiers. The rioting lasted for close to four days, during which
time the Panamanian National Guard made no effort to control the riot-
ers. All told, 18 Panamanians and 4 American soldiers were killed; 200 to
300 Panamanians and 150 Americans were injured. Citing "unprovoked
aggression," Panamanian President Rodolfo Chiari broke relations with
Washington and immediately renamed the 4th of July Avenue the "Avenue of the Martyrs."[31]

These periodic anti-U.S. riots prompted many key political leaders in
the United States to conclude that the United States needed to eventually
transfer control of the canal over to Panama lest the conditions for an
even more violent or revolutionary response erupt. They believed that
U.S. control of the canal was increasingly an anachronism from a more
imperialist period. It was time for a change. Senator Fulbright, in comments he made a year before the Dominican intervention, summed up
this position well:

> The basic problem . . . is the exercise of American control over a part of the
> territory of Panama in this age of intense nationalist and anti-colonialist
> feeling. . . . It seems to me entirely proper and necessary for the United

States to take the initiative in proposing new agreements that would redress some of Panama's grievances. . . . Surely, in a confrontation so unequal, it is not unreasonable to expect the United States to go a little further than half-way in the search for a fair settlement.[32]

But, as became overwhelmingly clear by the time of the debates over the ratification of the 1977 Panama Canal treaties, not all Americans shared this sentiment. The Pentagon, for one, viewed Panama as a strategic position in the world where, unlike most other places, U.S. bases could be legally located. Indeed, the Pentagon cared far more about the military bases than the canal itself.

President Johnson responded to the 1964 flag riots by appointing his Latin American adviser Thomas Mann to chair the Panama Review Group to address the growing controversy over the canal. But while the Johnson administration was willing to consider transferring the canal over to Panama, at this point it was still committed to maintaining the military bases. National Security Adviser McGeorge Bundy, for one, sent out a classified memo to the secretaries of defense and state urging that the new agreement "provide for continuation of U.S. military bases and facilities" inside the zone.[33]

Beginning in 1965, talks between the Johnson administration and Panamanian President Marco Robles led to the announcement in 1967 of three new treaties, ones that, while not ratified, eventually became the foundation for the successful 1977 treaties. The Johnson administration's overtures to Panama during this period on the whole demonstrate a willingness to lessen Washington's imperial presence in the region. This fact is worth considering when evaluating its motivations during the Dominican crisis, when many historians concluded that Washington's real motive was to prevent a liberal democratic regime in that island nation.

THE 1968 COUP AND THE RISE OF OMAR TORRIJOS

By the late 1960s, political developments in Panama were developing even faster than was Washington's strategic and political understanding of the canal. This in turn dramatically altered the political climate in which the two countries continued to negotiate revisions to the treaties. In 1968, two-time Panamanian president Arnulfo Arias was once again elected. The Harvard and Cambridge–trained Arias was the godfather of Panamanian politics, ruling intermittently as a fascist-leaning Axis sympathizer or democratic populist.[34]

Unwisely for his own political survival, on assuming office in October 1968, Arias immediately began purging the National Guard's leadership. Arias removed most of the general staff through forced retirements or assignments to "diplomatic exile." Lieutenant Colonel Omar Torrijos was told to leave El Salvador as a military attaché.[35] Within days of the inauguration, Torrijos launched a coup against Arias, who quickly found himself in the Canal Zone before heading to exile in Miami. Arias's latest presidency ended ten days, eleven hours, and forty-some minutes after it began.[36]

A new civilian-military junta was established, and newly scheduled elections were then canceled. Washington severed relations with the junta but restored them in less than a month. By early 1969, Torrijos had pushed aside any potential rivals and consolidated his firm grip on power. Arias loyalists launched a guerrilla campaign in the region of Chiriquí that lasted around a year. It was decimated by National Guard troops commanded by a young officer, Manuel Antonio Noriega. For the next eleven years, the Panamanian military dominated politics in Panama.

In December 1969, Torrijos felt confident enough in his position to afford taking a trip to Mexico City. Torrijos was in Mexico for only two days when a coup against him unfolded back in Panama. Some National Guard officers were concerned about Torrijos's supposed Communist leanings and increasingly dictatorial rule.[37] Torrijos and his loyal colleagues chartered a plane that they flew to El Salvador.

From there, Torrijos spoke over the phone with Noriega, who pledged his loyalty to the nervous leader. Noriega then instructed Torrijos to fly to the provincial city of David. When the plane was approaching in the early morning in David, Noriega gave the order to light torches and turn on the headlights of dozens of trucks along the runway. The plane landed safely. Advancing to the capital overland, Torrijos was securely back in power by the next day. Most important for Panama's subsequent history, Noriega had won Torrijos's loyalty and would now be a key member of Torrijos's growing "revolution."[38]

Torrijos's rule after the coup attempt shifted dramatically toward a nationalist, anti-imperialist form of populism. Almost always dressed in his trademark military fatigues, Torrijos at least rhetorically became a

champion of Panama's majority poor. Unlike the legions of white aristo-
cratic politicians who had led Panama previously—known as *rabiblancos*
in Panama—Torrijos presented himself as a man of the people. Soon Torrijos was being compared to nationalists such as Fidel Castro of Cuba and
Gamal Abdel Nasser of Egypt. One particularly astute observer described
Torrijos in the following manner:

> Basically, Torrijos was an inspired improviser with a great capacity for
> booze and small talk and little stomach for day-to-day administration. He
> was willing to shake up the country and its government, step on elite toes,
> bluff the gringos, and above all spend money freely. He was an old-
> fashioned nationalist who wanted Panama to have a bigger piece of the
> canal pie, but he was also a willful leader who sometimes used force and
> even murder to intimidate opponents and to stay in power.[39]

Initially, U.S. officials were largely pleased with Torrijos, viewing him
as a military man who would be more realistic and pragmatic about the
canal negotiations.[40] Washington also began to pump significant amounts
of money—around $3 million a year on top of its normal budget—into
Torrijos's National Guard, slowly helping to push it from a national security force to a full-fledged Latin American army.[41] Concerned about the
spread of communism in the region, U.S. policymakers overlooked the
fact they were creating a Frankenstein in Panama. The National Guard
and its future commander Noriega were incubated by the United States
during the Torrijos years.

THE PANAMA CANAL TREATIES

On consolidating his populist authoritarian rule following the failed 1969
coup attempt against him, Torrijos began to make the canal the overriding
issue of his regime. His often-quoted phrase "No quiero entrar en la hist-
oria, sino en el canal" (I don't want to enter into history, only into the
canal") demonstrated his unyielding commitment to this issue.[42] Torrijos
once called U.S. control of the canal a "stake in our heart."[43] Indeed, Torrijos proved to be a much tougher negotiator than Washington ever anticipated. His first deft move was to call for the UN Security Council to hold
a special session in Panama in March 1973 to discuss what was euphemis-
tically characterized as "problems of colonialism and dangers to peace in
Latin America."[44]

At the meeting, the Panamanian representative to the United Nations maneuvered to call a vote on a pro-Panama resolution on the status of the canal. Thirteen of the fifteen Security Council members voted for the resolution. Aside from Great Britain's abstention, only the United States vetoed the resolution—only its third since 1945—but Panama emerged with a moral victory. After the meeting, Panama's foreign minister Juan Antonio Tack remarked, "The United States has vetoed Panama, but the world has vetoed the United States."[45] The Security Council's maneuver allowed Torrijos to internationalize the canal issue, making it part of the broader focus on issues of national liberation and self-determination that were paramount during the 1970s.

In September 1973, President Richard Nixon appointed seasoned Latin America adviser Ellsworth Bunker to lead the U.S. delegation to the continuing talks over the canal.[46] Then, in February 1974, President Ford's secretary of state, Henry Kissinger, arrived at Tocumen international airport—he did not fly into the Canal Zone, a symbolic act that was not lost on the Panamanians—to continue discussions with his counterparts.[47]

Kissinger agreed to negotiate the canal on the basis of eight principles, including the recognition of Panamanians' sovereignty and a fixed date for the end of U.S. jurisdiction over the Canal Zone.[48] With the war in Vietnam, relations with China, and diplomacy in the Middle East on his agenda, Kissinger's trip to Panama demonstrates the importance this issue held at this time. It is striking to compare this to December 1999, when President Clinton's secretary of state, Madeleine Albright, did not even attend the ceremony marking the transfer of the canal over to Panama.

When Jimmy Carter took office in 1977, one of his first actions was to issue Presidential Review Memorandum 1, calling for the immediate review of the Panama policy.[49] There was a growing perception in Washington that an inability to resolve the canal issue diplomatically could lead to a situation where the United States would have to defend the canal militarily. Sending in troops to defend an "imperial" possession was not part of the new president's foreign policy image. And estimates cited 100,000 as the number of U.S. troops that would need to be deployed to defend the canal in a hostile environment.

Alternately, technological change meant that a growing number of ships could not fit in the canal, making the waterway less important economically. Moreover, the United States already had a two-ocean navy, while nuclear submarines and long-range missiles lessened the canal's strategic importance. There was also still hope that the United States could negotiate the extension of the U.S. bases even if the canal was handed over entirely.[50]

Carter firmly believed that warm relations with Panama were crucial to keeping the canal secure.[51] And for Panama, warm relations meant a new canal treaty. To pursue this policy goal, in 1977 Carter appointed Sol Linowitz to work alongside Bunker as America's chief negotiators. Privately, Secretary of State Cyrus Vance and National Security Adviser Zbigniew Brzezinski believed that there needed to be a viable resolution to the canal issue before the 1978 midterm elections.[52]

On September 7, 1977, Carter and Torrijos signed two treaties—the Panama Canal Treaty and the Neutrality Treaty—that addressed the governance of the canal, the status of the military bases, and the security of the canal after the handover at midnight, December 31, 1999.[53] The first treaty created a new Panama Canal commission that would control tolls and other revenues distributed between the United States and Panama. By this time, the Joint Chiefs of Staff had largely dropped its insistence on retaining bases in Panama after 1999, opening up room for treaty renegotiations.

The timing of the Panama Canal negotiations coincided with the 1976 U.S. presidential race, an overlap that ensured that the issue would become part of U.S. domestic politics. Above all, conservatives such as Republican presidential candidate Ronald Reagan, who battled President Ford for the party's nomination, used the issue to champion a more aggressive foreign policy and emphasize the unwillingness of certain leaders to stand up for key U.S. interests. In Reagan's words, the canal was a "sovereignty issue." In his famous words, "When it comes to the canal, we bought it, we paid for it, it's ours, and we should tell Torrijos and company that we're going to keep it."

Indeed, Reagan's denunciations of any treaty served as a rallying cry for conservatives following the Vietnam War. Critics of the negotiations cited several reasons why they opposed transferring the canal to Panamanian control. They argued that the United States was on strong legal grounds in that the Canal Zone was U.S. property, that Panama lacked the technical skills needed to run the canal, that Panama was politically unstable and therefore could not be relied on to maintain or defend the canal, and that the undemocratic Torrijos regime was in danger of turning Communist. A report written for a conservative think tank in 1977 summed up the view of many on the right:

> The future security and well-being of the United States are threatened by the administration's proposed abandonment of sovereignty over the Panama Canal and the Canal Zone. . . . A U.S. retreat from Panama would probably be the last nail in the coffin of the Monroe Doctrine. . . . If we will not stand fast in our own backyard, if we compromise and equivocate and retreat about an issue as vital as the Panama Canal and an area as strategic as the Caribbean, where will we stand?[54]

Essayist William Buckley was one conservative who supported the treaties, as he believed that the United States should leave Panama "while the initiative is still clearly our own. That is the way great nations act."[55] Yet, while most of the foreign policy establishment supported some sort of treaty, the American public opposed the treaties by a margin of two to one.[56]

The Panamanian people ratified the treaties by over a two-thirds margin on October 23, 1977. The Carter administration made an intensive public relations pitch in order to drum up domestic support for ratification of the treaties. In early February 1978, Senator Dennis DeConcini (D-Ariz.) added an amendment to the treaty that gave the United States the right to intervene if the canal was interfered with. Supporters of the treaties worried that DeConcini's move would make it seem as though Washington was setting up a scenario similar to the Soviets in Czechoslovakia in 1968—that the United States would intervene for any reason. Needless to say, the Panamanians were not pleased with the amendment, but it nonetheless remained in the treaty. Soon after, the Senate ratified the treaty by a vote of 68 to 32, just one more vote than the requisite two-thirds.[57]

In 1979, the Carter administration saw the first tangible benefit of the treaties when Torrijos returned a favor by providing sanctuary to the shah of Iran after he had been overthrown. By the time of his reelection campaign in 1980, however, Carter was unquestionably hampered by his support for the treaties in his failed race against the nation's soon-to-be first neoconservative president, Ronald Reagan.

THE RISE OF NORIEGA: 1968–1986

Starting as early as the late 1960s, Manuel Noriega deftly positioned himself vis-à-vis the U.S. intelligence community as an indispensable resource inside Panama. In 1967, Noriega took classes at the U.S. School of the Americas in the Canal, quickly ingratiating himself to U.S. officials with his seemingly unparalleled intelligence-gathering capabilities.[58] Contrary to the impressions that some observers have, Washington did not support Noriega in order to create an American puppet in Panama City; rather, the reason was more quotidian. The United States was looking for a reliable intelligence source, one it could count on to provide timely and accurate information of growing leftist guerrilla insurgencies, Cuba, and the increasingly important issue of narcotics trafficking.[59]

Noriega did all of that and more. Indeed, Noriega worked for the Americans, but he also worked for the Cubans and the Colombian drug lords and whoever else was willing to pay the price. In 1980, former Costa Rican president José Figueres was visiting Fidel Castro when Figueres commented that Castro was the best-informed man in the region. Castro responded, "No, Noriega is the best informed man. He knows everything the left and right are doing."[60] Some State Department officials called Noriega "rent-a-colonel,"[61] and he was known in the drug underworld as the "Caribbean Prostitute."[62]

By the early 1970s, Noriega had become chief of G-2, the National Guard's intelligence service. The United States helped train Noriega in intelligence and soon put him on the payroll. Over the next decade, Washington paid Noriega hundreds of thousands of dollars to be an ally in the seedy Central American intelligence world. He had become such a cherished resource to the U.S. intelligence community that by 1976, when American Ambler Moss took over as ambassador, he discovered that Noriega was the liaison for the CIA, FBI, Customs Service, and several military intelligence agencies.[63] Between 1973 and 1982, the United States provided the money for the training of 350 Panamanian intelligence officers.

During the 1970s and 1980s, Noriega established working relationships with high-ranking U.S. policymakers such as CIA Director William Casey and National Security Council staff member Oliver North. In December 1976, Noriega even met with then CIA Director George Bush at a private lunch hosted by the Panamanian ambassador in Washington. The Reagan administration also most likely attempted to use Noriega to help supply the Nicaraguan contras despite the fact that it knew the extent of Noriega's involvement in the drug trade.[64]

While the notion of working with Noriega seems outrageous today, in the context of the times the dealings are more understandable. For example, Noriega continued to arrest drug traffickers and send them to the United States. Since he was also working for Cuba, U.S. officials reckoned that Noriega would be a good source of information about a country that had been difficult for U.S. intelligence agencies to penetrate. In addition, in the 1970s at least, Torrijos, not Noriega, was the chief political figure in Panama. Noriega was all about intelligence, and at that time there was no reason to suspect that he would end up becoming the country's dictator. This all changed when Noriega dramatically increased his power after the disputed 1984 presidential elections.

What is also evident is that even through the mid-1980s, U.S. intelligence agencies continued to believe that Noriega's benefits outweighed his costs. As late as March 1987, Noriega was cooperating in major bilateral money-laundering investigations.[65] The 1987 annual report of the State Department's narcotics division certified that Panama had "fully cooperated" with antinarcotics matters. A 1978 letter from President Carter's Drug Enforcement Administration (DEA) director, Peter Bensinger, highlights the value that Noriega provided to the intelligence agencies. "[The DEA] very much appreciates all of your support and cooperation which you have extended to our agency during the last year," and he wished Noriega "very best regards for a happy and successful new year."[66] Amazingly, the DEA continued to send Noriega letters of support, known as "attaboy" letters, up until just a few years before the invasion.

THE 1984 ELECTIONS

In August 1981, Torrijos died in a plane crash that even today has still not been fully explained. While most blame poor weather conditions, others have cited Noriega's involvement or even the work of the CIA. Whatever the case, Panama's strongman was dead and the country's political future unclear. While we will likely never know Torrijos's ultimate plans, many believed that Torrijos had intended to hold elections in May 1984, setting Panama on a course toward greater democracy.

In March 1982, Noriega and two other officers ousted Colonel Florencio Flores, who had succeeded Torrijos as commander of the National Guard. The three coup plotters had worked about a plan whereby fellow plotter Lieutenant Colonel Rubén Paredes would become the National Guard commander but would subsequently resign from his military post and run for president. Noriega would then become commander until 1987. In August 1983, Noriega replaced him as commander as planned, and a week later Paredes announced his candidacy for the presidency.

But then, contrary to the secret plan, Noriega did not back Paredes in the election; instead, he threw his support behind Nicolás Ardito Barletta, a former vice president at the World Bank who had studied under then economics professor George Shultz at the University of Chicago.[67] Paredes's campaign withered, and he was soon ousted from the Guard. Noriega stood alone at the top of the Panamanian military. Before long he had promoted himself to the rank of brigadier general. Noriega quickly changed the name of the National Guard to the Panamanian Defense Forces (PDF). For the next five years, Noriega dominated all aspects of Panamanian life from his position as commander of the PDF. With no need to appoint himself as president, Noriega instead allowed political figures to act as president to lend a veneer of democratic legitimacy to his rule.

In a highly irregular election, Barletta defeated octogenarian Arnulfo Arias by less than 2,000 votes out of 600,000 counted. Despite clear evidence of foul play, Secretary of State Shultz attended Barletta's inauguration, and President Reagan received him at the White House.[68] For an administration that was deeply concerned about the spread of communism in the isthmus, they now had a government in Panama that they could work with. Barletta was a widely known technocrat, and Noriega was the undisputed king of intelligence. In 1985, however, Noriega had ousted Barletta, who had become increasingly critical of the military commander. Noriega replaced Barletta with first vice president Eric Arturo Delvalle, who was now slated to serve out the original term of office until 1989.[69]

Over the course of the next few years, a series of episodes served to highlight Noriega's increasingly despotic influence. In June 1987, for example, after being attacked by Noriega, retired Colonel Robert Díaz Herrera publicly announced on television that Noriega had fixed the 1984 presidential elections and was behind Torrijos's murder. Immediately, anti-Noriega protests began in Panama City; this would be a common sight for the next two and a half years.[70] The anti-Noriega umbrella group Civic Crusade was formed. Equally visible and much more vicious were the pro-Noriega special PDF forces—known as Dobermans—that harassed and intimidated protesters and other political opponents.[71]

On June 26, the U.S. Senate passed Resolution 239 by a vote of eighty-two to two that called for Noriega to step down pending the outcome of an investigation into Díaz Herrera's charges of election fraud. Noriega responded by turning the Dobermans loose on the U.S. embassy and consulate, an act that led some in Washington to conclude that a PDF assault on U.S. citizens or soldiers was a distinct possibility. During the fall of 1987, Congress passed a series of resolutions condemning Noriega and threatening economic sanctions if civil liberties were not respected in Panama.[72]

By the end of 1987, Noriega has become a painful thorn in the side of the Reagan administration. Any value that Noriega provided on the intelligence side was now outweighed by the damage he was causing to Reagan's credibility in Panama and in Washington. No one could deny that Washington had cultivated Noriega; the question now was how they would get rid of him.[73]

CONGRESS GETS TOUGH

Well before the Reagan administration imposed sanctions on the Noriega regime, certain members of Congress had been focusing on Noriega's illicit activities. In fact, between 1985 and 1987, the Reagan administration was playing catch-up to congressional critics such as dovish freshman Massachusetts Senator John Kerry and his conservative colleague Jesse Helms of North Carolina. Both Helms and Kerry persistently pressured the Reagan administration to do something about Noriega. Helms started the congressional attention in March and April 1986, when he conducted hearings on the issue over the objections of the administration.

Helms was committed to shedding light on Noriega's dirty work. A good part of the hearings focused on the murder of Hugo Spadafora, a confidant of Torrijos, a pro-Sandinista guerrilla, and a newly vocal critic of Manuel Noriega. In late 1985, Spadafora's decapitated body had been found in a U.S. mailbag near the border of Costa Rica.[74] Many believed that Noriega was behind the murder. One crucial motivation for Helms's condemnation of Noriega was that he wanted to demonstrate that Noriega was unfit to handle receiving the canal. According to one of his aides, "We want to turn the canal over to a viable, stable democracy, not a bunch of corrupt drug runners."[75]

Soon after Helms's hearings began, Kerry started his own investigation into drug trafficking in Panama. Over the course of the next two years, Kerry's Foreign Relations Subcommittee on Terrorism, Narcotics, and International Communication was the epicenter for congressional scrutiny of Noriega's dealings. What emerged from the investigations were an entire series of revelations about Noriega's dealings with Cuba, the contras, Colombian drug kingpins and guerrillas, and Panama's position as the money-laundering capital of the region.

A June 12, 1986, front-page article in the *New York Times* by investigative reporter Seymour Hersh amplified the congressional scrutiny of Noriega. Hersh, who made his name uncovering the My Lai massacre during the Vietnam War, wrote the article to coincide with Noriega's visit to the United States, where he was presented with a Panamanian medal of honor at the Inter-American Defense Board. Hersh argued that Noriega was tied to the killing of Spadafora, that he was involved in drug trafficking, and that "for the last fifteen years, he had been providing intelligence information simultaneously to Cuba and the United States."[76]

A SHIFT IN U.S. POLICY

Following the example of the "people power" movement in the Philippines that ousted autocratic leader Ferdinand Marcos in February 1986, many observers in Washington believed that civic, nonviolent opposition would eventually remove Noriega. The removal of Haiti's Jean-Claude "Baby Doc" Duvalier was another example. This logic explains the Reagan administration's decision to escalate the pressure against Noriega in early 1988. With Noriega already hated by an overwhelming majority of Panamanians, new measures were needed to break Noriega. In addition, the administration faced intense congressional pressure to remove Noriega from power. What is also readily apparent is that the growing drug concern in the United States meant that any national politician with any future had to demonstrate that he or she was doing something about drugs. For President Reagan, this meant removing Noriega.

The effort to dislodge the Panamanian strongman received a jolt on

February 5, 1988, when two grand juries, one in Tampa and the other in Miami, announced indictments against Noriega. The twelve-count Miami indictment accused Noriega of helping Colombia's notorious Medellín cartel ship more than two tons of cocaine through Panama in return for a payment of $4.5 million. One Miami attorney stated that "in plain language, he utilized his position to sell the country of Panama to drug traffickers."[77] The three-count Tampa indictment charged Noriega with attempts to smuggle more than one million pounds of marijuana into the United States. It also alleged that Noriega had agreed to allow more than $100 million in profits from drug sales to be laundered through Panama banks.[78] The cumulative sentences for Noriega, if convicted, were for 145 years in prison.[79]

Almost immediately, it became apparent that the indictments had not been well coordinated through the foreign policy bureaucracy. State Department officials learned of the indictments only a week before they were made public. One National Security Council aide complained that foreign policy was being made by the Justice Department; U.S. attorneys responded that they were indicting a criminal, not making foreign policy.[80]

There is no question that, while it might have had cosmetic appeal in terms of the war on drugs, the indictments were poor foreign policy. Most critical was that the United States did not have an extradition treaty with Panama, which meant that there was no ready legal mechanism to get Noriega to Florida. And even this hope was predicated on Noriega's being out of power, which was much wishful thinking at the time. As expected, Noriega responded to the indictments with his usual scorn, calling them "a joke and an absurd political movement."[81]

Reeling from the bungled indictments that same month, the Reagan administration sent Assistant Secretary of State Elliott Abrams to Miami to meet with President Delvalle in order to pressure him to fire Noriega. But Noriega quickly outmaneuvered Delvalle and had him removed from office. Noriega then had the National Assembly appoint Manuel Solís as president. However, Delvalle enacted some revenge on Noriega when his lawyers argued successfully in U.S. courts that Panama's government assets in the United States needed to be transferred to Delvalle's control since he was the legal president of the country.[82] While he was originally seen as a Noriega puppet, the Reagan administration turned Delvalle into something of a symbol of democracy in Panama after his removal.

The Reagan administration responded to Delvalle's removal by announcing a fresh round of economic sanctions against Noriega that barred U.S. companies from paying taxes to the Panamanian government and eliminated Panama's sugar quota. Over the course of the next two years, Panama's economy contracted dramatically. Gross domestic product fell by 17 percent in 1988 and 8 percent in 1989.[83] There was an initial belief that the sanctions were the last nail in Noriega's coffin, leading Elliott Abrams to proclaim on March 27 that Noriega was "hanging on by a thread." National Security Adviser Colin Powell said that the sanctions were having a "telling effect."[84]

But while the sanctions certainly hampered Panama's economy, Noriega was buoyed by limitless drug revenue and thus able to continue paying his 15,000 PDF members, a critical accomplishment, as his survival was overwhelmingly reliant on their support.[85] Furthermore, the sanctions were not universally applied, and many U.S. corporations easily found ways around them and continued to do business with the Noriega regime.

Then suddenly on May 11, 1988, the White House announced that in return for Noriega's retirement, the indictments would be dropped.[86] This plan confirms that at this point in time the Reagan administration's primary concern was removing Noriega, not eliminating the PDF as an institution. The episode was especially delicate for Bush, who was slipping in the polls against Democratic presidential contender Michael Dukakis. For candidate Bush, dropping an indictment against America's "number one drug thug" at the height of the drug concern was politically damaging. Bush responded that he would not "bargain with drug dealers . . . whether they're on U.S. or foreign soil."[87] Dukakis slammed Bush for his supposed longtime connection to Noriega. "How about telling us who in this administration was dealing with Noriega. Who was paying Noriega? Who was ignoring the fact that we knew he was dealing in drugs and making millions and we're still doing business with him?"[88]

Congress was also almost uniformly negative. On May 17, the Senate passed a nonbinding amendment stating that no negotiations by the United States with Noriega should be made that "involve the dropping of the drug-related indictments against him."[89] Senator Robert Dole (R-Kans.) said that the White House was sending the "wrong signal" on drugs. Dole said that he supported efforts to remove Noriega but "not at the cost of undermining our war on drugs . . . [with this indictment] we have said that under certain circumstances we'll negotiate with leniency for those who are responsible, directly or indirectly, for the addiction and death of our children." Senator Pete Wilson (R-Calif.) opined that a deal with Noriega was akin to cutting "a deal with the devil."[90] By the end of May, the White House quietly withdrew the offer.

The Reagan administration's pressure against Noriega was not working. In May, Reagan had announced that Noriega "must go," but he was still firmly in command in Panama. The administration continued to receive criticism from Congress over what was now increasingly considered a fiasco. Senator Alfonse D'Amato (R-N.Y.), for one, accused the Pentagon and Joint Chiefs of being "cowards" for not being more aggressive against Noriega.[91]

With Noriega in power and the sanctions not working sufficiently, during the summer of 1988 a rupture emerged within the administration about what to do next regarding Noriega. The State Department believed that a more muscular approach was needed and that Washington should start considering a plan for a military intervention, such as a commando-style raid, to nab Noriega. The Pentagon, on the other hand, was more cautious, as the generals worried that a military operation could easily lead to a hostage situation. According to one White House official who participated in the discussions, "The diplomats wanted a muscular military policy. The soldiers, who would have to do the fighting, wanted negotiations with Noriega."[92]

The dispute between State and the Pentagon became a battle of wills and bureaucratic prowess between Abrams and Joint Chiefs of Staff Chairman Admiral William Crowe. Crowe told Reagan that 50,000 Americans could not be guarded in Panama, thus making an invasion a recipe for disaster. Vice Admiral Jonathan Howe represented Crowe at interagency meetings and attempted to counter Abrams's criticisms that the Pentagon was overly cautious. Abrams countered that the PDF was not a military but more like a crooked police force. "The PDF is like a Mississippi police force in the 1960s. It's vicious, corrupt, and incompetent. It is a group that never carried out a military operation."[93] George Shultz, for one, at this point did not buy the idea that a huge invasion force was needed and instead believed that a small force could go in and grab Noriega.

THE MAY 1989 ELECTIONS

By mid-1988, the United States was involved in a low-intensity war with Noriega's forces. From February 1988 to May 1989, over 600 incidents involving harassment of U.S. civilians and troops were reported, including several instances when U.S. servicemen were detained and beaten. As during the Grenada crisis, U.S. policymakers were greatly concerned about the potential for a Tehran-style hostage situation. At the same time, the CIA supported numerous unsuccessful attempts to oust Noriega. Washington was perfectly willing to use covert means to get at Noriega, but at this moment the emphasis was almost exclusively focused on Noriega himself.

In 1989, newly inaugurated president Bush faced a difficult scenario in Panama. Although he had easily defeated Dukakis in the 1988 presidential election, on taking office Bush still had to confront his putative image as a "whimp," constantly played up by the media. After eight years as vice president under the rhetorically dramatic and strong-willed Reagan, the press portrayed Bush as a lightweight, a characterization that spilled over into the perception of his handling of foreign policy.

One of Bush's first acts as president was to approve a number of covert operations aimed at Noriega. He also supported Congress's move to transfer $10 million through the National Endowment for Democracy to the opposition groups and candidates who were planning to run against Noriega's handpicked candidate in the May 1989 presidential elections.[94] When news of the transfer reached Panama, however, Noriega pounced on the revelation. A pro-Noriega newspaper ran a headline referring to the main opposition candidate: "Bush Buys Endara with $10 Million so He Will Provide Military Bases and Revise Treaties."[95] It is interesting to note that Noriega's claim about the motivations behind U.S. policy was the same one that many U.S. critics made following the 1989 invasion.

The May 7 presidential elections took place in a climate of heightened tensions. Most independent observers thought that the ticket led by pragmatic Arnulfo Arias acolyte Guillermo Endara and his two vice presidential candidates, Guillermo "Billy" Ford and Ricardo Arias Calderón, would win easily.[96] But few knew what to expect from Noriega, who was backing his handpicked candidate Carlos Duque. Despite massive fraud that included stealing ballot boxes in broad daylight, exit polls conducted by the Catholic Church had 55.1 percent for Endara and 39.5 percent for

Duque. Even areas such as El Chorrillo, the grindingly poor neighborhood where the PDF headquarters known as La Comandancia was located, voted overwhelmingly against Duque, an affront that Noriega apparently avenged during the invasion.

Duque claimed victory, though, a move that sparked howls of protests from the opposition and international observers. That there were so many foreigners present for the elections was no mistake, as the Bush administration had "flooded Panama with international observers" to ensure that Noriega could not commit foul play.[97] Former president Jimmy Carter was in Panama with a delegation and announced that "the government is taking the election by fraud. It's robbing the people of Panama of their rights." Another former president, Gerald Ford, remarked that he "never thought the fraud would be this blatant. These people are absolutely shameless." Duque responded by denouncing the fraud accusations as a "desperate" attempt to use "disinformation to alter a legitimate triumph."[98] Noriega quickly canceled the elections and installed his crony Francisco Rodríguez as president.

A few days later, the opposition organized a rally of thousands of protestors near La Comandancia. Yielding clubs and firing shots, Noriega's PDF Dobermans and his vigilante, Cuba-trained "Dignity Battalions" attacked the marchers, including Billy Ford, who emerged from a vehicle soaked in his bodyguard's (who had just been killed) blood. Shocking images of Noriega's henchmen beating up opposition candidates were piped across the world. Noreiga's treachery was now on display for the world to see.

Bush responded by declaring that the United States "will not recognize or accommodate a regime that holds power through force and violence at the expense of the Panamanian people's right to be free."[99] Ambassador Arthur Davis was immediately recalled. Bush also ordered an additional 2,000 troops to Panama, a move that was only reluctantly agreed to by Joint Chiefs chairman Crowe. Bush then announced a seven-point plan intended to remove Noriega through a combination of pressure and incentives. The points included greater regional diplomacy with the Organization of American States (OAS), more diplomatic and economic sanctions, and preventive measures such as encouraging U.S. companies to send dependents back to the United States.[100]

BUSH INCREASES THE PRESSURE AGAINST NORIEGA

During the spring and summer of 1989, the National Security Council's Policy Coordinating Group met regularly to discuss Panama policy.[101] There was a growing sentiment that more forceful action was needed. While some top officials still preferred the commando-style option or no operation at all, a full-scale invasion was becoming increasingly popular. The interagency discussion led to the distribution of policy document NSD-17 issued on July 22. It ordered the canal-based U.S. Southern Command (SOUTHCOM) to increase its patrols and training fights in and around Panama. At the time of NSD-17, tension between U.S. forces and the PDF escalated dramatically. Part of this was due to Bush's decision to increase the frequency and size of U.S. military operations in the Canal Zone.

Operations such as Purple Storm and Sand Fleas were intended as a show of military force and political resolve that would, it was hoped, intimidate Noriega. In August alone, SOUTHCOM conducted eleven military exercises in the Canal Zone. These maneuvers had the added utility of helping mask the start of any real invasion. In fact, on the night of December 19, Noriega mistook the real invasion for a practice exercise.

As pressure on Noriega increased, President Bush decided that a change of U.S. command was needed in Panama. He replaced General Fred Woerner—some at SOUTHCOM called him the "Whimp-com" commander—who had been in the position since 1987 with General Maxwell R. Thurman. Woerner had always been cautious about any operation against Noriega, a position that did not fit with the administration's increasingly hawkish stance. While largely an administrative general, Thurman was known as "Maxatollah" or "Mad Max." He was an indefatigable worker who had no patience for thugs like Noriega.[102] Some critics cited the fact that Thurman did not speak Spanish. One supporter quipped, "MacArthur didn't have to speak Korean to plan the Inchon invasion."[103]

On September 30, Thurman assumed his command in Panama just about the same time that Colin Powell was promoted over other more senior officers to replace Crowe as chairman of the Joint Chiefs of Staff.[104] Powell, who had previously opposed an invasion, now told Thurman that he must be ready to "take down" not just Noriega but the entire PDF as well. According to Powell,

I thought that what we would have to do eventually was take it all down. We would really have to take the PDF down or else you couldn't solve the problem. And I came into office with that mindset. There were lots of budding Noriegas throughout the PDF and to take Tony out just wouldn't do it.[105]

American objectives in Panama had changed dramatically. By late October, the Bush administration began revising its previous war plan, Blue Spoon, to make it reflect a massive invasion, one that would take out the U.S.-nurtured PDF in a matter of hours or days. This change in planning had enormous implications for U.S. policy objectives in Panama. A pinprick strike to abduct Noriega was out. Regime change was in.

At the start of October, the wife of PDF major Moisés Giroldi notified SOUTHCOM that her husband was planning a coup against Noriega and that he wanted U.S. help. It has been reported that Giroldi decided to inform SOUTHCOM of his intentions soon after a party where Noriega gave Giroldi an order in front of other guests that he and his fellow officers were to shoot down all U.S. military aircraft.[106] On receiving the news about the revolt, SOUTHCOM commanders contacted the Pentagon, and Secretary of Defense Dick Cheney authorized Noriega's arrest if revolting officers turned him over to them. Thurman went ahead and positioned units near La Comandancia just in case. He also ordered attack helicopters to fly above the capital.[107] Yet all this was for nothing, as Washington ultimately decided not to get directly involved in the coup.

On October 3, the coup began, and before long Giroldi had Noriega in custody inside La Comandancia. Giroldi went on national radio to announce the rebellion. Strangely, he did not mention what had happened to Noriega, a sign for many that he was still not fully in control. Amazingly, Giroldi allowed Noriega to use the telephone, and Noriega immediately called one of his mistresses for help. She alerted the notorious Battalion 2000 (named for the year that Panama would assume control of the canal) troops located at the Rio Hato base about forty miles outside the capital. Correctly believing that rebels would block an overland route, the pro-Noriega forces commandeered several airplanes at an airbase near Rio Hato and flew to Panama City. By early afternoon that same day, they had freed Noriega. Giroldi was soon dead, and his family sought asylum in the Canal Zone. The coup was over.

Senior officials in the Bush administration were adamant that they were not caught off guard by the coup.[108] There was no doubt that the United States had not done much to aid the rebels; the open question was whether this neglect was intentional. There was also question as to whether the rebels had unsuccessfully attempted to turn Noriega over to SOUTH-COM. Cheney, Powell, and Thurman all publicly stated that they did not trust the rebels. According to Thurman, the coup plan was "ill-conceived, ill-motivated, and ill-fed."[109] Powell apparently also told Thurman during the crisis that getting rid of Noriega was "something that had to be done on a U.S. timetable."[110] During congressional testimony, Cheney argued that

> we had serious doubts about whether or not this was a legitimate coup attempt or whether it was an effort by General Noriega to seek to involve the United States in ways that would be embarrassing by sucking us into coup-plotting with someone who was a Noriega crony.[111]

Others, however, were not so generous. Criticism quickly emerged that the American inaction during the coup proved that Bush was all talk and no action. Reflecting the bipartisan consensus against Noriega, Senators D'Amato, Helms, and Kerry conducted a joint press conference as the coup was still unfolding, making it clear in no uncertain terms that they wished to see it succeed. One Democratic congressman went so far as to say that the result from the coup "makes Jimmy Carter look like a man of resolve. There's a resurgence of the whimp factor." Even one of Noriega's confidants revealed that "the rebels did their share, but the Americans didn't do theirs. The Americans wanted a white-glove coup, American style. The U.S. behaved like a lady in a whorehouse."[112] Bush responded by criticizing the "instant hawks" that were appearing from where there used to be "feathers of a dove." "Some of it's political," Bush added, and "some of it's the understandable frustrating [sic] they feel about this man staying in office."[113]

Observers also criticized Bush for doing too much. Larry Birns of the Council on Hemispheric Affairs said that the United States should be "out of the business of installing and taking other governments out" and that "history shows that against unspeakable odds, a population, if it has suffi-cient resolve, will get rid of its oppressor."[114] As we will see, the Panama case is actually one where the taking out of Noriega by the United States ended up being a quick and lasting way for Panama to get rid of its oppressor. And even if the Panamanian people had removed Noriega themselves, it was more than likely that someone who was far from democratic would have replaced him. Even Giroldi, the ringleader of the October coup, held an instinctive suspicion and dislike of civilian politicians.

The three months following the revolt were by far the most intense in U.S.–Panama relations since the public feud with Noriega began two years earlier. In early November, Bush approved an additional $3 million to fund covert operations in Panama, although the CIA was still prevented from attempting to assassinate Noriega. Noriega responded to the coup in his own way: cracking down on domestic opposition. Political opponents were jailed, tortured, and killed. American and PDF troops continuously traded shots inside the Canal Zone.[115]

Then, in a surprise move on December 15, Noriega removed Rodríguez as president and installed himself as the "Maximum Leader of National Liberation." Noriega then declared before the Panamanian legislature that Panama was in a "state of war" with the United States. While yielding a machete, he opened his speech with a "word of praise and thanks to the just and merciful God of the universe, as Jehovah, as Allah, as Yahweh, as Buddha, as the universal conscience of the soul." He continued that the U.S. military had

> launched psychological attacks and have carried out a plan to poison minds by inventing all sorts of lies and trying by every means to win the minds of the weakest. We have resisted, and no we must decide to advance in our land to strengthen our internal front to improve our resistance and advance toward an offensive of creativity and development in the generational project of the new republic. . . . Render unto Caesar what is Caesar's, to God what is God's, and to the Panamanians what is Panama's.[116]

THE INVASION OF PANAMA

Events took an even greater turn for the worse the next evening, when four U.S. officers driving in Panama City took a wrong turn near a checkpoint at La Comandancia. Troops of the PDF and members of the Dignity Battalion attempted to get the officers to leave the vehicle. Dozens of PDF troops rushed the car while the soldiers sped off. Guards immediately opened fire on the car. Bullets hit three of the men, killing twenty-four-year-old Marine Lieutenant Roberto Paz. Paz was the first American soldier killed in Panama since Washington and Noriega had begun their undeclared war. That same night, a Navy lieutenant and his wife were stopped at the same roadblock, where they were detained, most likely because the PDF troops thought that they had witnessed the shooting. They were blindfolded and roughed up, and the wife was threatened with rape before they were released four hours later.[117]

The next day was Sunday, December 17, and Bush met for ninety minutes with his senior advisers, including Powell, Cheney, National Security Adviser Brent Scowcroft, and Vice President Dan Quayle to discuss the Panama situation. Bush believed that he could no longer let Noriega call the shots in this feud. During the meeting, Bush asked if a limited operation would be able to get Noriega. Bush also asked about the number of casualties, the potential for a hostage situation, diplomatic consequences, and whether the operation would end up like the Iran hostage rescue mission.

Unlike the Grenada operation, the Panama invasion was undertaken following the Goldwater-Nichols Defense Reorganization Act of 1986. The operational fiasco in Grenada prompted this legislation, which was the largest military command reform since the National Security Act of 1947.[118] In an effort to streamline command and control operations, Goldwater-Nichols designated the chairman of the Joint Chiefs of Staff to be the president's principal military adviser; it also made the chairman responsible for contingency plans.[119] Goldwater-Nichols thus gave Colin Powell unprecedented flexibility and control to plan and implement the invasion of Panama.

During this critical White House meeting, three military options were placed on the table: an Entebbe-style commando raid supported by conventional troops from the Canal Zone, the use of 12,000 or so U.S. troops stationed in the zone to launch an assault on the PDF, or a full invasion using the 12,000 "local" troops plus another 12,000 flown in from the United States. Powell advocated the full-invasion option, one that he argued would guarantee the elimination of both Noriega and "Noriega-ism." Powell also mentioned that a massive force would lessen the time the PDF had to seize hostages.

While the decision to launch the invasion had been brewing in the president's mind ever since early October, the most recent events, such as the Paz killing, had infuriated him. At the same time, some of Bush's advisers did not think that the Paz killing represented enough of a "smoking-gun incident" that was needed to justify an invasion of this magnitude. At the end of the meeting, however, Bush had made his decision. The United States would launch a full-scale invasion of Panama. Bush apparently ended the meeting by saying, "This guy is not going to lay off. . . . It will only get worse. Ok, let's do it."[120] At that time, the full invasion was still called Blue Spoon until a U.S. commander remarked that Americans would not understand such a silly name. Thus, the invasion became known as Operation Just Cause. Two days later, the invasion was ready to go.

American commanders viewed Panama as a target with a bull's-eye, and that was Panama City. They wanted to isolate and seize La Comandancia as quickly as possible. Other key objectives were to secure the Tocumen international airport just outside the city and to nab Noriega. In the months leading up to the invasion, a six-person U.S. intelligence group held a twenty-four-hour "Noriega watch" in an attempt to track his every movement; rehearsal raids were conducted.[121] If AWACS planes or other intelligence outlets discovered Noriega attempting to escape the country by air, then AC-130 gunships and F-16 fighters were to intercept his aircraft and force it to land.

While the PDF forces numbered around 13,000 troops, only about 4,000 were estimated to be combat ready. Just Cause had two broad objectives: protect American lives and installations and capture Noriega and eliminate the PDF; the other was to replace Noriega's regime with the democratic government of Endara and rebuild the PDF. As we will see, both of these objectives were met.

On the afternoon of December 19, Rangers from Fort Lewis, Washington, and Fort Stewart, Georgia, began leaving for Panama in a few dozen C-130 transport planes. When it was all done, roughly 10,000 troops, ferried in around 200 planes from the United States, joined the others already in Panama. That same day, John Bushnell, the U.S. embassy's deputy chief of mission, invited Guillermo Endara, Billy Ford, and Ricardo Arias Calderon to dinner at Howard Air Force Base. While it was not unusual for the three men to visit the Canal Zone, this time it was to inform them that the invasion was under way. At Howard, General Thurman briefed them on the mission and offered them the opportunity to assume their elected offices. They agreed, and just before midnight they were soon sworn in as the "legitimate" government of Panama.

By 10:00 P.M. on the night of December 19, U.S. intelligence had picked up reports that the PDF had an idea of H-Hour, the time of the start of the mission. Then, at midnight, PDF headquarters sent out a message: "They're coming. The ballgame is at 1 A.M. Report to your units . . . drag your weapons and be prepared to fight."[122] It is also believed that the Cuban operatives were logging the number of C-130s flying to Panama at one every ten minutes. From that number, they then estimated the tonnage and troop numbers entering the country.

But Noriega still believed that this was a bluff, that Bush would not dare risk a full-scale invasion just to capture him. He was wrong. Just before 1:00 A.M. on the morning of December 20, U.S. Special Forces struck key PDF installations throughout Panama. Four Navy SEALs had already been killed during an operation.[123] The battle for Panama had begun.

Two pilots flew F-117 Stealth fighters to the PDF base at Rio Hato, where they dropped one 20,000-pound bomb each within 150 yards of the PDF's 6th and 7th Rifle Company barracks to confuse the occupants just before the Rangers of Task Force Red parachuted into the area. While the bombs succeeded in terrifying the PDF troops, they also roused them out of bed, which made them better prepared to battle the landing Rangers. Some 1,300 Rangers jumped over Rio Hato, and over the next forty-five minutes they were joined by an additional 2,700 troops from the 82nd Airborne in what became the largest U.S. airborne operation since World War II.[124] While the PDF troops at Rio Hato were quickly defeated, the jump had its costs. The Rangers dropped from an extremely low altitude carrying 100-pound packs. Four were killed, and 86 formed part of an "orthopedic nightmare" with broken legs and ankles.[125]

Right after the Special Forces had begun operation, Task Force Bayonet led the main assault on La Comandancia. Assisted by helicopter gunships, three battalions rolled through downtown Panama City to seize the PDF headquarters and protect the U.S. embassy. The PDF forces at La Comandancia resisted for about three hours before surrendering. For the rest of the day, there were skirmishes in Panama City but no serious fighting with the PDF. In just a couple of hours, the battle for Panama had ended.[126]

In a briefing to the press, Colin Powell did point out that there had been "considerable burning" near La Comandancia. The issue of the tremendous fires that burned the El Chorrillo neighborhood to the ground became quite controversial over the next several months. A dispute arose as to whether U.S. shooting had started the fires or whether Noriega's Dignity Battalions lit them in a fit of spite, punishing the majority of residents who had voted against Noriega's candidate in the May elections.

One particularly effective operation was called Ma Bell. American Special Forces called PDF garrison commanders and instructed them to look out their windows at the circling AC-130H Spectre gunships. They then told the commanders that if they did not surrender, the gunships would start unloading their cannons, capable of shooting 2,500 rounds per minute, to demolish the structure. During the invasion, more than 1,000 PDF soldiers surrendered in Ma Bell operations.

After PDF headquarters were secured, attention quickly turned to the Marriott Hotel, where it was believed a hostage situation was taking place. The PDF had already taken two American executives away from the hotel, and there was concern that Dignity Battalions were searching the hotel for Americans. Pilots from American Airlines sent out a plea for help from the hotel. At one point, Powell phoned Thurman and told him, "You've got to have a plan. Tell me when it's [the Marriott Hotel] going to be taken."[127] By 10:00 P.M., the 82nd Airborne had cleared the hotel, and the Americans were safe.

Powell was also concerned about the pro-Noriega radio station that still had not been taken off the air. The station Radio Nacional continued to function all day on December 20, broadcasting news about American "atrocities" and giving assurances that Noriega was still in command of the resistance. At 7:00 P.M., a Delta Force commando team stormed the building. Right then, the broadcaster announced, "The invader's helicopter is on top of the building." A few minutes later, the station was broadcasting music.[128]

The ease of the military operations in Panama enabled Powell by the night of the first day to focus more on the political side of the operation. In particular, this meant producing an outcome in Panama that remained in line with the mission's overall objectives, such as installing Endara and eliminating the PDF. Both Powell and Joint Staff Director General Tom

Kelley highlighted a "two-pronged" psychological warfare campaign to win support for Endara and to get the roaming fighters to quit.

This campaign came into action on December 22, when the 96th Civil Affairs Battalion landed in Panama with the task of establishing a police force, distributing emergency food, and supervising Panamanian contractors cleaning up the city.[129] It was also charged with the sensitive task of helping to develop "grassroots" efforts to sell the Endara government to the Panamanian public. On December 22, Endara formally abolished the PDF and announced the creation of an organization called the Fuerza Publica. By early 1990, the troops who had arrived from the United States began leaving Panama. By 1991, U.S. troop levels in Panama were below the pre–May 1989 number of 10,000.

While Powell had his eye on the medium- and even long-term economic and political reconstruction, by the second day widespread outbreaks of looting became a much more immediate and pressing problem, one that U.S. officials believed threatened to diminish Just Cause's initial success. Roaming bands of Dignity Battalions were looting thousands of businesses in Panama City with seeming impunity. Could it be, some pundits questioned, that the United States had won the war in just a few hours but could not control the peace? There is no question that U.S. planners had not properly prepared for the power vacuum left behind when the PDF collapsed so quickly. Estimates of the economic losses were in the hundreds of millions of dollars. Yet by December 26, order had been generally restored to the streets of the capital, and, while economically devastating, the looting did not escalate into anything more serious. Still, half the looted stores remained closed as late as May 1990.

One major criticism of the operational component of the invasion came from the U.S. media, which, similar to the Grenada crisis, complained that they had arrived in Panama after most of the fighting had ended. Bush had approved the creation of a Pentagon-organized media pool that consisted of Washington-based reporters or those already based in Panama. The order for them to mobilize for action came at 7:30 P.M. on December 19 after the evening news had ended. The media pool then took off from Andrews Air Force Base outside Washington four hours later and did not arrive in Panama until early morning. Pentagon spokesman Pete Williams accepted blame for the delay in granting access.[130]

It is also true, though, that the brevity of the fighting meant that there was not much time to get the reporters before the hostilities had already ceased. All told, 23 American soldiers were killed and 323 wounded; around 300 PDF troops were killed and roughly 300 Panamanian civilians killed (although around 200 of these were estimated to have been part of the Dignity Battalions).[131]

APPREHENDING NORIEGA

Another embarrassment for the administration was that after the first day, U.S. forces had still not located Noriega. Powell told the press that "we'll chase him and we will find him. I'm not quite sure he's up to being chased around the countryside by Army Rangers, Special Forces and light infantry units."[132] Pentagon officials did not miss the opportunity to announce, however, that at Noriega's residence at Fort Amador, they had located pornography, a portrait of Hitler, voodoo paraphernalia, and 100 pounds of cocaine. (The cocaine later turned out to be corn flour.) Raiding troops also discovered an attaché case fitted with a submachine gun, $3 million in U.S. currency, stacks of opera compact discs, and a wine cellar with Israeli wines and French cognac.[133]

Noriega had learned about the invasion while he was spending the night with a prostitute at a hotel near Panama City. It is believed that one of his bodyguards was waiting outside the hotel when he saw U.S. paratroopers landing at a nearby airstrip. He called La Comandancia, but no one answered because they had their hands full with the U.S. assault on the compound. Noriega then fled the hotel. Over the next five days, more than forty Special Forces operations across the country were conducted aimed at apprehending Noriega. They all failed, but some just barely. At one seaside villa on the Pacific coast, a team found lit cigarettes and warm coffee.[134] By now, the Bush administration had placed a $1 million bounty on Noriega's head.

On Christmas Eve, officials at the Vatican embassy in Panama City sent a car to meet Noriega at a secret location and bring him back to the embassy. After being on the run for four days, Noriega appeared to have decided that an attempt at political asylum was his last and only chance to escape a prison cell in the United States. Dressed only in running shorts and a T-shirt and carrying two AK-47 rifles, Noriega entered the embassy. When Cheney was informed that Noriega had just surfaced at the Vatican embassy, he apparently told Powell to not "let that guy out of the compound." The State Department immediately contacted the Vatican in Rome and requested that it not grant political asylum to Noriega. Back on the ground near the embassy compound, Major General Marc Cisneros negotiated with the embassy officials in an attempt to broker a deal that would lead to Noriega leaving the compound peacefully. Yet negotiations initially did not bring much progress toward a resolution of the standoff.

The next day, General Thurman ordered that rock music be blasted at the embassy around the clock. Songs such as "I Fought the Law (and the Law Won)" and "Voodoo Child" formed part of a psychological operation to get Noriega to conclude that surrendering to the Americans was better than listening to the music all day. Quickly, though, the music strategy became a political liability, especially since Vatican officials complained that it was driving them crazy too.

As the days passed and Noriega remained inside, a surreal scene began to take place outside the compound.[135] Panamanians routinely congregated to shout slogans against Noriega—"Death to Hitler" or "Justice for the Tyrant"—and to hand flowers to Americans keeping watch.[136]

After over a week in the embassy, Papal Nuncio Monsignor José Sebastián Laboa convinced Noriega that there were no other options but to give himself up. On January 3, dressed in his military uniform and carrying a Bible, Noriega walked out of the front of the embassy, where U.S. troops immediately apprehended him. He was finally in their hands; however, the question remained as to whether the United States had the legal right to arrest Noriega and take him out of Panama.

A few days before the attack, the administration had gone public with a "clarification" of the law that forbade U.S. military personnel from conducting police work both at home and abroad. A change in the law allowed the military to arrest persons overseas wanted by a U.S. warrant. To be sure, one cannot imagine a scenario where a country as small as Panama could ever use the same reasoning to justify the apprehension and trial of an American arrested on American soil. Nonetheless, this paved the way for the military to attempt to seize Noriega during the invasion. Ultimately, though, U.S. DEA agents brought Noriega to Miami. On the flight, Noriega is reported to have given his autograph to some of the U.S. agents. That same night, thousands of celebrating Panamanians packed the six-lane Calle Cincuenta in Panama City.

POSTINVASION

On the morning of December 20, President Bush went on national television to address the American people regarding the invasion that was still under way. He told the public that Noriega declared "his military dictatorship to be in a state of war" with the United States that represented an "imminent danger" for Americans in Panama. Stating that he had no higher obligation than to protect the lives of American citizens, Bush decided to invade after "reaching the conclusion that every other avenue was closed."[137]

Similar to Reagan during the Grenada operation, the next day Bush sent a letter to Speaker of the House Thomas Foley (D-Wash.) and President Pro Tempore Robert Byrd (D-W.Va.) "consistent" with the War Powers Resolution justifying the invasion for the reasons of protecting American lives, defending the canal, bringing Noriega to justice, and promoting democracy in Panama.[138] Interestingly, in an indication that the Bush administration was concerned about the perceived international legitimacy of the operation, the letter also invoked the self-defense provision of article 51 of the UN Charter.[139]

One critical aspect that factored into the decision to invade that President Bush did not emphasize was that, at least implicitly, the administration wanted the invasion to be seen as a victory in the "war on drugs." Administration officials wasted little time in claiming that money laundering would be a thing of the past in post-Noriega Panama. William J. Bennett, Bush's "Drug Czar," told reporters that Panama "has been used as a sanctuary, a vacation spot, a banking center for traffickers, a place to go when the heat is turned up. I believe Panama is unlikely to be used in that capacity in the future."[140]

Yet if there was one justification for the invasion that did not stand up to the test of time, it was the one that claimed that removing Noriega would send a devastating blow to the international drug-trafficking business. In an example of how pervasive this thinking had become in the United States, the father of one solider killed in Panama was quoted as saying that he supported the invasion because "the drugs Noriega was dealing were killing American kids, and now maybe that'll stop."[141]

REACTIONS TO THE INVASION

The American public responded overwhelmingly positively to the invasion. A January 1 poll reported that 80 percent of Americans believed that the invasion was justified. President Bush's approval rating soared to 76 percent, one of the highest for a president since Vietnam.[142] Perhaps even more important for Bush, the invasion appeared to allow him to solidify his position as a strong commander in chief. Panamanians were even more enthusiastic about the invasion than Americans. A CBS–New York Times poll found that 92 percent of them supported the invasion.[143] When Dan Quayle visited Panama on January 29, 1990, he was repeatedly mobbed by supportive crowds. During one church service, the people chanted, "Viva Quayle," and held signs that read, "Gringos Don't Go Home. Clean Panama First." Assistant Secretary of State for Inter-American Affairs Bernard Aronson remarked that in Panama "you could feel a sense of liberation in the air."[144] On *ABC News*'s "This Week," new president Endara stated that the Panamanian people thought of the operation as being

> more a liberation than an invasion. . . . After seeing the paramilitary organizations working and the more than 80,000 arms that Noriega distributed among his cronies and thugs, I am convinced now that U.S. action was necessary for establishing freedom and democracy in Panama. Without U.S. help, we couldn't have done it ourselves. This is the opinion of a very, very high percentage of the Panamanian people. We are thankful to the United States.[145]

The sermon given by a prominent Panamanian priest on Sunday, January 21, expressed that

> the Lord remembered us and directed a change of course toward the road of liberation, justice, and freedom. At that point the jurists become embroiled in arguments over whether it was as invasion, an intervention, or an act of aggression. Those people faithful to God, in their own way, with their logic very often outside of the lawyer's terminology, believe that it was an invasion, but not an invasion of Panama. Because Panama was two nations, or one nation and one country and an anti-country because there were exiles who had to leave the country. But here, within our country, we felt exiled. Exiled from justice. Exiled from liberty. It was an exile. The country was divided between a corrupt country, that country with bellicose strength, that country with the power of destruction, and the other country, the country which felt annihilated before so much, so many weapons, so much expulsion, so much disarray, torture, and imprisonment.

Therefore, the invasion was against the anti-country, against the corruption. And Noriega and his men didn't believe in what they said. All of that
fanfare of shouting and slogans—at first shot, all of them fled like rabbits.
All that which was not fictitious, all of that collapsed and the true country
now starts to take its first difficult and costly steps towards its reconquest:
A free country with justice and liberty. . . . There is no pie left, because
Noriega ate the whole pie.[146]

The priest, however, did not miss the opportunity to add that the United
States "aided, created, and increased the power of Noriega's absurd army,
such that, this isn't a present given to us but, ethically and morally, it justly
is a restitution."

The overwhelming support from people in the United States and Panama did not mean that President Bush was out of the woods with regard
to criticisms of the invasion. Even though a majority of the members of
the body supported the invasion, several members of Congress stridently
attacked the administration for its decision. Senator Ted Kennedy (D-
Mass.) argued that the United States did not have the right to

roam the hemisphere, bringing dictators to justice or installing new governments by force or other means. Surely, it is a contradiction in terms and a
violation of America's best ideals to impose democracy by the barrel of a
gun in Panama or any nation.

Kennedy also stated that it was "difficult to deny" that the invasion had
"cost more lives than it saved" and that "historians will eventually tally
these costs and judge the wisdom of the action. Already, however, this feel
good invasion does not feel so good any more."[147] Kennedy also asked for
the UN resolution that "strongly deplored" the invasion to be included in
the congressional record. In a comment that mirrored how members of
Congress had compared Grenada to the Soviet invasion of Afghanistan,
Representative Don Edwards (D-Calif.) intimated that with the invasion,
the United States had forfeited its moral legitimacy:

I wonder how we would feel if the Soviets said that they were going to take
over neighboring Finland, because they do not like the way the government
runs, or they're disturbed that a Russian has been killed while walking down
one of the streets of a Finnish city.[148]

Several months after the invasion, critics jumped on the fact that Senator Jesse Helms had brought up the issue of not transferring the canal over to Panama at the scheduled December 1999 because of claimed instability in the country. Yet, while Helms no doubt had his own concerns and wishes, there is no evidence that the Bush administration ever acted on his suggestion. If anything, it tried to downplay Helms's position so as not to create a controversy that would detract from the invasion's enormous military success and political popularity.[149]

The reaction from around the world was largely negative. The previously mentioned UN General Assembly resolution condemning the invasion passed 75 to 20 with 40 abstentions. The United States, Great Britain, and France used their vetoes to block a resolution criticizing the invasion as a majority of the Security Council members had voted in favor.[150] An OAS resolution "deeply regretted" the invasion and called for an "immediate withdrawal" of foreign troops.[151]

Writing two years after the invasion, former Costa Rican president and Nobel Peace Prize winner Oscar Arias wrote that the invasion brought back memories of the Big Stick and that the United States

> must learn that the use of force is never a good substitute for the strength of reason. . . . They must realize that war and intervention produce no winners, and that constructive and lasting relations cannot be based upon mistrust and resentment.[152]

Alan Garcia, the populist Peruvian president, flew the Panamanian flag above the presidential palace in Lima and said that "it will stay up there until the Yankee troops get out of Panama." Garcia also promised that "once the carnival of the invasion is over, the protests will start, and American troops are not going to solve the internal economic crisis."[153]

Most scholarly criticisms of the invasion rested on the argument that the invasion was illegal because it violated Panama's sovereignty. One critic listed Bush's justifications for the war and stated that they were "political arguments, not legal ones. In fact, they are a resurrection of the Roosevelt Corollary."[154] To a certain extent, this is an apt observation. While the administration did its utmost to justify the invasion in terms of international law, its defense was largely political.

In addition to legal critiques, many critics believed that the U.S. legacy of heavy-handedness and general disregard for promoting democracies abroad would in the long run ensure a negative outcome in Panama. They pointed out that in late December when Endara went to meet the diplomatic corps for the first time, he did so in a vehicle provided to him by the U.S. embassy. Endara and his cabinet also spent the first several days after the invasion working out of the Foreign Ministry because the Presidential Palace was in the hands of U.S. authorities.[155] The suggestion behind these criticisms was clear: that the United States had effectively assumed control of Panama and that the Endara was largely a puppet president.

An opinion editorial in the *New York Times* concluded that "except for the death, destruction, and diversion it brought, 'Operation Just Cause' was as phony as its name." It added that if Bush had "kept his cool" and acted more like Mikhail Gorbachev "vis-à-vis his former satellites in Eastern Europe [that] General Noriega would sooner or later have been overthrown by his own people."[156] In fact, the notion that the Panamian people would have eventually removed Noriega and that this would have been more salubrious for Panama gained increasing credence among invasion critics. Michael Massing wrote in the *New York Review of Books* that

> a policy of disengagement might enable General Noriega to hang on to power longer than would otherwise be the case. But such a strategy, by leaving Panama's political future to the Panamanians themselves, would provide a much more solid foundation for the development of democracy. And, not least, it would leave intact the principle of non-intervention.[157]

Writing in the *Wall Street Journal*, Hodding Carter argued that the Endara "regime" was "little more than a still-born gesture toward democracy, a brief way-station along the road to renewed control by the PDF."[158] A list of sixty-nine American citizens signed an advertisement in the *New York Times* stating, "We object to the idea we can impose democracy on another nation." Another advertisement chastised the Bush administration for "Gun Barrel Democracy."[159] Articles appeared with headlines such as "U.S. Played God in Panama and Created Its Own Devil," "It May Prove Difficult to Let Panama Get On with Its Life," and "The Intervention That Misfired."

Most of the initial criticisms of the invasion centered on its legality or

THE INVASION OF PANAMA, 1989

future ability to promote democracy. Yet by the summer of 1990, voices began to emerge that argued that there were more nefarious reasons behind the U.S. decision to invade. If the Bush administration's justifications for the invasion—protecting lives, defending the canal, or supporting democracy—were lies, then there had to be another reason for the invasion. Their answer: to allow the United States to rewrite the 1977 treaties in order to maintain the military bases and control over the canal well past the December 31, 1999, handover date.

For example, a *NACLA Report on the Americas* wrote that a "more compelling argument [for the invasion] is that the United States sought to guarantee access to its military bases after 2000, when the treaties require their removal."[160] An "independent inquiry" of the U.S. invasion did not even feel compelled to prove that the invasion was driven by the need to modify the canal treaties; rather, it needed only to explain to its readers why the United States thought that changing the treaties was so critical:

> To explain why the United States would go so far as to invade Panama to change the treaties, it is necessary to understand Panama's strategic military significance for the entire region . . . careful observers of U.S. foreign policy know that U.S. support for dictatorial and corrupt governments in other countries in Central America indicates that there must be some other motivation to explain the Bush administration's decision to go to war. Ample evidence reveals that the U.S. government and the Pentagon planned to overthrow the Panamanian government and replace it with a dependent and subservient regime(s) which could renegotiate the key provisions of the 1977 Panama Canal treaties.[161]

We now know, of course, that the United States never even attempted to change the treaties. In another instance, a paid advertisement that ran in the magazine *The Nation* signed by over 100 "well-known Americans" included the statement,

> The truth is that the U.S. aggression in Panama is a major escalation of military intervention in the whole region. The goal is to continue U.S. domination . . . "Yanqui imperialism" as people all over Latin America name it. . . . We can and must mount a far more powerful resistance to the horror of U.S. imperialist crime. The oppressed people of Panama, Latin America, and the world expect nothing less.[162]

Another key criticism claimed that it was really U.S. helicopter gunships that set El Chorrillo ablaze. The often-cited "inquiry" wrote that, in
reference to the residents of Panama City who had been made homeless
because of the fighting, 18,000 "war refuges" were "stuffed in concentration camps." While certainly not comfortable, these "concentration
camps" were actually hangars on U.S. air bases.[163] What is more, while
U.S. bullets most likely led to at least some of the destruction of the neighborhood, interviews with many residents of the El Chorrillo revealed that
they believed that Noriega's men were likely responsible for many of the
fires that destroyed their homes. According to a Spanish priest who
worked and lived in the area, "The fire was something deliberate, intentional and premeditated . . . people in the neighborhood saw members of
the Dignity Battalions throwing grenades to start the fire and pouring gas-
oline to spread it."[164]

Critics also claimed that the Pentagon had covered up the number of
Panamanian civilians killed in the invasion. On January 10, 1990, the Pentagon announced that there had been 220 unarmed civilians killed. This
number was immediately attacked by figures such as former Attorney
General Ramsey Clark, who claimed that it was a "conspiracy of silence"
to hide the extent of the civilian death toll number.[165]

The American investigative television program *60 Minutes* ran a seg-
ment on the Pentagon's supposed cover-up of civilian deaths. It cited
4,000 civilians killed; other groups put the number at 8,000. The docu-
mentary *Panama Deception*, which won the Academy Award for best doc-
umentary, reported that thousands were killed and uncritically inter-
viewed Panamanian residents who claimed that the U.S. troops used
weapons with lasers that made its victims disappear. Soon critics were citing "thousands and thousands" of civilians killed, often buried in
unmarked mass graves. Even in 2004, fifteen years after the invasion,
mainstream sources continue to report these types of numbers. The
United Methodist Church's General Board of Global Ministries wrote that

the invaders withheld all information concerning the number of people
killed or injured, as well as figures for property damage. The number of
dead is estimated at between 4,000 and 10,000.[166]

An exhaustive 1992 report by the Investigations Subcommittee of the
House Armed Services Committee was met with little fanfare. The report

concluded that a very large proportion of the "civilian dead" were in fact members of Dignity Battalions. One reason for this was that only 13 percent of the civilians dead were women and children. Working with numbers provided by a number of independent human rights organizations, the report estimated that the total civilian dead (including Dignity Battalion members) was around 300, and a "reasonable estimate" of the numbers of "innocent bystanders" killed during Just Cause was "almost certainly less than 100."[167] While it did not receive credit at the time, the Pentagon provided the most accurate statistics for civilian deaths during the invasion. In fact, it overreported them.

POSTINVASION REDEVELOPMENT AND DEMOCRACY

Manuel Noriega's arrival at the Vatican embassy signaled the end of Just Cause. The U.S. operation in Panama was now called Promote Liberty. From December 26 to January 3, U.S. civil affairs troops helped distribute 1,660 tons of food and 218 tons of medical supplies. It also created a camp at Balboa High School for some 5,000 persons left homeless by the fighting.[168] Promote Liberty was the U.S. government's largest nation-building exercise since Vietnam. The American team included accountants, city planners, postal workers, pharmacists, insurance underwriters, legal experts, economists, and engineers, among others.[169] In addition to repairing damage from the invasion, projects included school repair, reforestation, and national park protection.

The invasion also led to the end of U.S. economic sanctions. Washington immediately released the Panamanian government's assets held in the United States. But the task confronting the Endara government was daunting: under Noriega, Panama's foreign debt had surged to $5.5 billion, and the nation owed accrued interest payments of $700 million. This makes it all the more remarkable that Panama's gross domestic product grew by 4 percent in 1990 and 6 percent in 1991. Inflation stayed under 2 percent.

In late January 1990, President Bush announced a $1 billion package for Panama.[170] Forty million dollars was earmarked for emergency relief for homeless Panamanians, including several million dollars to build houses for El Chorrillo residents.[171] The U.S. Agency for International Development promised $6,500 for each family made homeless by the invasion. The aid was unfortunately slow in coming—twelve years after the invasion, residents of El Chorrillo continued to complain that the

United States and successive Panamanian governments had neglected their needs. However, they did not express any nostalgia for Noriega.[172]

Panama's General Assembly opened on March 1, 1990, to tremendous support from the Panamanian people. But while he initially enjoyed meteoric public approval ratings, President Endara's support dropped precipitously a few years into office. By the end of 1991, Endara's approval rating was only 10 percent.

One fear was that Endara's weakness would allow for the old populist-military politics to reemerge in Panama. Fortunately, however, this did not happen. The Torrijos-based PRD did return but this time reconstituted as a democratic party. In May 1994, Panama held a historic "Costa Rican" election: free, fair, and peaceful. For the first time since 1960, the popular vote dictated the country's presidential succession, and, more important, the PRD-led opposition and its candidate Ernesto "El Toro" Perez Balladares won, and the incumbent Endara government agreed to honor the results. According to one Panamanian newspaper editor,

> Never before after an election in Panama has there been such tranquility or has been seen a transition team working so harmoniously; never before has the winning candidate received so much support from his adversaries . . . [continuing] we Panamanians have matured in the ethics of our politics; we have decidedly begun to live in a democratic era.[173]

In the postinvasion era, Panama did experience some threats to its nascent democracy. In March 1990, a shadowy pro-Noriega 20th of December Movement took responsibility for tossing a grenade into a crowded disco that killed a U.S. serviceman and wounded twenty-seven others. The group also conducted several attacks at U.S. installations, but nothing significant ever came of their actions, and they quickly ceased operating.

A December 1990 coup attempt from an embittered former PDF officer that required 400 U.S. troops to quell was another instance that threatened to rattle Panama's newly found democracy.[174] Yet despite these sorts of coup attempts and other violent acts, Panamanian democracy began putting down deep roots.

In addition, as agreed in the Panama Canal Treaties ratified by both countries in 1977, the U.S. transferred sovereignty of the Canal Zone to Panama in December 1999. Today, the U.S. military bases are gone. Perhaps the greatest irony of the results of the invasion is that since the transfer there has been an increasing desire within Panama for the U.S. military to *return* to its former military bases given their tremendous economic impact on the local economy. Instead of the normal cries of "Yankee Go Home!" one occasionally hears "Yankee Come Back!"

However, while the past fifteen years since the U.S. invasion have made up a remarkably positive and unprecedented era in Panama's political history, Panama is not a utopia. The U.S. invasion irrevocably removed Noriega and the PDF, and a democracy followed in its wake, but corruption, poverty, frustration, and, yes, drug trafficking remain in Panama. Yet one must certainly ask the question as to what Panama might look like today if the United States had not invaded or even if it had invaded but solely to apprehend Noriega.

NOTES

1. This point was made in R. M. Koster and Guillermo Sanchez, *In the Name of the Tyrants, Panama: 1968–1990* (New York: Norton, 1990).

2. See Eytan Gilboa, "The Panama Invasion Revisited: Lessons for the Use of Force in the Post Cold War Era," *Political Science Quarterly* 110, no. 4 (1995–1996): 539–40.

3. See Georges A. Fauriol, "The Shadow of Latin America Affairs," *Foreign Affairs* (1989/1990): 116.

4. "Reason and Law Reject Our Panama Invasion," *New York Times*, January 2, 1990.

5. John Major, *Prize Possession: The United States and the Panama Canal, 1903–1979* (Cambridge: Cambridge University Press, 1993), 378.

6. Charles Maechling Jr., "Washington's Illegal Invasion," *Foreign Policy*, no. 79, 113.

7. For an insightful take on the political implications of Bush's decision to invade, see "Civilization's Limits," *Wall Street Journal*, December 22, 1989.

8. For more on this point, see Paul Gigot, "Get Ready to Use Democracy's Gunboats Again," *Wall Street Journal*, December 21, 1989.

9. Michael L. Conniff, *Panama and the United States: The Forced Alliance* (Athens: University of Georgia Press, 1992), 20.

10. David N. Farnsworth and James W. McKenney, *U.S.-Panama Relations, 1903–1978: A Study in Linkage Politics* (Boulder, Colo.: Westview Press, 1983), 15.

11. Farnsworth and McKenney, *U.S.-Panama Relations*, 17.

12. Koster and Sánchez, *In the Name of the Tyrants*, 386.

13. Quoted in Koster and Sánchez, *In the Name of the Tyrants*, 387.

14. Conniff, *Panama and the United States*, 64.

15. Conniff, *Panama and the United States*, 64.

16. Major, *Prize Possession*, 34.

17. Quoted in Major, *Prize Possession*, 34. Roosevelt told the second quotation to his biographer twelve years later.

18. See Frederick W. Marks, *Velvet on Iron: The Diplomacy of Theodore Roosevelt* (Lincoln: University of Nebraska Press, 1979).

19. Koster and Sánchez, *In the Name of the Tyrants*, 19.

20. Quoted in Koster and Sánchez, *In the Name of the Tyrants*, 383.

21. E. H. Kahn, "Letter from Panama," *The New Yorker*, August 16, 1976, 64–74.

22. Thomas Donnelly, Margaret Roth, and Caleb Baker, *Operation Just Cause: The Storming of Panama* (New York: Lexington Books, 1991), 3–7; Koster and Sánchez, *In the Name of the Tyrants*, 21.

23. Quoted in Major, *Prize Possession*, 58.

24. William H. Drohan, "When All the Bills Came Due: The Development of U.S.-Panamanian Relations through 1989," in Bruce W. Watson and Peter G. Tsouras, eds., *Operation Just Cause: The U.S. Intervention in Panama* (Boulder, Colo.: Westview Press, 1991), 20.

25. Quoted in Association of the Bar of the City of New York, *Report on: The Use of Armed Force in International Affairs: The Case of Panama*, June 1992. The 1936 Hull-Alfaro Treaty raised the annuity to $430,000 to offset the devaluation of the U.S. dollar in 1933. Article III of the treaty stipulated that the Canal Zone was sovereign territory of Panama under jurisdiction of the United States. See Donald Mabry, "Panama's Policy toward the United States: Living with Big Brother," in Watson and Tsouras, *Operation Just Cause*, 5.

26. Conniff, *Panama and the United States*, 76–85.

27. The 1955 treaty increased the annuity paid for the canal and eliminated the discriminatory wage differential that favored U.S. employees of the Canal Company. See Association of the Bar of the City of New York, *The Use of Armed Force in International Affairs: The Case of Panama*, June 1992.

28. Conniff, *Panama and the United States*, 85.

29. Mabry, "Panama's Policy toward the United States: Living with Big Brother," 6.

30. Farnsworth and McKenney, *U.S.-Panama Relations*, 35.

31. Conniff, *Panama and the United States*, 96.

32. Quoted in Major, *Prize Possession*, 327.

33. McGeorge Bundy, "Policy toward Present and Future of the Panama Canal," National Security Action Memoranda No. 323, January 8, 1965 (declassified May 23, 1978), www.lbjlib.utexas.edu/johnson/archives.hom/NSAMs/nsam323.asp (accessed June 3, 2003).

34. Koster and Sánchez, *In the Name of the Tyrants*, 58.

35. John Dinges, *Our Man in Panama: How General Noriega Used the United States—and Made Millions in Drugs and Arms* (New York: Random House, 1990), 43.

36. Koster and Sánchez, *In the Name of the Tyrants*, 79.

37. Conniff, *Panama and the United States*, 126.

38. Dinges, *Our Man in Panama*, 127.

39. Conniff, *Panama and the United States*, 126.

40. Drohan, "When All the Bills Came Due," 20.

41. Koster and Sánchez, *In the Name of the Tyrants*, 58.

42. Quoted in Dinges, *Our Man in Panama*, 78.

43. Quoted in Dinges, *Our Man in Panama*, 73.

44. Quoted in Dinges, *Our Man in Panama*, 78.

45. Quoted in Conniff, *Panama and the United States*, 130.

46. The State Department had requested that Nixon resume treaty talks since 1971. Robert Anderson, who had led the 1965–1967 talks, once again presided until Bunker took over. See Conniff, *Panama and the United States*, 130.

47. Farnsworth and McKenney, *U.S.-Panama Relations, 1903–1978*, 137.

48. Association of the Bar of the City of New York, *The Use of Armed Force in International Affairs*.

49. Drohan, "When All the Bills Came Due," 8.

50. By 1975, only 16 percent of U.S. import/export tonnage passed through the canal. See Drohan, "When All the Bills Came Due," 8.

51. Rebecca L. Grant, "Operation Just Cause and the U.S. Policy Process," *RAND Publication Series* 199 (1990): 5.

52. Major, *Prize Possession*, 136; Cyrus Vance, *Hard Choices: Critical Years in America's Foreign Policy* (New York: Simon & Schuster, 1983), 141.

53. During the transition, a U.S.-chartered corporation, the Panama Canal Commission, would run the canal. Until 1990, its director and a majority of the governing board would be U.S. citizens. After that, the director would be Panamanian, nominated by the Panamanian government and confirmed by the U.S. Senate. The treaty also maintained the right of the United States to defend the canal militarily.

54. Quoted in Major, *Prize Possession*, 327.

55. Quoted in Major, *Prize Possession*, 345.

56. Farnsworth and McKenney, *U.S.-Panama Relations, 1903–1978*, 174, 247.

57. Major, *Prize Possession*, 353.

58. Michael Massing, "The Intervention That Misfired," *The Nation*, May 21, 1988, 708.

59. Seymour Hersh, "The Creation of a Thug," *Life*, March 1990, 81–93; Gilboa, "The Panama Invasion Revisited," 541.

60. Quoted in Frederick Kempe, *Divorcing the Dictator: America's Bungled Affair with Noriega* (New York: G. P. Putnam's Sons, 1990), 109.

61. Quoted in Kempe, *Divorcing the Dictator*, 159.

62. Kevin Buckley, *Panama: The Whole Story* (New York: Simon & Schuster, 1991), 21.

63. Kempe, *Divorcing the Dictator*, 83.

64. David Hoffman, "Noriega Drug Questions Ignored," *Washington Post*, April 9, 1989.

65. Linda Robinson, "Dwindling Options in Panama," *Foreign Affairs* (1989/ 1990): 187.

66. Quoted in Michael R. Hathaway, "The Role of Drugs in the U.S.-Panama Relationship," *Operation Just Cause: The U.S. Intervention in Panama*, ed. Bruce W. Watson and Peter G. Tsouras (Boulder, Colo.: Westview Press, 1990), 32.

67. Gilboa, "The Panama Invasion Revisited," 542.

68. David Norman Miller, "Panama and U.S. Policy," *Global Affairs*, 4, no. 3 (summer 1989): 128–47.

69. Grant, "Operation Just Cause and the U.S. Policy Process," 10.

70. Díaz Herrera had been out of the PDF inner circle after he participated in a

coup against Noriega when Noriega was in France at the time of the Spadafora murder
in 1986. Díaz Hererra was the third participant in the 1982 plot to remove Flores.
Noriega was supposed to step down in 1987 so that Díaz Herrera could take over the
PDF.

71. Linda Drucker, "Washington Cries Uncle," *Commonweal*, July 15, 1988,
391–92; see also Richard Millett, "Looking beyond Noriega," *Foreign Policy*, no. 71,
50.

72. Hathaway, "The Role of Drugs in the U.S.-Panama Relationship," 39.

73. In 1987, Congress cut of $26 million in assistance to Panama. The World Bank
also halted the disbursement of existing loans.

74. Gilboa, "The Panama Invasion Revisited," 542.

75. Quoted in Carla Anne Robbins, "Drug King? Spy? Not I, Says General Noriega;
Is Panama Run by a Military 'Mafia'?," *U.S. News and World Report*, July 27, 1986, 36.

76. Seymour M. Hersh, "Panama Strongman Said to Trade in Drugs, Arms, and
Illicit Money," *New York Times*, June 12, 1986.

77. Quoted in Philip Shenon, "Noriega Indicted by U.S. for Links to Illegal
Drugs," *New York Times*, February 6, 1988.

78. Joe Pichirallo, "Noriega Given Offer to Drop Drug Charges," *Washington Post*,
May 12, 1988.

79. In the Miami indictment, Noriega was one of fifteen codefendants. Others
included several big Colombian drug cartel leaders.

80. Grant, "Operation Just Cause and the U.S. Policy Process," 20.

81. Quoted in Dinges, *Our Man in Panama*, 295.

82. Robinson, "Dwindling Options in Panama," 187. An unsuccessful coup
against Noriega in March forced U.S. officials to acknowledge that they had overestimated the strength of the opposition to Noriega within PDF ranks.

83. For a comprehensive report on the sanctions, see appendix I to "GAO Review
of Economic Sanctions against Panama," Statement of Frank C. Conahan, Assistant
Comptroller General for National Security and International Affairs, before the House
Committee on Foreign Affairs, July 26, 1989 (GAO/T-NSIAD-89-4).

84. Lou Cannon, "Anti-Noriega Sanctions Are Having 'Telling Effect' White
House Says," *Washington Post*, April 6, 1988.

85. "Gunning for Noriega," *The Economist*, December 23, 1989.

86. The May announcement represented the culmination of several months of
secret dealings with members of Noriega's regime.

87. David Hoffman, "Bush Splits with Reagan on Handling of Noriega," *Washington Post*, May 19, 1988.

88. Quoted in Kempe, *Divorcing the Dictator*, 336. At this point, polls had Dukakis
ahead of Bush by ten points.

89. Quoted in Gilboa, "The Panama Invasion Revisited," 549.

90. Quoted in Helen Dewar, "Dole Warns against Dropping Noriega Case," *Washington Post*, May 17, 1988.

91. Quoted in Gilboa, "The Panama Invasion Revisited," 549.

92. Quoted in Robert Pear, "The Noriega Fiasco: What Went Wrong," *New York
Times*, May 30, 1988.

93. Quoted in Kempe, *Divorcing the Dictator*, 299.

94. Waltraud Queise Morales, "U.S. Intervention and the New World Order: Les-

sons from Cold War and Post Cold War Cases," *Third World Quarterly* 15, no. 1 (March 1994): 77.

95. Lindsey Gruson, "Panama Says U.S. Aids Opponents in Effort to Break Canal Treaties," *New York Times*, April 25, 1989.

96. The opposition coalition was known as ADOC (Alliance of Democratic Civilian Opposition). Endara was from Arnulfo Arias's party, Arias from the Christian Democrats, and Ford from Molirena. The pro-Noriega coalition was a group of eight parties known as Colina (National Liberation Coalition). See Robinson, "Dwindling Options in Panama."

97. Author interview with Bernard Aronson, former assistant secretary of state for inter-American affairs, October 19, 2004.

98. All quoted in Lindsey Grunson, "Noriega Stealing Election, Carter Says," *New York Times*, May 9, 1989.

99. George Bush, "Remarks at a Question and Answer Session with Reporters on the Situation in Panama," May 11, 1989, *Public Papers of the Presidents of the United States: George Bush, 1989–1993*, vol. 1 (Washington, D.C.: U.S. Government Printing Office, 1990).

100. See Gilboa, "The Panama Invasion Revisited," 553; Grant, "Operation Just Cause and the U.S. Policy Process," 29; author interview with Bernard Aronson, former assistant secretary of state for inter-American affairs, October 19, 2004.

101. The interagency group included Bernard Aronson from the State Department, William Price from the National Security Council, Richard Brown from Defense, and Brigadier General David C. Meade for the U.S. Army, Joint Staff.

102. "Maxatollah," *The Economist*, January 6, 1990, 26.

103. Quoted in Buckley, *Panama*, 192.

104. Ronald H. Cole, "Operation Just Cause: The Planning and Execution of Joint Operations in Panama," Joint History Office, Office of the Chairman of the Joint Chiefs of Staff, Washington, D.C., 1995, 12.

105. Quoted in Donnelly et al., *Operation Just Cause*, 53.

106. Buckley, *Panama*, 196.

107. Ivan Musicant, *The Banana Wars: A History of United States Military Intervention in Latin America from the Spanish American War to the Invasion of Panama* (New York: Macmillan, 1990), 395.

108. "The Panama Coup," *Christian Science Monitor*, October 6, 1989.

109. Quoted in Cole, "Operation Just Cause," 15.

110. Quoted in Gilboa, "The Panama Invasion Revisited," 556.

111. Senate Joint Hearing before the Committee on Armed Services and the Select Committee on Intelligence, 101st Cong., 1st sess., October 6 and 17 and December 22, 1989, 29. For more on the controversy over the October coup, see Benjamin Crosby, "Rethinking Policy on Panama," *Christian Science Monitor*, October 24, 1989; Godfrey Sperling Jr., "Panama Coup Was No Bay of Pigs," *Christian Science Monitor*, October 24, 1989; David Hoffman, "Bush Attacks Critics of Response to Coup," *Washington Post*, October 14, 1989; John Huge, "Getting Noriega," *Christian Science Monitor*, October 11, 1989; Lucia Mouat, "Lessons from a Failed Coup," *Christian Science Monitor*, October 10, 1989.

112. Quoted in Kempe, *Divorcing the Dictator*, 392.

113. Quoted in Hoffman, "Bush Attacks Critics of Response to Coup."

114. Quoted in Maureen Dowd, "Bush, under Fire, Defends Role in Panama Crisis," *New York Times*, October 7, 1989.

115. Colonel William C. Bennett, "Just Cause and the Principles of War," *Military Review*, March 1991, 2–12.

116. Manuel Noriega, "Noriega's Speech before the National Assembly of Corregimiento Representatives, 15 December 1989," Translation. Printed in U.S. Department of Commerce, Foreign Broadcast Information Service. LAT-89-21.

117. Cole, "Operation Just Cause," 27.

118. See *Operation Just Cause: A Preliminary Assessment*, House of Representatives, 101st Cong., 2nd sess., *Congressional Record* 136, no. 8 (February 5, 1990).

119. Cole, "Operation Just Cause," 27.

120. Quoted in Cole, "Operation Just Cause," 30; Donnelly et al., *Operation Just Cause*, 99.

121. See Bennett, "Just Cause and the Principles of War."

122. Quoted in Cole, "Operation Just Cause," 34.

123. Of the nineteen U.S. servicemen killed in action, ten were from the Special Forces. See *Operation Just Cause: A Preliminary Assessment*.

124. Ronald H. Cole's study of Operation Just Cause is by far the most comprehensive unclassified document on the operation.

125. Buckley, *Panama*, 239.

126. At 7:30 A.M., a Ranger assault cleared the Tocumen airport and opened it up for reinforcements from the 82nd Airborne. See Peter Huchthausen, *America's Splendid Little Wars: A Short History of U.S. Military Engagements, 1975–2000* (New York: Viking, 2003), 119.

127. Quoted in Cole, "Operation Just Cause," 34; for more on the hostage situation at the Marriott Hotel, see Richard Millett, "The Aftermath of Intervention: Panama 1990," *Journal of Interamerican Studies and World Affairs* 32, no. 1 (spring 1990): 1–15.

128. Author translation from Spanish. Quoted in Koster and Sánchez, *In the Name of the Tyrants*, 377.

129. Author phone interview with Michael P. Peters, commander of 96th Civil Affairs Battalion (Airborne), November 15, 2004.

130. Alex Jones, "Fighting in Panama: The Press; Editors Says Journalists Were Kept from Action," *New York Times*, December 22, 1989.

131. Musicant, *The Banana Wars*, 417.

132. Quoted in Michael R. Gordon, "Fighting in Panama: The Chief of Staff; Vital for the Invasion; Politically Attuned General," *New York Times*, December 25, 1989.

133. Joseph B. Treaster, "The Palace: In Noriega's Home, Décor Paints a Picture of Extravagance," *New York Times*, December 25, 1989.

134. Donnelly et al., *Operation Just Cause*, 105.

135. Donnelly et al., *Operation Just Cause*, 364.

136. The invasion was not without its series of embarrassing moments. On December 28, U.S. troops surrounded the residence of the Cuban ambassador to Panama after they had received intelligence that the pro-Noriega operatives had received asylum there. The next day, U.S. troops ransacked the residence of the Nicaraguan ambassador to Panama. While small arms were found at the Nicaraguan ambassador's home, the move was clearly a violation of diplomatic immunity. See Larry Rohter, "After

Noriega: Panama City; Impasse over Noriega Persists, but Order Returns to the Streets," *New York Times*, December 27, 1989.

137. George Bush, "Address to the Nation Announcing U.S. Military Action in Panama," 20 December 1989, *Public Papers of the United States*, vol. II (Washington, D.C.: U.S. Government Printing Office, 1990).

138. George Bush, "Letter to the Speaker of the House of Representatives and the President Pro Tempore of the Senate on the United States Military Action in Panama," December 21, 1989, *Public Papers of the United States*, vol. II.

139. Maechling, "Washington's Illegal Invasion," 13.

140. Quoted in Richard L. Berke, "Fighting in Panama: The Drug War; Washington Hopes to Close a Trafficking Haven," *New York Times*, December 21, 1989.

141. Quoted in Craig Wolff, "Fighting in Panama: The Survivors; For Military Families, Worry, Grief, and Pride," *New York Times*, December 23, 1989.

142. Michael Oreskes, "Approval of Bush, Bolstered by Panama, Soars in Poll," *New York Times*, January 19, 1990.

143. Steve C. Ropp, "Panama: The United States Invasion and Its Aftermath," *Current History* 90, no. 554 (March 1991): 112; Brook Larmer, "Panamanians Applaud Invasion," *Christian Science Monitor*, December 29, 1989.

144. Quoted in House Foreign Affairs Committee, *Hearing on U.S. Policy toward Panama*, February 6, 1990, 101st Cong., 2nd sess., 1990, Federal News Service, Lexis-Nexis.

145. Quoted in Robert Pear, "Quayle Gets Warm Welcome in Panama," *New York Times*, January 29, 1990.

146. Quoted in "Report on Visit to Panama, January 19 to January 22, 1990," 101st Cong., 2nd sess., *Congressional Record* 136, no. 3 (January 25, 1990).

147. Kennedy quoted in "The Panama Invasion," 101st Cong., 2nd sess., *Congressional Record* 136, no. 1 (January 23, 1990).

148. Edwards quoted in "The Panama Invasion," 101st Cong., 2nd sess., *Congressional Record* 136, no. 1 (February 7, 1990).

149. Senate Foreign Relations Committee, *Hearing on the Situation in Panama*, 101st Cong., 2nd sess., *Congressional Record* 136, no. 1 (January 25, 1990).

150. On the Security Council, the Soviet Union, China, Algeria, Colombia, Ethiopia, Malaysia, Nepal, Senegal, and Yugoslavia voted yes. The United States, Great Britain, and France voted no. Finland abstained. On January 17, 1990, the United States vetoed a resolution declaring the U.S. forces' search of the Nicaraguan ambassador's house to be a violation of international law. See David E. Pitt, "Panama's New Chief to Ask U.S. Aid," *New York Times*, January 18, 1990.

151. They were UN Resolution 44/420 and OAS Resolution #534 (800/89). See "The Panama Invasion," 101st Cong., 2nd sess., *Congressional Record* 136, no. 10 (February 7, 1990).

152. Oscar Arias, "A New Opportunity for Panama," *Harvard International Review* 13, no. 3 (spring 1991): 25–29.

153. Quoted in James Brooke, "Peruvian Still Outraged by Invasion of Panama," *New York Times*, January 14, 1990.

154. Maechling, "Washington's Illegal Invasion," 6.

155. Larry Rohter, "It May Prove Difficult to Let Panama Get On with Its Life," *New York Times*, December 31, 1989.

156. John B. Oakes, "Bush in Panama: A Tragicomedy," *New York Times*, January 26, 1990.

157. Michael J. Massing, "New Trouble in Panama," *New York Review of Books*, May 17, 1990, 43.

158. Hodding Carter III, "U.S. Played God in Panama and Created Its Own Devil," *Wall Street Journal*, January 4, 1990.

159. See "Panama Invasion Still Concerns Many Americans," 101st Cong., 2nd sess., *Congressional Record* 136, no. 57 (May 9, 1990).

160. "Panama: Reagan's Last Stand," *NACLA Report on the Americas* 22, no. 4 (1990): 11; John Dinges, "General Coke?," *NACLA Report on the Americas*, 22, no. 4 (1990): 20.

161. Independent Inquiry of the U.S. Invasion of Panama, *The U.S. Invasion of Panama: The Truth behind Operation "Just Cause"* (Boston: South End Press, 1991), 5.

162. See "Panama Invasion Still Concerns Many Americans" (Extension of Remarks).

163. Author phone interview with Michael P. Peters, commander of 96th Civil Affairs Battalion (Airborne), November 15, 2004.

164. Quoted in Larry Rohter, "Residents Say Force Loyal to Noriega Set Fire to Neighborhood in Reprisal," *New York Times*, December 29, 1989.

165. David E. Pitt, "The Invasion's Civilian Toll: Still No Official Count," *New York Times*, January 10, 1990.

166. See United Methodist Church General Board of Global Ministries, Panama Country Profile, http://gbgm-umc.org/country_profiles/country_history.cfm?Id = 117 (accessed June 23, 2004).

167. House Investigations Committee of the Committee on Armed Services, *The Invasion of Panama: How Many Innocent Bystanders Perished?*, 102nd Cong., 2nd sess., July 7, 1992, 1–2.

168. Author phone interview with Michael P. Peters, commander of 96th Civil Affairs Battalion (Airborne), November 15, 2004.

169. Massing, "The Intervention That Misfired," 708.

170. By the end of 1992, $368 million had been disbursed, including $40 million for emergency relief and $113 million for economic recovery activities. See "Fact Sheet: Panama 2 Years after Operation Just Cause," *U.S. Department of State Dispatch* 3, no. 6 (February 10, 1992), 96.

171. Robert Pear, "US$1 Billion of Aid to Panama Announced," *New York Times*, January 26, 1990; see also "Urgent Assistance for Democracy in Panama Act of 1990," Public Law 101-243 (H.R. 3952), February 14, 1990.

172. David Gonzalez, "12 Years Later, Scars of the U.S. Invasion Remain," *New York Times*, November 3, 2001.

173. Quoted in Margaret E. Scranton, "Panama's First Post-Transition Election," *Journal of Interamerican Studies and World Affairs* 37, no. 1 (spring 1995): 69.

174. Ropp, "Panama," 112.

Conclusion

It has been over fifteen years since the United States sent military forces into Panama, the most recent of the three interventions covered in this book. Yet the passage of time has still not allowed us to get a fuller understanding of these historical events or the lessons that we should take away from them. To take one case, today U.S. motives for intervening in Grenada are routinely characterized as being cynical or even disingenuous. Noted political scientist Peter Smith writes in one of the most widely read textbooks on U.S.–Latin American relations that President Ronald Reagan's invocation of a Communist threat in Grenada seemed "patently absurd."[1] In 2004, a *BBC News* report written in the aftermath of Reagan's death included that the 1983 Grenada invasion was widely "dismissed as a clumsy stunt."[2] Journalism professor Mark Danner warned that Iraq in 2003 was not Lebanon in 1983, a country "from which the United States could sail away and invade Grenada."[3]

Yet these types of interpretations tend to overlook the historical evidence that suggests that the decisions to intervene were driven by a variety of motivating factors, a reality that makes it harder to categorize them so easily. On the contrary, the evidence suggests that these decisions were based on credible threats either to American national security or to the lives of American citizens. Presidents Lyndon Johnson, Reagan, and George H. W. Bush were each confronted with a security crisis in America's traditional backyard. Along with their advisers, these presidents knew that a decision not to act was just as significant as a decision to act. In each case, the intelligence was at best imperfect, but this did not excuse them from the responsibility of determining the U.S. responses to these crises.

These leaders ordered American "boots on the ground" in order to determine the outcome of the situation. This fact alone poses many problems in our evaluation of these actions, as most scholars view American boots on the ground as an automatically harmful event, one that reinforces the desire of the United States to dominate the region. From this perspective, and given the cited track record of U.S. overt and covert activities in Latin America, U.S. intervention is rarely if ever justified or beneficial, no matter what strategic, democratic, or humanitarian rhetoric a particular administration might use to justify the operation.

One problem with this approach is that we often study the definitive cases of deleterious American actions—again, the Bay of Pigs and efforts to overthrow Arbenz and Allende are the often-cited examples—in order to support our broader conclusions about the nature of American involvement in the region. Yet we must be careful not to derive our broader historical conclusions from only certain American interventions or other sorts of episodes.

If anything, the events studied in this book attempt to provide us with more empirical evidence to help us characterize U.S. involvement in Latin America during the Cold War. This is not to argue that particular conclusions about the invasion of Grenada or Panama somehow negate other instances of American involvement. Rather, we must be open to all the evidence, whether or not it reinforces or undermines our preestablished views on the topic.

GUNBOAT DEMOCRACY?

As we have seen, the existence of perceived security threats greatly helps explain what motivated American officials to decide to intervene in these three cases. Yet any comprehensive study of U.S. foreign policy must at least consider what has occurred in those countries following the initial interventions. It is thus significant that currently the people of the Dominican Republic, Grenada, and Panama enjoy some of the most competitive and representative political systems in Latin America. Freedom House, an organization that rates the level of democracies in countries around the world, currently places Panama and Grenada alongside Japan and well above Argentina, Mexico, and South Korea. The Dominican Republic is ranked alongside Brazil and Thailand.

Freedom House ranks countries on a scale from 1 to 7, going from "free" to "partly free" to "not free." Before the invasion, Grenada was ranked a 5, and after 1983 it began a steady drop down to its present score of 1.5. Panama is similar: at the height of Noriega's reign, the country's score was 7; after the invasion, it moved down to 1.5. These scores indicate that both countries are now some of the freest in the world.[4] The Dominican Republic's score of 2.5 in 2004 puts it in the "free" category.

To be sure, the rankings of one American nongovernmental organization do not represent an exhaustive analysis of the state of democracy in these three countries. While certainly not ideal, the index remains a relatively easy and straightforward way to get a rough idea of the state of democracy in any particular country. For example, few would argue that many of the countries listed in 2003 as "unfree" (e.g., North Korea and Burma) were actually legitimate democracies.

It is certainly not the intention of this book to argue that American intervention in these episodes was the sole factor that led to stronger democracies. Much more research on the postintervention democratic practices and institutions is required before we can draw more definitive conclusions. Yet the historical record suggests that in all three outcomes, democratic institutions emerged stronger than before the interventions. In addition, the instances of full-scale invasion—Grenada and Panama—are also the two cases where democracy emerged the strongest. That is, contrary to what is normally accepted about American interventions, from these cases democracy remains strongest where the United States intervened the most.

Now one can argue that all three countries would still be democratic today if the United States had not intervened. This certainly might have been the case, but we know that democracy could also have easily taken much longer to put down deep roots.

As was alluded to in the introduction, much of the academic and policy critiques of the U.S. use of force during the past thirty years are firmly grounded in the Vietnam War experience. Stated simply, the "Vietnam syndrome" is the belief that U.S. interventions overseas invariably lead to moral disgust at home and strategic failure abroad. However, these critiques often fail to consider numerous foreign policy actions since Vietnam, ones that yielded drastically different lessons learned. That is, the cases studied in this book in part provide counterweights to the Vietnam syndrome interpretation of American interventions.

In our conventional study of these three interventions, we often describe them by repeating the regular litany about "stunts," "shams," and "deceptions." Thus, for example, when writing Ronald Reagan's eulogy, BBC referred back to the "sham" in Grenada; yet, if it is a sham, then what is made of the fact that Grenada's democratically elected prime minister attended the funeral?[5] Or what do we conclude when on June 16, 2004, the Grenadian Parliament approved a motion commemorating Reagan's "significant role in restoring peace and democracy."[6] We must also consider almost the entire population of Grenada who turned out to cheer President Reagan's visit to the island a couple of years after the invasion.

To be sure, this is not to say that Washington can never be the source of malfeasance; on the contrary, the United States a long and well-documented history of heavy-handed involvement in Central America and the Caribbean. Yet, for example, just because one concludes from the evidence that the United States was wrong to overthrow Jacobo Arbenz in Guatemala in 1954 does not automatically make the Dominican, Grenada, and Panama interventions equally wrong or immoral.

The apparent disconnect between what many critics continue to claim for U.S. motives and what actually occurred sheds crucial light on the larger question of the impetus behind the use of armed force. In addition to the Dominican Republic, Grenada, and Panama, the cases of Bosnia and Kosovo in the 1990s are instances where American power has also been used for the net benefit of the citizens of the involved countries. The Bosnia and Kosovo examples are more clear-cut instances of humanitarian interventions, as the lives of hundreds of thousands of civilians were at stake.

Yet the interventions discussed in this book reveal that, when the circumstances are appropriate, military intervention (such as a semihostile intervention such as the Dominican case, a full-scale invasion similar to Grenada and Panama, or something else) might effectively address the crisis at hand or at least be more preferable to a policy of inaction. In other words, there might not even need to be a severe humanitarian crisis at hand for a U.S. intervention to be necessary—or even legitimate.

UNDERSTANDING POLICYMAKERS' DECISIONS

During the Cold War, many intellectuals criticized various U.S. policies—examples include Vietnam and U.S. nuclear policy in Europe—to the extent that just from listening to the public discourse of a Martian landing on earth in 1988 or so might have concluded that the United States was equally or even more evil than its Soviet counterpart. In other words, critics have often tended to focus almost exclusively on what they see as the sordid defects of American power in the international system.

This is certainly that case for the study of U.S. policy toward Latin America. "Guatemala 1954" and "Chile 1973" became the mantras by which we pass down our understanding of U.S. motivations, actions, and outcomes. American interventions or destabilization efforts invariably led to dictatorships, repression, or the continuation of an exploitative status quo. The Dominican, Grenada, and Panama episodes were often by extension lumped alongside these others or overlooked entirely.

As observers, one mistake often made is to assume the worst about the motives and abilities of U.S. administrations and policymakers, that U.S. officials were likely bumbling, racist, and ignorant. What we fail to consider as much is that policymakers must act quickly on imperfect information and, above all, take responsibility for their actions. President Clinton's defense secretary, William Cohen, made this point strongly during his testimony to the September 11th Commission in 2004. When asked about his decision to bomb a suspected terrorist facility in Sudan that turned out to be a civilian facility, Cohen explained,

> this particular facility [al Shifa], according to the intelligence we had at that time, had been constructed under extraordinary security circumstances, even with some surface-to-air missile capability or defense capabilities; that the plant itself had been constructed under these security measures; that the—that the plant had been funded, in part, by the so-called Military Industrial Corporation; that bin Laden had been living there; that he had, in fact, money that he had put into this Military Industrial Corporation; that the owner of the plant had traveled to Baghdad to meet with the father of the VX program; and that the CIA had found traces of EMPTA nearby the facility itself. According to all the intelligence, there was no other known use for EMPTA at that time other than as a precursor to VX.
>
> Under those circumstances, I said, "That's actionable enough for me," that that plant could, in fact, be producing not baby aspirin or some other pharmaceutical for the benefit of the people, but it was enough for me to say we're going to take—we should take it out, and I recommended that.
>
> Now, I was criticized for that, saying, "You didn't have enough." And I

put myself in the position of coming before you and having someone like
you say to me, "Let me get this straight, Mr. Secretary. We've just had a
chemical weapons attack upon our cities or our troops, and we've lost several hundred or several thousand, and this is the information, which you
had at your fingertips—you had a plant that was built under the following
circumstances; you had a manager that went to Baghdad; you had Osama
bin Laden, who had funded, at least, the corporation; and you had traces of
EMPTA; and you did what? You did nothing?" Is that a responsible activity
on the part of the Secretary of Defense? And the answer is pretty clear.

So I was satisfied, even though that still is pointed as a mistake—that it
was the right thing to do then. I believe—I would do it again based on that
kind of intelligence.[7]

Cohen's comments reveal the tremendous political and moral responsi-
bilities that policymakers must contend with when deciding how to
respond to complex and fast-moving events; the implications of their
actions are equally enormous. We owe it to those who accept these bur-
dens to understand the environment in which decisions are made. We
must be aware that it is always infinitely easier to criticize after the fact
than it is to decide at the present. Policymakers never have the benefit of
hindsight to guide their decisions.

This of course does not mean that we should be blindly deferential
toward policymakers' decisions and actions; instead, we should attempt to
put ourselves in the shoes of those who we are studying, critically but
modestly analyzing events through the same lens that the policymakers
used. Now once we have seen events through these lenses, then we should
feel at liberty to criticize where criticism is warranted. But we do a disser-
vice to our understanding of the complexity of decision making if we do
not first get into the minds of those making these fateful decisions.

The overwhelming majority of Americans who go into public service
are well-intentioned, serious individuals who are committed to carrying
out U.S. foreign policy to the best of their abilities. Make no mistake,
American officials have committed terrible wrongs and made egregious
errors. As Reinhold Niebuhr has taught us, evil can be committed during
the exercise of power no matter how noble the intentions may be.[8] Thus,
we must be careful never to assume that American policies and operations
are automatically justified because our policymakers had "good intentions."

Nevertheless, the end of the Cold War and the implosion of communism as a global rival to Western liberalism now allow us to place into
greater context much of the perfidy the United States committed during
this era. American policymakers' decisions and intentions were not always
virtuous, but the spread of liberal democracy around the world in recent
decades suggests that the United States must have been doing something
right. There are certainly many in the Dominican Republic, Grenada, and
Panama who would agree.

NOTES

1. Peter Smith, *Talons of the Eagle: Dynamics of U.S.-Latin American Relations*
(Oxford: Oxford University Press, 2000), 181.

2. *BBC News*, "Reagan's Mixed White House Legacy," June 8, 2004.

3. Mark Danner, "Iraq: The New War," *New York Review of Books*, September 25,
2003, 91.

4. See Freedom House, www.freedomhouse.org/ratings/allscore04.xls. The rankings start in 1973, so the Dominican Republic's score before and after the intervention
cannot be evaluated.

5. "Dignitaries That Attended Reagan's Funeral," *Wall Street Journal*, June 11,
2004.

6. Loren Brown, "Grenada Parliament Honors Ronald Reagan," Associated Press,
June 17, 2004.

7. Quoted in Stephen F. Hayes, "There They Go Again," *The Weekly Standard*,
June 28, 2004.

8. Reinhold Niebuhr, *The Irony of American History* (New York: Charles Scribner's
Sons, 1952), 1–42.

Bibliography

PUBLIC INTERVIEWS

Author phone interview with Seth Tillman, Fulbright staff member on the Senate Foreign Relations Committee, July 17, 2003.

Author interview with Pat Holt, staff member on the Senate Foreign Relations Committee, July 18, 2003.

Author phone interview with Kenneth Dam, deputy secretary of state, July 18, 2004.

Author interview with Craig Johnstone, deputy assistant secretary of state for the Caribbean, July 2, 2004.

Author interview with Langhorne Motley, assistant secretary of state for inter-American affairs, October 5, 2004.

Author interview with Bernard Aronson, assistant secretary of state for inter-American affairs, October 19, 2004.

Author interview with Tony Gillespie, executive assistant secretary of state for the Caribbean, November 17, 2004.

Author phone interview with Michael P. Peters, commander of 96th Civil Affairs Battalion (Airborne) (1989), November 15, 2004.

Author interview with Cpt. Burdett Thompson, 1st Brigade of 82nd Airborne, March 1, 2005.

Author phone interview Vice Admiral Jonathan Howe, Joint Chiefs of Staff, March 2005.

GOVERNMENT DOCUMENTS

Bundy, McGeorge. "Policy toward Present and Future of the Panama Canal." National Security Action Memoranda No. 323. January 8, 1965 (declassified May 23, 1978), www.lbjlib.utexas.edu/johnson/archives.hom/NSAMs/nsam323.asp (accessed June 3, 2003).

Bush, George H. W. Address to the Nation Announcing United States Military Action in Panama. December 20, 1989.

———. *Public Papers of the Presidents of the United States: George Bush, 1989–1993,* vol. 2. Washington, D.C.: U.S. Government Printing Office, 1990.

Carter, Jimmy. "Human Rights and Foreign Policy Speech." 1977. *Basic Readings in*

Democracy, United States Information Agency, http://usinfo.state.gov/usa/infousa/facts/democrac/demo.htm (accessed August 20, 2004).

———. "Human Rights/Presidential Directive/NSC-30." February 17, 1978. Jimmy Carter Library, www.jimmycarterlibrary.org/documents/pd30.pdf (accessed August 20, 2004).

Cole, Ronald H. "Operation Just Cause: The Planning and Execution of Joint Operations in Panama." Washington, D.C.: Office of the Chairman of the Joint Chiefs of Staff, Joint History Office, 1995.

———. "Operation Urgent Fury: The Planning and Execution of Joint Operations in Grenada." Washington, D.C.: Office of the Chairman of the Joint Chiefs of Staff, Joint History Office, 1997.

Cranton, Senator Alan, Senator Alana Simpson, Senator John McCain, and Speaker of the House Jim Wright. "Question and Answers with Congressional Leadership Following Their Meeting with President Bush." May 11, 1989. Federal News Service.

Dodd, Christopher. "Press Conference with Senator Christopher Dodd, Jose Blandon, Panamanian Defector on the Panamanian Situation." October 3, 1989. Federal News Service.

Dominican Republic. Declassified Documents Reference System. Farmington Hills, Mich.: Gale Group, 2003.

Grenada. Declassified Documents Reference System. Farmington Hills, Mich.: Gale Group, 2003.

Gregorsky, Frank. "The Liberation of Grenada: The Enslavement of Democrats." *Congressional Record*, November 16, 1983. Extension of Remarks, 33221–22.

Helms, Senator Jesse, Senator John Kerry, Senator Alfonse D'Amato, Juan Sosa, and Jose Blandon. "Press Conference in the Senate Press Gallery on the Panamanian Situation." October 3, 1989. Federal News Service.

Johnson, Lyndon. "The Cabinet Meeting of June 18, 1965." Executive Office of the President, The Presidential Document Series, Minutes and Documents of the Cabinet Meetings of President Johnson (1963–1969), Primary Sources in U.S. Presidential History, Lexis-Nexis.

Lawler, Daniel, and Carolyn Yee, eds., and Edward C. Keefer, gen. ed. *Foreign Relations, 1964–1968: Dominican Republic; Cuba; Haiti; Guyana.* Washington, D.C.: U.S. Government Printing Office, 2005.

Mann, Thomas C. "The Dominican Crisis: Correcting Some Misconceptions." *Department of State Bulletin* 53 (November 8, 1965): 730–38.

———. "The Dominican Crisis: The Hemispheric Acts." U.S. Department of State, 1965.

———. "U.S. Policy toward Communist Activities in Latin America: Pro and Con." *Congressional Digest*, November 19, 1965, 260.

Meeker, Leonard C. "The Dominican Situation in the Perspective of International Law." *Department of State Bulletin* 53, no. 1359 (July 12, 1965): 60–65.

Motley, Langhorne A. "The Decision to Assist Grenada." *Current Policy* 541 (January 24, 1984): 1–4.

Noriega, Manuel. "Noriega's Speech before the National Assembly of Corregimiento Representatives, 15 December 1989." Translation. Printed in U.S. Department of Commerce, Foreign Broadcast Information Service. LAT-89-21.

Reagan, Ronald. "America's Commitment to Peace." Address to the Nation, October 27, 1983. *Department of State Bulletin* 83, no. 2081 (December 1983): 1–5.

————. "Evil Empire Speech." June 8, 1982. Fordham Modern History Sourcebook, www.fordham.edu/halsall/mod/1982reagan1.html (accessed August 20, 2004).

————. "National Security Decision Directive 75." January 17, 1983. Federation of American Scientists Intelligence Resource Program, www.fas.org/irp/offdocs/nsdd/nsdd-075.htm (accessed August 20, 2004).

————. *Public Papers of the Presidents of the United States, January 1 to July 2, 1982.* Washington, D.C.: U.S. Government Printing Office, 1983.

Rusk, Dean, "Situation in the Dominican Republic." *Department of State Bulletin* 45, no. 1174 (December 25, 1961): 1054–55.

Urgent Assistance for Democracy in Panama Act of 1990. Public Law 101-243 (H.R. 3952). February 14, 1990.

U.S. Congress. *Congressional Record.* 89th Cong., 1st sess., 1965. Volumes unknown, 1965. Washington, D.C.

U.S. Congress. House. Committee on Armed Services. The Invasion of Panama: How Many Innocent Bystanders Perished? 102nd Cong., 2nd sess., July 7, 1992. Committee Print no. 11.

U.S. Congress. House. Committee on Armed Services, Reports from the Honorable Samuel S. Stratton, the Honorable Elwood H. (Bud) Hillis, and the Honorable Ronald V. Dellums, on their November 5–6, 1983, visit to Grenada with Speaker's fact-finding mission. 98th Cong. 1st sess., November 15, 1983.

U.S. Congress. House. Committee on Foreign Affairs. Statement of Frank C. Conahan, Assistant Comptroller General for National Security and International Affairs. Appendix I to "GAO Review of Economic Sanctions against Panama," July 26, 1989 (GAO/T-NSIAD-89-4).

U.S. Congress. House. Committee on Foreign Affairs. U.S. Military Actions in Grenada: Implications for U.S. Policy in the Eastern Caribbean: Hearing before Committee on Foreign Affairs. 98th Cong., 1st sess., November 2, 3, and 16, 1983.

U.S. Congress. House. Committee on Foreign Affairs. United States Policy toward Grenada. 97th Cong., 2nd sess., June 15, 1982.

U.S. Congress. House. Committee on Foreign Affairs. U.S. Policy toward Panama. 101st Cong., 2nd sess., February 6, 1990. Federal News Service, Lexis-Nexis.

U.S. Congress. House. Committee on Foreign Relations. Grenada War Powers: Full Compliance Reporting and Implementation. H.J. Res. 402. 98th Cong., 1st sess., October 27, 1983.

U.S. Congress. House. Communication from the President of the United States Transmitting a Report on the Deployment of United States Armed Forces to Grenada, October 26, 1983. 98th Cong., 1st sess., 1983. H. Doc. 98-125.

U.S. Congress. House. Operation Just Cause: A Preliminary Assessment. 101st Cong., 2nd sess., 1990. *Congressional Record* 136, no. 8. Lexis-Nexis.

U.S. Congress. House. "Panama Invasion Still Concerns Many Americans. 101st Cong., 2nd sess., 1990. *Congressional Record* 136, no. 57, May 9, 1990. Extension of Remarks. Lexis-Nexis.

U.S. Congress. House. *Sense of Congress concerning Operation Just Cause in Panama.* 101st Cong., 2nd sess. *Congressional Record* 136, no. 10, February 7, 1990.

U.S. Congress. House. "Serious Questions Remain over Panama Invasion." 101st

Cong., 2nd sess. *Congressional Record* 136, no. 12, February 20, 1990. Extension of Remarks.

U.S. Congress. House. The War Powers Resolution: Relevant Documents, Correspondence, Reports. 98th Cong., 1st sess., 1983. Committee Print.

U.S. Congress. Senate. Committee on Armed Services and Select Committee on Intelligence. 1989 Events in Panama. 101st Cong., 1st sess., October 6 and 17 and December 22, 1989.

U.S. Congress. Senate. Committee on Foreign Relations. Hearing on the Situation in Panama, 101st Cong., 2nd sess., 1990. *Congressional Record* 136, no. 1. Lexis-Nexis.

U.S. Congress. Senate. Committee on Foreign Relations. Situation in the Dominican Republic and Other Documents. Executive Sessions of the Senate Foreign Relations Committee, vol. 4077-02. 89th Cong., 1st sess., 1965. Declassified in 1990.

U.S. Congress. Senate. Foreign Relations Committee. The Panama Invasion. 101st Cong., 2nd sess. *Congressional Record* 136, no. 1 (January 23, 1990).

U.S. Congress. Senate. The Panama Invasion. 101st Cong., 2nd sess., 1990. *Congressional Record* 136. Lexis-Nexis.

U.S. Congress. Senate. Report on the Visit to Panama, January 19 to January 22, 1990. 101st Cong., 2nd sess., 1990. *Congressional Record* 136, no. 3.

U.S. Department of Defense. "Special Briefing regarding the Military Action in Panama." December 20, 1989. Federal News Service.

———. "Special Briefing regarding Panama." December 20, 1989. Federal News Service.

U.S. Department of State Bulletin. *Grenada: Collective Actions by the Caribbean Peace Force* 83, no. 2081 (December 1983): 67–82.

———. "Message of President Eisenhower." Vol. 43, no. 1107 (September 12, 1960): 412.

———. Statements by President Lyndon Johnson. "U.S. Acts to Meet Threat in Dominican Republic." Vol. 52, no. 1351 (May 17, 1965): 738–48.

———. "U.S. Expresses Concern over Events in Dominican Republic." Vol. 45, no. 1173 (December 18, 1961): 1003.

U.S. Department of State. "The Larger Importance of Grenada." *Current Policy* 526 (November 4, 1983): 1–3.

U.S. Departments of State and Defense. *Grenada: A Preliminary Report.* Washington, D.C. (December 16, 1983).

U.S. Department of State Dispatch. *Fact Sheet: Panama after Operation Just Cause* 2, no. 5 (February 4, 1991).

———. *Fact Sheet: Panama 2 Years after Operation Just Cause* 3, no. 6 (February 10, 1992), EBSCOhost (accessed May 9, 2003).

U.S. General Accounting Office. National Security and International Affairs Division. "Letter to Andrew Jacobs, Jr." September 13, 1990, 1–2 (GAO/NSIAD-90-279FS).

Weinberger, Caspar. "The Uses of Military Power." Address at the National Press Club, Washington, D.C., November 28, 1984.

White House Office of the Press Secretary. Statement by the Press Secretary. December 20, 1989. Federal News Service.

Woodward, Robert F. "U.S. Seeks Withdrawal of OAS Action on Trade with Dominican Republic." *Department of State Bulletin* 45, no. 1171 (December 4, 1961): 929–32.

NONGOVERNMENTAL DOCUMENTS

Association of the Bar of the City of New York. *The Use of Armed Force in International Affairs: The Case of Panama.* June 1992.

Center for Strategic Studies. *Dominican Action 1965 Intervention or Cooperation?* Special Report Series, No. 2. Georgetown University, Washington, D.C. July 1966.

Central American and Caribbean Program. School of Advanced International Studies. *Report on Panama.* Findings of the Study Group on United States-Panamanian Relations. Occasional Paper No. 13. Johns Hopkins University. April 1987.

Freedom House. Freedom Table 1972 to 2003, www.freedomhouse.org/ratings/allscore04.xls.

Grant, Rebecca L. "Operation Just Cause and the U.S. Policy Process." *RAND Publication Series* 199 (1990).

Lind, William S. *Report to the Congressional Military Caucus: The Grenada Operation.* Washington, D.C.: Military Reform Institute, April 5, 1984.

United Methodist Church General Board of Global Ministries. Panama Country Profile, http://gbgm-umc.org/country_profiles/country_history.cfm?Id = 117 (accessed June 23, 2004).

BOOKS

Adkin, Mark. *Urgent Fury: The Battle for Grenada.* Lexington, Mass.: Lexington Books, 1989.

Aker, F. *Breaking the Stranglehold: The Liberation of Grenada.* Gun Owner's Foundation, 1984.

Atkins, G. Pope, and Larman C. Wilson. *The Dominican Republic and the United States: From Imperialism to Transnationalism.* Athens: University of Georgia Press, 1998.

Beck, Robert. *The Grenada Invasion: Politics, Law, and Foreign Policy Decisionmaking.* Boulder, Colo.: Westview Press, 1993.

Beschloss, Michael. *Searching for Glory: Johnson's White House Tapes.* New York: Simon & Schuster, 2001.

Blachman, Morris J., William M. Leogrande, and Kenneth Sharpe, eds. *Confronting Revolution: Security through Diplomacy in Central America.* New York: Pantheon Books, 1986.

Boot, Max. *The Savage Wars of Peace Small Wars and the Rise of American Power.* New York: Basic Books, 2002.

Bracey, Audrey. *Resolution of the Dominican Crisis, 1965: A Study in Mediation.* Washington, D.C.: Institute for the Study of Diplomacy, Edmund A. Walsh School of Foreign Service, Georgetown University, 1980.

Brown, Seyom. *Faces of Power: Constancy and Change in Foreign Policy from Truman to Clinton.* New York: Columbia University Press, 1994.

Buckley, Kevin. *Panama: The Whole Story.* New York: Simon & Schuster, 1991.

Burrowes, Reynold. *Revolution and Rescue in Grenada: An Account of the US-Caribbean Invasion.* Westport, Conn.: Greenwood Press, 1988.

Carothers, Thomas. *In the Name of Democracy: US Policy toward Central America during the Reagan Years.* Berkeley: University of California Press, 1991.

Chester, Eric Thomas. *Rag-Tags, Scum, Riff-Raff, and Commies: The U.S. Intervention in the Dominican Republic, 1965–1966*. New York: Monthly Review Press, 2001.

Conniff, Michael L. *Panama and the United States: The Forced Alliance*. Athens: University of Georgia Press, 1992.

Dinges, John. *Our Man in Panama: How General Noriega Used the United States—and Made Millions in Drugs and Arms*. New York: Random House, 1990.

Donnelly, Thomas, Margaret Roth, and Caleb Baker. *Operation Just Cause: The Storming of Panama*. New York: Lexington Books, 1991.

Dujmovic, Nicholas. *The Grenada Documents: Window on Totalitarianism*. Washington, D.C.: Fletcher School of Law and Diplomacy, 1988.

Dunn, Peter M., and Bruce Watson, eds. *American Intervention in Grenada: The Implications of "Urgent Fury."* Boulder, Colo.: Westview Press, 1985.

Ellison, Herbert J., and Jiri Valenta, eds. *Grenada and Soviet/Cuban Policy: Internal Crisis and US/OECS Intervention*. Boulder, Colo.: Westview Press, 1986.

Farnsworth David N., and James W. McKenney. *U.S.-Panama Relations, 1903–1978: A Study in Linkage Politics*. Boulder, Colo.: Westview Press, 1983.

Ferguson, James, *Grenada: Revolution in Reverse*. London: Monthly Review Press, 1990.

Finnemore, Martha. *The Purpose of Intervention*. Ithaca, N.Y.: Cornell University Press, 2003.

Fishel, John T., and Max G. Manwaring. *Toward Responsibility in the New World Order: Challenges and Lessons of Peace Operations*. London: F. Cass, 1998.

Freedman, Lawrence. *Kennedy's Wars: Berlin, Cuba, Laos, and Vietnam*. New York: Oxford University Press, 2000.

Gellman, Irwin. *Good Neighbor Diplomacy: United States Policies in Latin America, 1933–1945*. Baltimore: Johns Hopkins University Press, 1979.

Geyelin Philip. *Lyndon B. Johnson and the World*. New York: Praeger, 1966.

Gilmore, William C. *Grenada Intervention: Analysis and Documentation*. New York: Facts on File, 1984.

Gleijeses, Piero. *The Dominican Crisis: The 1965 Constitutionalist Revolt and American Intervention*. Baltimore: Johns Hopkins University Press, 1978.

———. *Shattered Hope: The Guatemalan Revolution and the United States, 1944–1954*. Princeton, N.J.: Princeton University Press, 1991.

Guevara Mann, Carlos. *Panamanian Militarism: A Historical Interpretation*. Athens: Center for International Studies, Ohio University, 1996.

Haass, Richard. *Intervention*. Washington, D.C.: Carnegie Endowment Press, 1994.

Hahn, Walter F., ed. *Central America and the Reagan Doctrine*. Washington, D.C.: United States Strategic Institute, 1987.

Halberstam, David. *War in a Time of Peace: Bush, Clinton and the Generals*. New York: Scribner, 2001.

Healy, David. *Drive to Hegemony: The United States in the Caribbean, 1898–1917*. Madison: University of Wisconsin Press, 1988.

Huchthausen, Peter. *America's Splendid Little Wars: A Short History of U.S. Military Engagements, 1975–2000*. New York: Viking, 2003.

Independent Inquiry of the U.S. Invasion of Panama. *The U.S. Invasion of Panama: The Truth behind Operation "Just Cause."* Boston: South End Press, 1991.

Johnson, Lyndon Baines. *The Vantage Point: A Time of Testing: Crises in the Caribbean.* New York: Holt, Rinehart and Winston, 1971.

Kagan, Robert. *A Twilight Struggle: American Power and Nicaragua, 1977–1990.* New York: Free Press, 1996.

Kempe, Frederick. *Divorcing the Dictator: America's Bungled Affair with Noriega.* New York: G. P. Putnam's Sons, 1990.

Kolko, Gabriel. *Confronting the Third World, US Foreign Policy, 1945–1980.* New York: Pantheon Books, 1988.

Koster, R. M., and Guillermo Sanchez. *In the Name of the Tyrants, Panama: 1968–1990.* New York: Norton, 1990.

Krasner, Stephen. *Sovereignty: Organized Hypocrisy.* Princeton, N.J.: Princeton University Press, 1999.

Kryzanek, Michael J. "The Dominican Intervention Revisited: An Attitudinal and Operational Analysis." In *United States Policy in Latin America: A Quarter Century of Crisis and Challenge, 1961–1986,* edited by John Martz. Lincoln: University of Nebraska Press, 1988, 135–56.

Kryzanek, Michael J. *US-Latin American Relations.* 2nd ed. New York: Praeger, 1990.

LaFeber, Walter. *Inevitable Revolutions: The United States in Central America.* New York: Norton, 1983.

LaRosa, Michael, and Frank O. Mora, eds. *Neighborly Adversaries: Readings in U.S.-Latin American Relations.* Lanham, Md.: Rowman & Littlefield, 1999.

Lee, Russell, and Albert Mendez. *Grenada 1983, Men at Arms Series, 159.* London: Osprey Publishing, 1985.

Leiken, Robert S., and Barry Rubin, eds. *The Central American Crisis Reader.* New York: Summit Books, 1987.

Lewis, Gordon K. *Grenada: The Jewel Despoiled.* Baltimore: Johns Hopkins University Press, 1987.

Lowenthal, Abraham F. *The Dominican Intervention.* Cambridge, Mass.: Harvard University Press, 1972.

McPherson, Alan. *Yankee No!: Anti-Americanism in US-Latin American Relations.* Cambridge, Mass.: Harvard University Press, 2003.

Major, John. *Prize Possession: The United States and the Panama Canal, 1903–1979.* Cambridge: Cambridge University Press, 1993.

Marcus, Bruce, et al. *Maurice Bishop Speaks: The Grenada Revolution and Its Overthrow 1979–1983.* New York: Pathfinder Press, 1984.

Martin, John Bartlow. *Overtaken by Events: The Dominican Crisis from the Fall of Trujillo to the Civil War.* New York: Doubleday, 1966.

Mecham, J. Lloyd. *The United States and Inter-American Security, 1889–1960.* Austin: University of Texas Press, 1961.

Mitchell, Nancy. *The Danger of Dreams: German and American Imperialism in Latin America.* Chapel Hill: University of North Carolina Press, 1999.

Molineu, Harold. *U.S. Policy toward Latin America: From Regionalism to Globalism.* Boulder, Colo.: Westview Press, 1986.

Musicant, Ivan. *The Banana Wars: A History of United States Military Intervention in Latin America from the Spanish American War to the Invasion of Panama.* New York: Macmillan, 1990.

Niebuhr, Reinhold. *The Irony of American History*. New York: Charles Scribner's Sons, 1952.

O'Shaughnessy, Hugh. *Grenada: Revolution, Invasion, and Aftermath*. London: Hamish Hamilton, 1984.

Oye, Kenneth, Donald Rothchild, and Robert Leiber, eds. *Eagle Entangled: U.S. Foreign Policy in a Complex World*. New York: Longman, 1978.

Palmer, Bruce. *Intervention in the Caribbean: The Dominican Crisis of 1965*. Lexington: University Press of Kentucky, 1989.

Pastor, Robert A. *Exiting the Whirlpool: U.S. Foreign Policy toward Latin America and the Caribbean*. 2nd ed. New York: Westview Press, 2001.

———. *Whirlpool: U.S. Foreign Policy toward Latin America and the Caribbean*. Princeton, N.J.: Princeton University Press, 1992.

Payne, Anthony, Paul Sutton, and Tony Thorndike. *Grenada: Revolution and Invasion*. New York: St. Martin's Press, 1984.

Pike, Frederick B. *FDR's Good Neighbor Policy: Sixty Years in Generally Gentle Chaos*. Austin: University of Texas Press, 1995.

Rabe, Stephen G. *Eisenhower and Latin America: A Foreign Policy of Anticommunism*. Chapel Hill: University of North Carolina Press, 1988.

———. *The Most Dangerous Area in the World: John F. Kennedy Confronts Revolution in Latin America*. Chapel Hill: University of North Carolina Press, 1999.

Schlesinger, Arthur. *A Thousand Days: John F. Kennedy and the White House*. New York: Houghton Mifflin, 1965.

Schlesinger, Stephen, and Stephen Kinzer. *Bitter Fruit: The Untold Story of the American Coup in Guatemala*. Garden City, N.Y.: Doubleday, 1982.

Schoonmaker, Herbert G. *Military Crisis Management: U.S. Intervention in the Dominican Republic, 1965*. New York: Greenwood Press, 1990.

Schoultz, Lars. *Beneath the United States: A History of U.S. Policy toward Latin America*. London: Harvard University Press, 1998.

———. *Human Rights and U.S. Policy towards Latin America*. Princeton, N.J.: Princeton University Press, 1981.

Scott, James M. *Deciding to Intervene: The Reagan Doctrine and American Foreign Policy*. Durham, N.C.: Duke University Press, 1996.

Seabury, Paul, and Walter McDougall, eds. *The Grenada Papers*. San Francisco: Institute for Contemporary Studies, 1984.

Searle, Chris. *Grenada: The Struggle against Destabilization*. New York: Writers & Readers Publishing, 1984.

Shultz, George P. *Turmoil and Triumph: My Years as Secretary of State*. New York: Charles Scribner's Sons, 1993.

Slater, Jerome. *Intervention and Negotiation: The United States and the Dominican Revolution*. New York: Harper and Row, 1970.

Smith, Gaddis. *The Last Years of the Monroe Doctrine, 1945–1999*. New York: Hill & Wang, 1994.

Smith, Peter. *Talons of the Eagle: Dynamics of U.S.-Latin American Relations*. Oxford: Oxford University Press, 2000.

Szulc, Tad. *Dominican Diary*. New York: Delacorte Press, 1965.

Thorndike, Tony. *Grenada: Politics, Economics, and Society*. London: Frances Pinter, 1985.

Tiwathia, Vijay. *The Grenada War: Anatomy of a Low-Intensity Conflict.* New Delhi: Lancer International, 1987.

Vance, Cyrus. *Hard Choices: Critical Years in America's Foreign Policy.* New York: Simon & Schuster, 1983.

Watson, Bruce W., and Peter G. Tsouras, eds. *Operation Just Cause: The U.S. Intervention in Panama.* Boulder, Colo.: Westview Press, 1991.

Wiarda, Howard. *Democracy and Its Discontents: Development, Interdependence, and U.S. Policy in Latin America.* Lanham, Md.: Rowman & Littlefield, 1995.

Yates, Lawrence A. *Power Pack: U.S. Intervention in the Dominican Republic, 1965–1966.* Fort Leavenworth, Kans.: Combat Studies Institute, U.S. Army Command and General Staff College, 1988.

Zakaria, Fareed. *From Wealth to Power: The Unusual Origins of America's World Role.* Princeton, N.J.: Princeton University Press, 1998.

ARTICLES

Adar, Korwa Gombe, and Catherine I. Harries. "Dual Nature of Sovereignty and Its Application to Foreign Policy Making: The Case of the U.S. Intervention in the 1980s." *Journal of Third World Studies* 10 (fall 1993): 323–42.

Ames, Ramses. "The United Nations' Reactions to Foreign Military Interventions." *Journal of Peace Research* 31, no. 4 (1994): 425–44.

Arias, Oscar. "A New Opportunity for Panama." *Harvard International Review* 13, no. 3 (spring 1991): 25–28.

Bell, Wendell. "The Invasion of Grenada: A Note on False Prophecy." *Yale Review* 75 (October 1986): 564–88.

Bender, J. B. "Dominican Intervention: The Facts." *National Review*, February 8, 1966, 112–14.

Bennett, William C. "Just Cause and the Principles of War." *Military Review*, March 1991, 2–13.

Bernheim, Roger. "Drama in the Caribbean." *Swiss Review of World Affairs*, July 1965, 3–4.

Berryman, Phillip. "Just Cause Examined." *Commonweal* 117, no. 4 (February 23, 1990): 103–5.

Bethel, Paul. "Dominican Intervention: The Myths." *National Review*, February 8, 1966, 107–11.

Black, George. "T.R.'s Invention." *The Nation*, June 5, 1989, 760–61.

Blade, William R. "The Reagan Doctrine." *Strategic Review* 14, no. 1 (winter 1986): 21–29.

Block, Marcia, and Geoff Mungham. "The Military, the Media, and the Invasion of Grenada." *Contemporary Crises* 13 (June 1989): 91–127.

Bolger, Daniel P. "Operation Urgent Fury and Its Critics." *Military Review* 66, no. 7 (July 1986): 57–69.

Bosch, Juan. "The Dominican Revolution." *New Republic*, July 24, 1965, 19–21.

Brands, H. W., Jr. "Decisions on American Armed Intervention: Lebanon, Dominican Republic, and Grenada." *Political Science Quarterly* 102, no. 4 (winter 1987–1988): 607–24.

Busch, Andrew E., and Elizabeth Spalding. "1983: Awakening from Orwell's Nightmare." *Policy Review* (fall 1993): 71–75.

Connell-Smith, Gordon, "The OAS and the Dominican Crisis." *The World Today* 21, no. 6 (June 1965): 229–36.

Danner, Mark. "Iraq: The New War." *New York Review of Books*, September 25, 2003, 88–91.

Diebel, T. L. "Bush's Foreign Policy: Mastery and Inaction." *Foreign Policy*, no. 84 (fall 1991): 3–23.

Dinges, John. "General Coke?" *NACLA Report on the America* 22, no. 4 (1990) 20–22.

Dore, Isaak I. "The U.S. Invasion of Grenada: Resurrection of the 'Johnson Doctrine'?" *Stanford Journal of International Law* 20 (spring 1984): 173–89.

Draper, Theodore. "A Case of Defamation: U.S. Intelligence versus Juan Bosch." *New Republic*, February 19, 1966, 13–19.

———. "A Case of Defamation: U.S. Intelligence versus Juan Bosch-II." *New Republic*, February 26, 1966, 15–18.

———. "The Dominican Crisis." *Commentary* 40, no. 6 (December 1965): 33–68.

———. "The New Dominican Crisis." *The New Leader*, January 31, 1966, 3–8.

———. "The Roots of the Dominican Crisis." *The New Leader*, May 24, 1965, 3–18.

Drucker, Linda. "Washington Cries Uncle." *Commonweal*, July 15, 1988, 391–92.

The Economist. "Ask the Grenadians." October 29, 1983, 13.

———. "Grenada; The Love Waves Stopped Working." March 17, 1979, 66.

———. "Grenada; More Light." November 5, 1983, 39.

———. "Gunning for Noriega." December 23, 1989, 29–30.

———. "Licensed to Kill?" November 5, 1983, 13.

———. "Maxatollah." January 6, 1990, 26.

———. "Power Needs Clear Eyes." October 29, 1983, 9.

———. "Say Something, If Only Goodbye." March 10, 1984, 31.

———. "The Priming of the Grenada Grenade." October 29, 1983, 17.

———. "Why the Sledgehammer Hit the Nutmeg." October 29, 1983, 41.

Falcoff, Mark. "Kissinger and Chile: The Myth That Will Not Die," *Commentary*, November 1, 2003, www.aei.org/include/news_print.asp?newsID=19385 (accessed June 23, 2004).

Fauriol, Georges A. "The Shadow of Latin America Affairs." *Foreign Affairs* 69, no. 1 (1990): 116–34.

Felten, Peter G. "The Path to Dissent: Johnson, Fulbright, and the 1965 Intervention in the Dominican Republic." *Presidential Studies Quarterly* 26, no. 4 (fall 1996): 1009–18.

Felton, John. "Congress Reels under Impact of Marine Deaths in Beirut, Invasion of Grenada." *Congressional Quarterly Weekly*, October 29, 1983, online (access date unknown).

Fenwick, Charles. "The Dominican Republic: Intervention or Collective Self-Defense." *American Journal of International Law* 60, no. 1 (January 1966): 64–67.

Ferguson, Yale H., "The Dominican Intervention of 1965: Recent Interpretations." *International Organization* 27, no. 4 (autumn 1973): 517–48.

Fields, Maj. Damon (USC), Lt. Col Bill Pope (USAF), and Lt. Col Sharon Patrick (USA). "Adventures in Hispaniola." *Proceedings* (U.S. Naval Institute), September 2002, 60–64.

Furlong, William L. "Panama: The Difficult Transition towards Democracy." *Journal of Interamerican Studies and World Affairs* 35, no. 3 (autumn 1993): 19–64.

Gilboa, Eytan. "The Panama Invasion Revisited: Lessons for the Use of Force in the Post Cold War Era." *Political Science Quarterly* 110, no. 4 (1995–1996): 539–62.

Hakim, Peter. "From Cold War to Cold Shoulder? The US in Central America." *Harvard International Review* 13, no. 3 (spring 1991): 4–6.

Hardt, D. Brent. "Grenada Reconsidered." *Fletcher Forum* 11 (summer 1987): 277–308.

Hayes, Stephen F. "There They Go Again." *The Weekly Standard*, June 28, 2004, 24–27.

Hersh, Seymour. "The Creation of a Thug." *Life*, March 1990, 81–93.

Isaacson, Walter. "Weighing the Proper Role." *Time*, November 7, 1983, 42–62.

Jentleson, Bruce W. "The Pretty Prudent Public: Post Post-Vietnam American Opinion on the Use of Military Force." *International Studies Quarterly* 36 (1992): 49–74.

Jentleson, Bruce W., and Rebecca L. Britton. "Still Pretty Prudent: Post-Cold War American Public Opinion on the Use of Military Force." *Journal of Conflict Resolution* 42, no. 4 (August 1998): 395–417.

Kahn, E. H. "Letter from Panama." *The New Yorker*, August 16, 1976, 64–74.

Kenworthy, Eldon. "Grenada as Theater." *World Policy Journal* 1, no. 3 (spring 1984): 635–51.

Kirkpatrick, Jeane J. "The U.N. and Grenada: A Speech Never Delivered." *Strategic Review* 12 (winter 1984): 11–18.

Kohut, Andrew, and Robert C. Toth. "Arms and the People." *Foreign Affairs* 73, no. 6 (November/December 1994): 45–61.

Leogrande, William M. "From Reagan to Bush: The Transition of U.S. Policy towards Central America." *Journal of Latin American Studies* 22, no. 3 (October 1990): 595–621.

Levitin, Michael J. "The Law of Force and the Force of Law: Grenada, the Falklands, and Humanitarian Intervention." *Harvard International Law Journal* 27 (spring 1986): 621–57.

Lowenthal, Abraham F. "The United States and the Dominican Republic: Background to Intervention." *Caribbean Studies* 10, no. 2 (July 1970): 30–55.

Maechling, Charles, Jr. "Washington's Illegal Invasion." *Foreign Policy*, no. 79 (summer 1990): 113–33.

Massing, Michael. "The Intervention That Misfired." *The Nation*, May 21, 1989, 708–10.

———. "New Trouble in Panama." *New York Review of Books*, May 17, 1990, 43–49.

Meernik, James. "United States Military Intervention and the Promotion of Democracy." *Journal of Peace Research* 33, no. 4 (1996): 391–402.

Miller, David Norman. "Panama and U.S. Policy." *Global Affairs* 4, no. 3 (summer 1989): 128–47.

Millett, Richard. "The Aftermath of Intervention: Panama 1990." *Journal of Interamerican Studies and World Affairs* 32, no. 1 (spring 1990): 1–15.

———. "Looking beyond Noriega." *Foreign Policy*, no. 71 (summer 1988): 46–63.

Moore, John Norton. "Grenada and the International Double Standard." *American Journal of International Law* 78 (January 1984): 145–68.

Morales, Wiltraud Quiese. "US Intervention and the New World Order: Lessons from

Cold War and Post-Cold War Cases." *Third World Quarterly* 15, no. 1 (March 1994): 77–102.

Moss, Ambler H., Jr. "War-Torn Panama Slowly Pulls Itself Together." *Harvard International Review* 13, no. 3 (spring 1991): 22–24.

Motley, James Berry. "Grenada: Low-Intensity Conflict and the Use of U.S. Power." *World Affairs* 146, no. 3 (winter 1983–1984): 221–38.

NACLA Report on the Americas. "Panama: Reagan's Last Stand." Vol. 22, no. 4 (1990): 11.

Nash, James. "What Hath Intervention Wrought? Reflections on the Dominican Republic." *Caribbean Review* 14, no. 4 (1985): 7–11.

Peceny, Mark. "Two Paths to the Promotion of Democracy during U.S. Military Interventions." *International Studies Quarterly* 39, no. 3 (September 1995): 371–401.

Plank, John N. "The Caribbean: Intervention, When and How." *Foreign Affairs* (October 1965): 37–48.

Rettie, John. "A Hungary in the Caribbean?" *New Statesman*, May 7, 1965 (page unknown).

Riggs, Ronald M. "The Grenada Intervention: A Legal Analysis." *Military Law Review* 109 (summer 1985): 1–81.

Robbins, Carla Anne. "Drug King? Spy? Not I, Says General Noriega; Is Panama Run by a Military 'Mafia'?" *U.S. News and World Report*, July 27, 1986, 36.

Robinson, Linda. "Dwindling Options in Panama." *Foreign Affairs* 68, no. 5 (1989): 187–205.

Rogers, William D., and Kenneth Maxwell. "Fleeing the Chilean Coup: The Debate over U.S. Complicity." *Foreign Affairs* (January/February 2004): www.foreignaffairs.org/20040101faresponse83116/william-d-rogers-kenneth-maxwell/fleeing-the-chilean-coup-the-debate-over-US-complicity.html (accessed July 19, 2004).

Ropp, Steve C. "Explaining the Long-Term Maintenance of a Military Regime: Panama before the U.S. Invasion." *World Politics* 44, no. 2 (January 1992): 210–34.

———. "Panama: The United States Invasion and Its Aftermath." *Current History* 90, no. 554 (March 1991): 113–16, 130.

———. "Things Fall Apart: Panama after Noriega." *Current History* 92, no. 572 (March 1993): 102–5.

Rubner, Michael. "The Reagan Administration, the 1973 War Powers Resolution, and the Invasion of Grenada." *Political Science Quarterly* 100, no. 4 (winter 1985/1986): 627–47.

Rumage, Sarah A. "Panama and the Myth of Humanitarian Intervention in U.S. Foreign Policy: Neither Legal nor Moral, Neither Just nor Right." *Arizona Journal of International and Comparative Law* 10 (1993): 1–76.

Schlesinger, Arthur, Jr. "The Lowering Hemisphere." *The Atlantic*, January 1970, www.theatlantic.com (accessed August 2, 2004).

Scranton, Margaret E. "Consolidation after Imposition: Panama's 1992 Referendum." *Journal of Interamerican Studies and World Affairs* 35, no. 3 (fall 1993): 65–102.

———. "Panama's First Post-Transition Election." *Journal of Interamerican Studies and World Affairs* 37, no. 1 (spring 1995): 69–100.

Shearman, Peter. "The Soviet Union and Grenada under the New Jewel Movement." *International Affairs* 61, no. 4 (autumn 1985): 661–73.

Shultz, George. "Terrorism in the Modern World." *Survival* 27, no. 1 (January/February 1985): 30–35.

Slater, Jerome. "Democracy vs. Stability: The Recent Latin America Policy of the United States." *Yale Review* (winter 1966): 169–81.

Tuomala, Jeffrey C. "Just Cause: The Thread That Runs So True." *Dickinson Journal of International Law* 13 (fall 1994): 1–67.

Vaky, Viron P. "Hemispheric Relations: Everything Is Part of Everything Else." *Foreign Affairs* 59, no. 3 (1980): 617–47.

Wagenheim, Kurt. "Talking with Juan Bosch." *The New Leader*, February 28, 1966, 7–10.

Waters, Maurice. "The Law and Politics of a U.S. Intervention: The Case of Grenada." *Peace and Change* 14, no. 1 (January 1989): 65–105.

Weeks, John, and Andrew Zimbalist. "The Failure of Intervention in Panama: Humiliation in the Backyard." *Third World Quarterly* 11, no. 1 (January 1989): 1–27.

Weinberger, Caspar W. "U.S. Defence Strategy." *Foreign Affairs* (summer 1986): 684–86.

Wells, Henry. "Turmoil in the Dominican Republic." *Current History* 50, no. 293 (January 1966): 14–20.

Whittle, Richard. "Objectives Achieved, Reagan Says: Congress Examines Causes, Costs of Grenada Operation." *Congressional Quarterly Weekly* (November 5, 1983), online (access date unknown).

Wiarda, Howard J. "The United States and the Dominican Republic: Intervention, Dependency, and Tyrannicide." *Journal of Interamerican Studies and World Affairs* 22, no. 2 (May 1980): 247–59.

Will, George F. "The Price of Power." *Newsweek*, November 7, 1983, 142.

Will, W. Marvin, "From Authoritarianism to Political Development in Grenada: Questions for U.S. Policy." *Studies in Comparative International Development* 26, no. 3 (fall 1991): 29–58.

Williams, Gary. "Prelude to an Intervention: Grenada 1983." *Journal of Latin American Studies* 29, no. 1 (February 1997): 131–69.

Wilson, Larman. "The Monroe Doctrine, Cold War Anachronism: Cuba and the Dominican Republic." *Journal of Politics* 28, no. 2 (May 1966): 322–46.

Index

ABOUT THE AUTHOR

Russell Crandall is associate professor of political science at Davidson College. He is author of *Driven by Drugs: United States Policy toward Colombia*. He is coeditor of *The Andes in Focus: Security, Democracy, and Economic Reform* and *Mexico's Democracy at Work: Political and Economic Dynamics*. In 2004–2005, Crandall served as director for Western Hemisphere initiatives at the National Security Council and special assistant to the deputy director for counterterrorism (J-5) at the Joint Chiefs of Staff. From 2002–2004, he served as a special advisor to the assistant secretary of defense for international security affairs.